# MUSH!
## SLED DOGS WITH ISSUES

WRITTEN BY
### GLENN EICHLER

ART BY
### JOE INFURNARI

:01

First Second
NEW YORK & LONDON

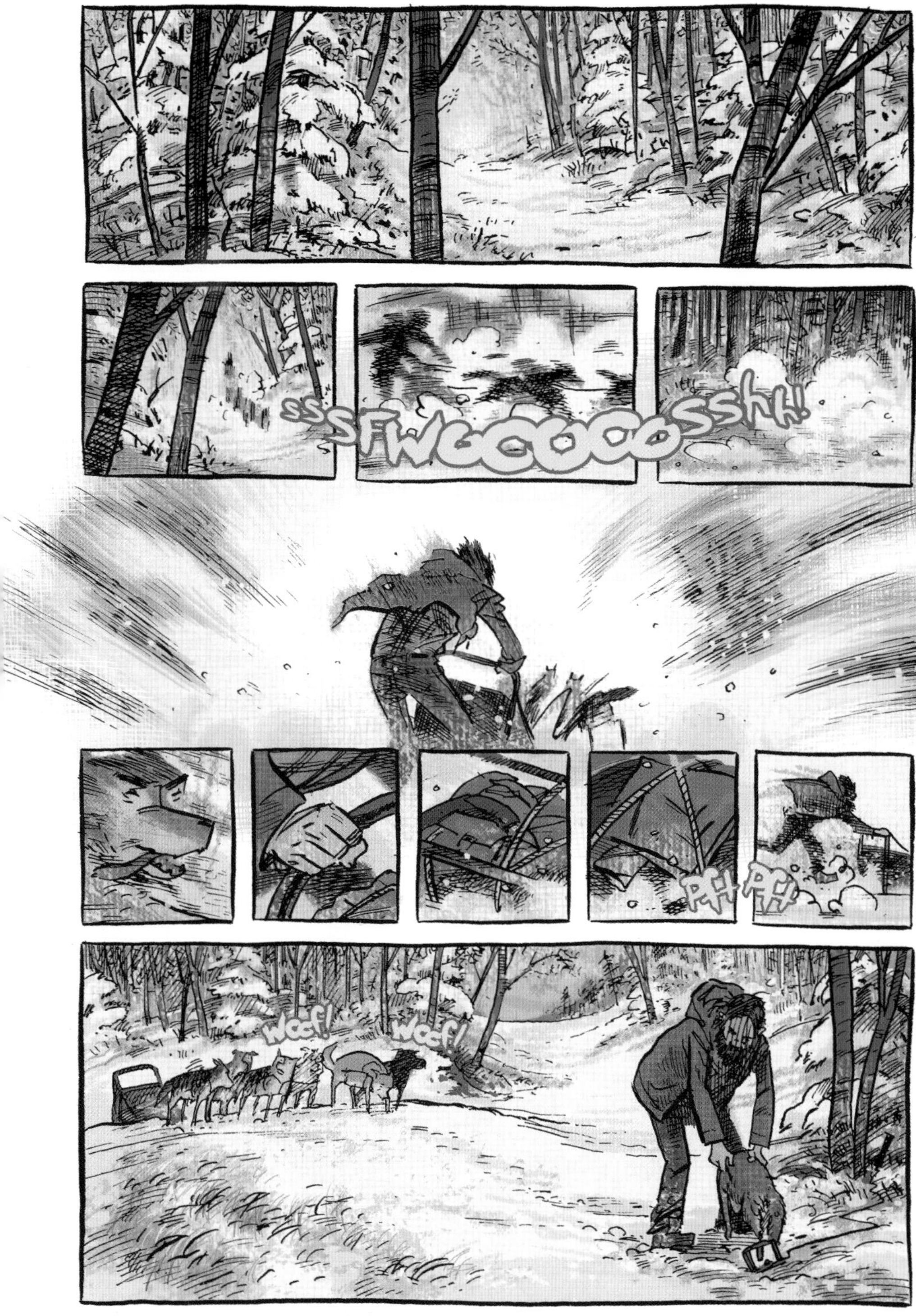

SSSFWOOOOOOSSHH!
PFF PFF
WOOF!
WOOF!

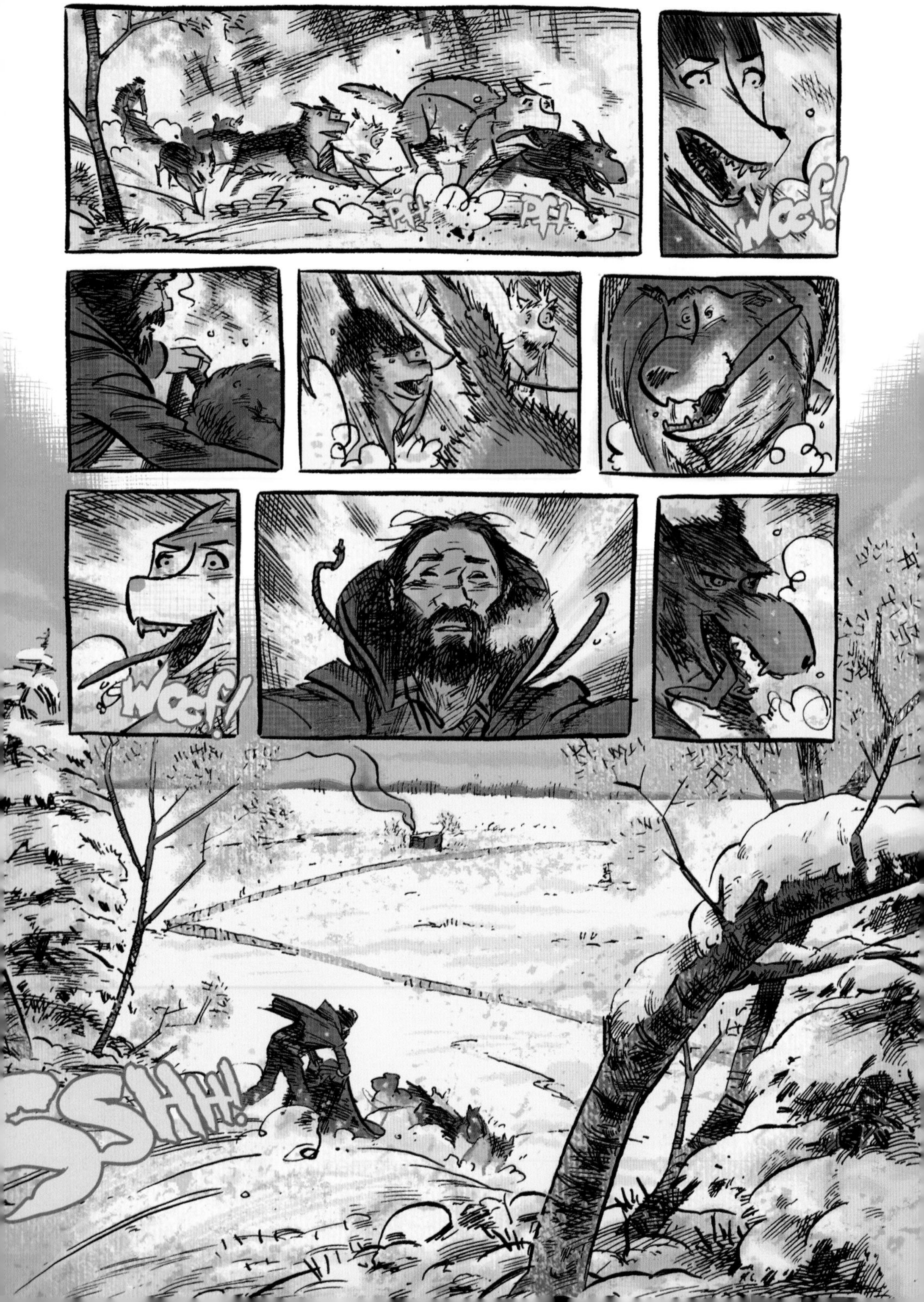
Pff!
Pff!
Woof!
Woof!
SHH!

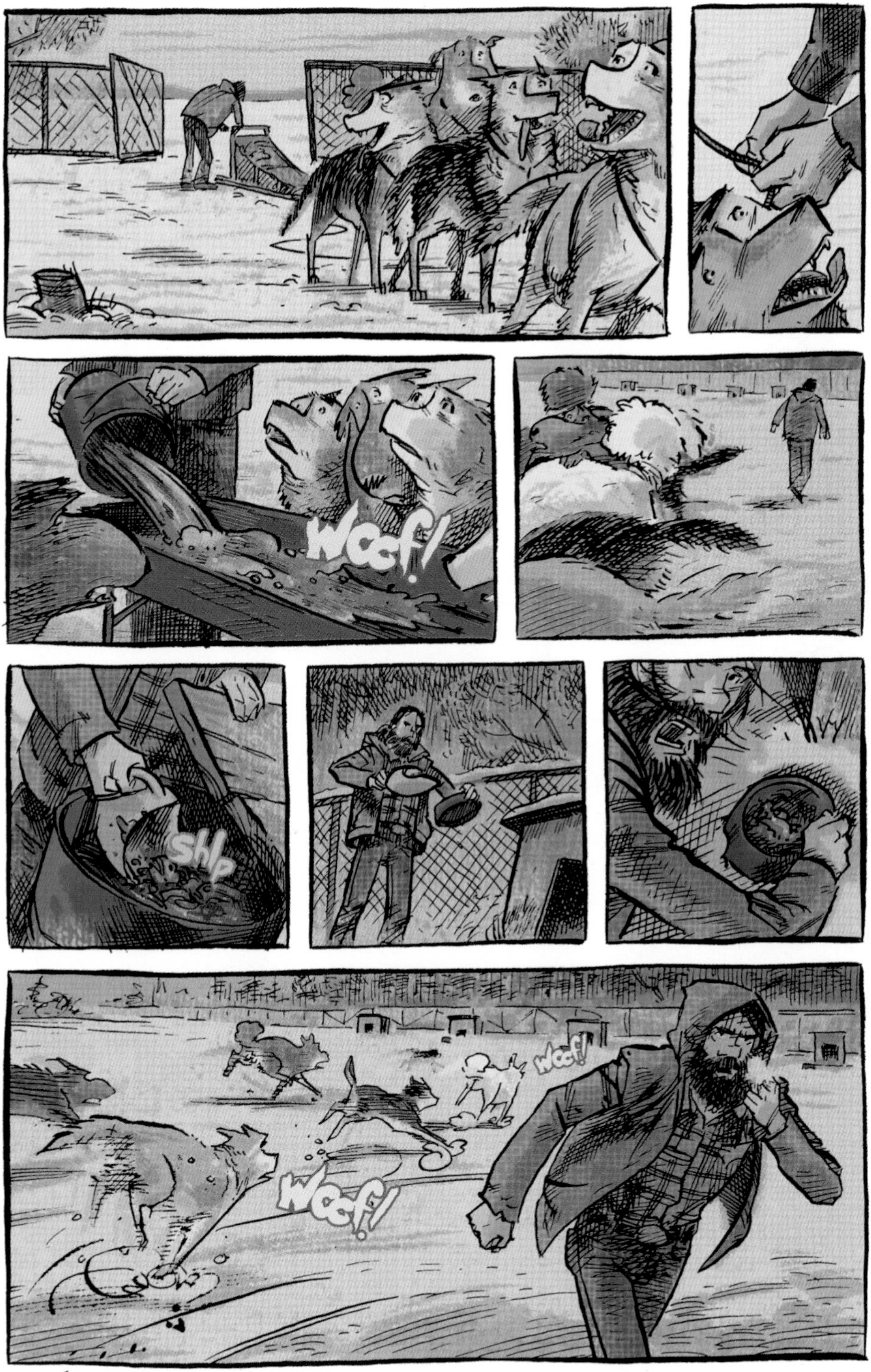
Woof!
shlp
Woof!
Woof!

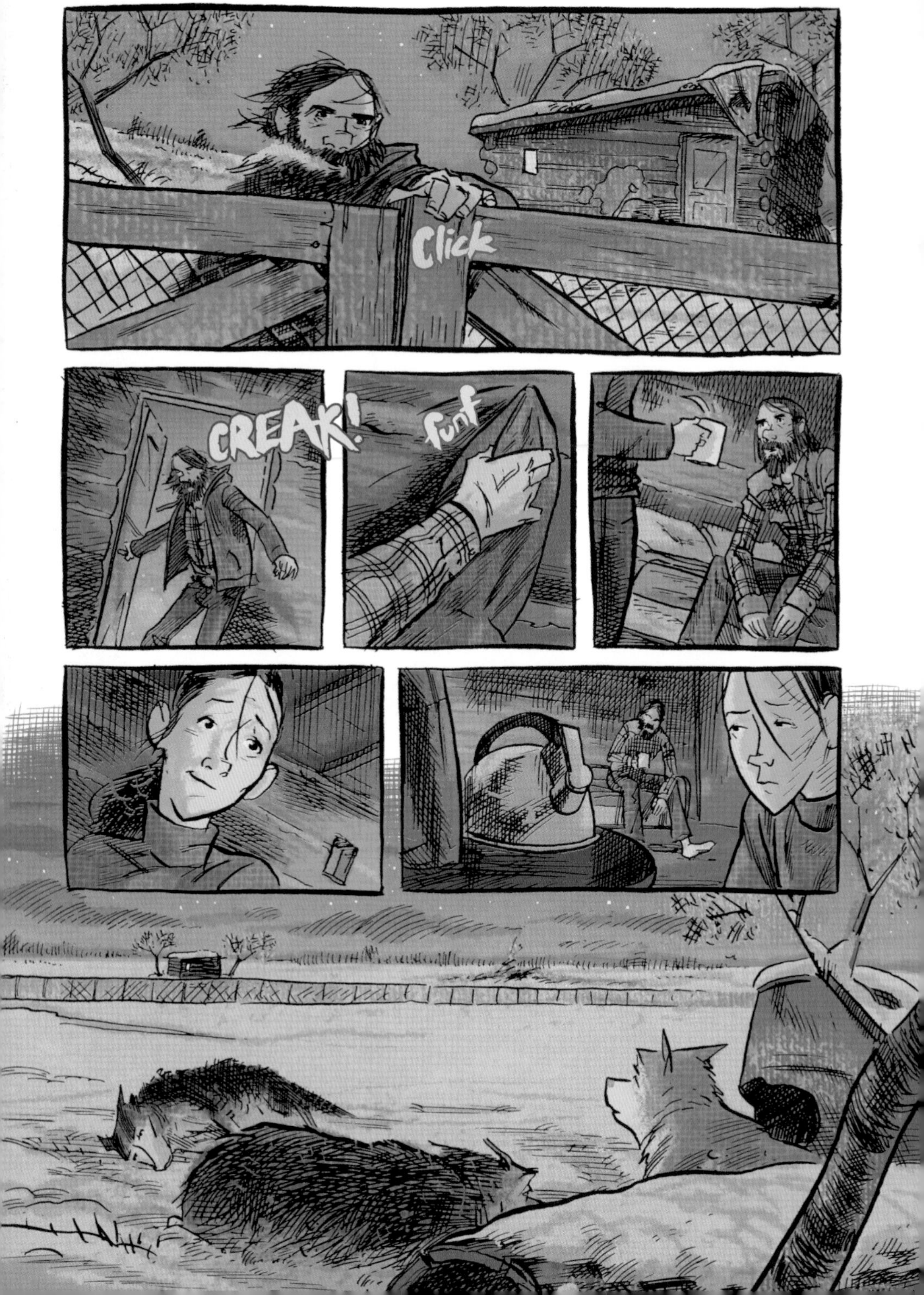
Click
CREAK!
funf

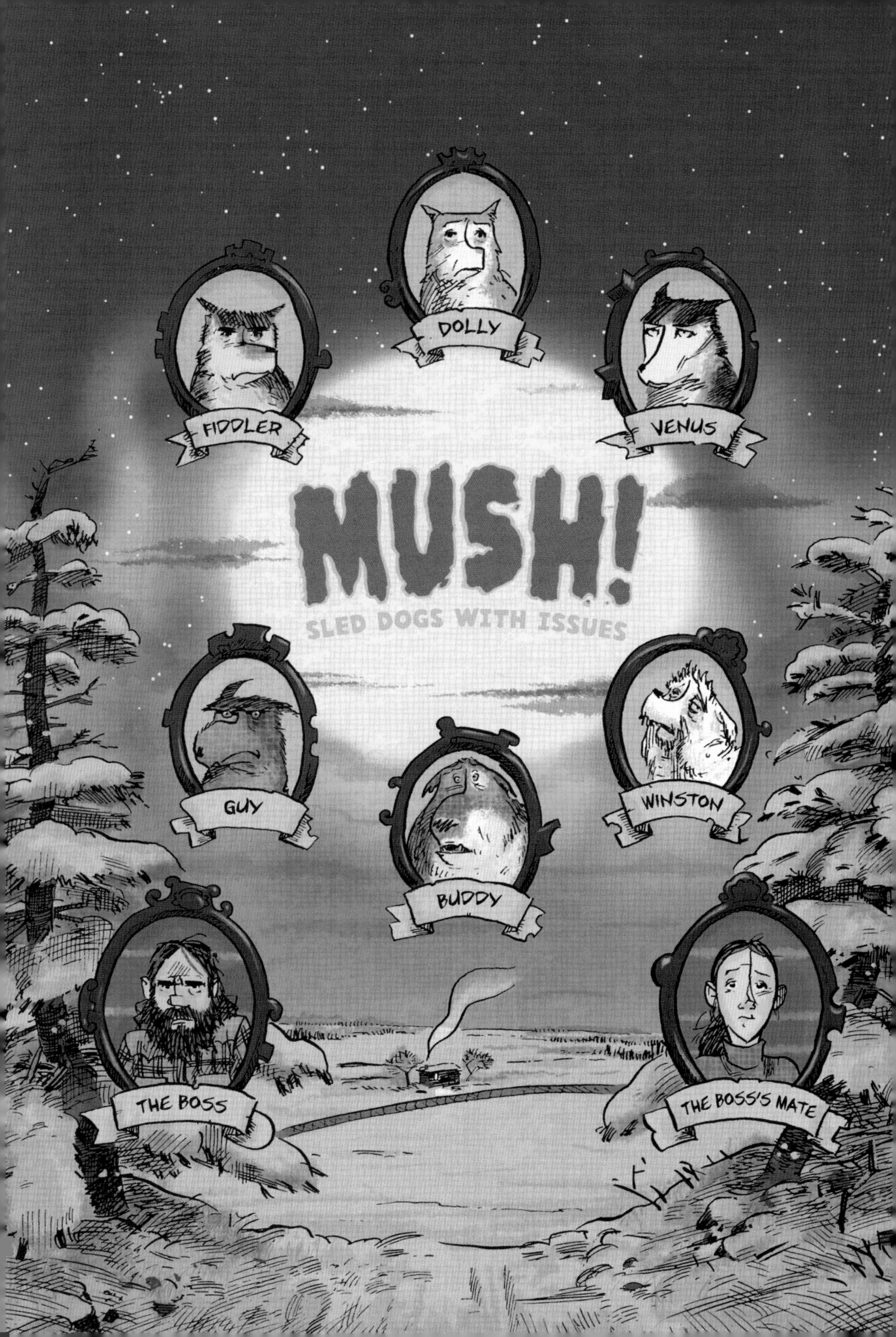
DOLLY
FIDDLER
VENUS
MUSH!
SLED DOGS WITH ISSUES
GUY
WINSTON
BUDDY
THE BOSS
THE BOSS'S MATE

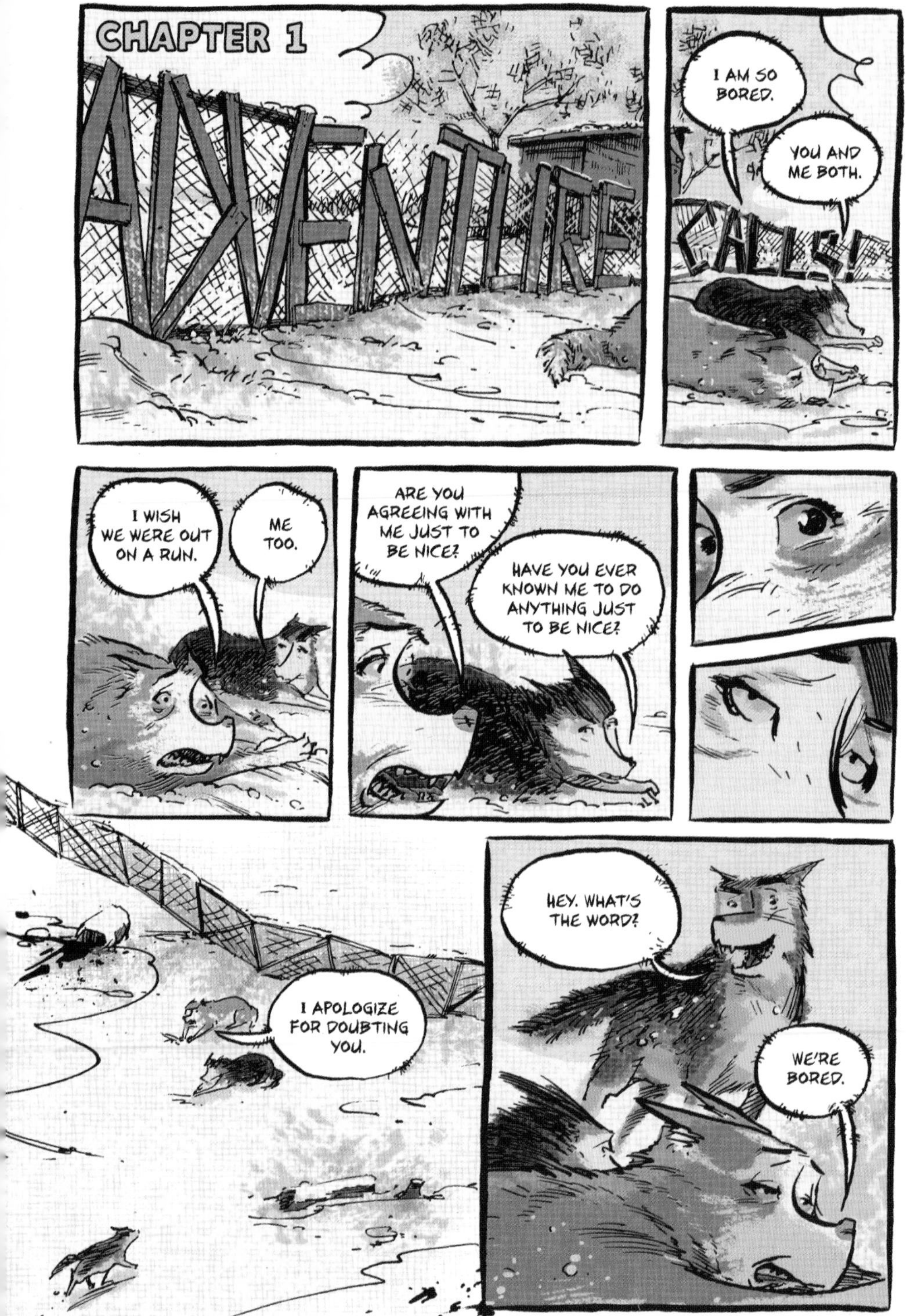
CHAPTER 1
ADVENTURE
CALLS!
I AM SO BORED.
YOU AND ME BOTH.
I WISH WE WERE OUT ON A RUN.
ME TOO.
ARE YOU AGREEING WITH ME JUST TO BE NICE?
HAVE YOU EVER KNOWN ME TO DO ANYTHING JUST TO BE NICE?
I APOLOGIZE FOR DOUBTING YOU.
HEY. WHAT'S THE WORD?
WE'RE BORED.

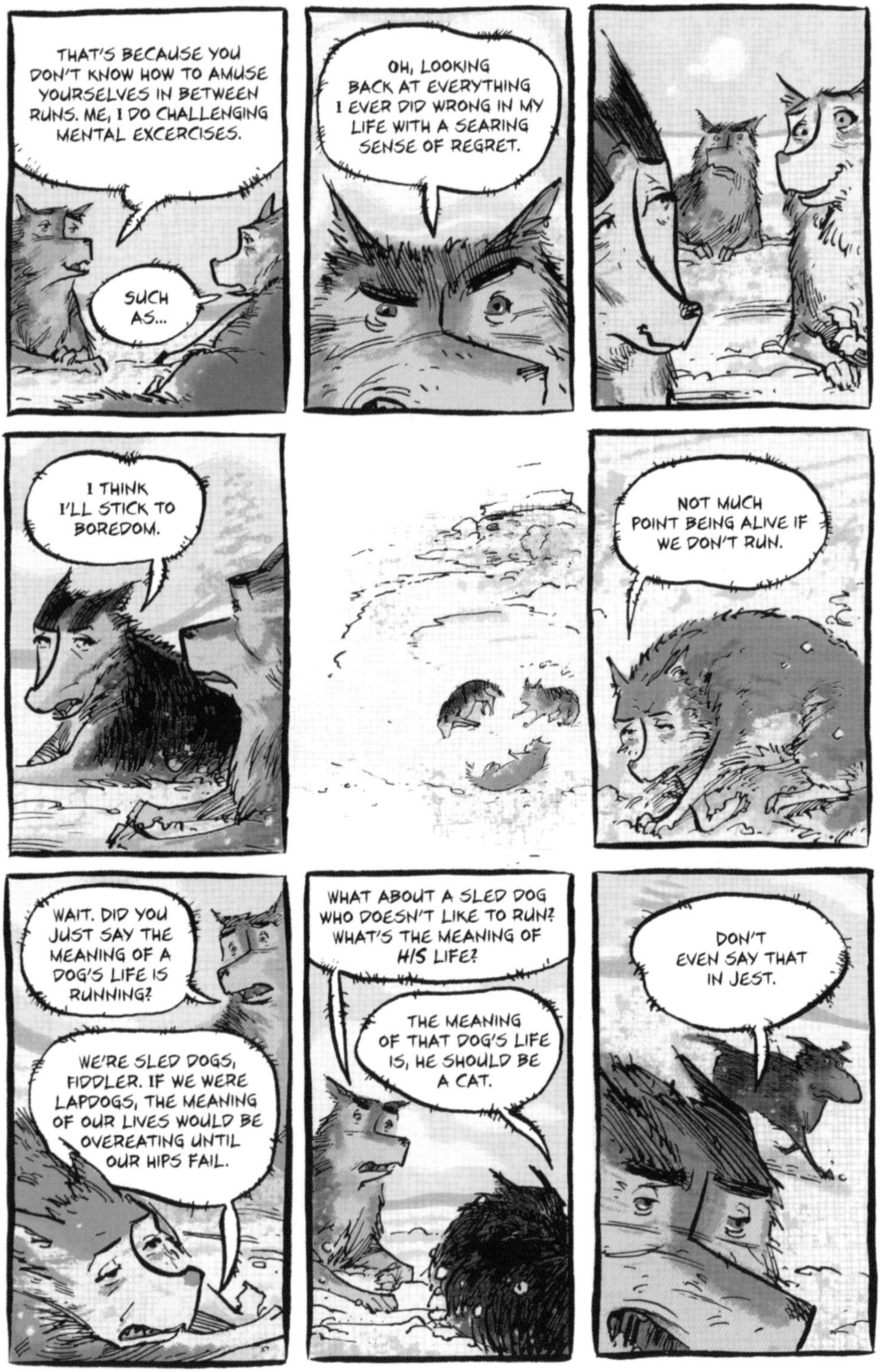
THAT'S BECAUSE YOU DON'T KNOW HOW TO AMUSE YOURSELVES IN BETWEEN RUNS. ME, I DO CHALLENGING MENTAL EXCERCISES.
SUCH AS...
OH, LOOKING BACK AT EVERYTHING I EVER DID WRONG IN MY LIFE WITH A SEARING SENSE OF REGRET.
I THINK I'LL STICK TO BOREDOM.
NOT MUCH POINT BEING ALIVE IF WE DON'T RUN.
WAIT. DID YOU JUST SAY THE MEANING OF A DOG'S LIFE IS RUNNING?
WE'RE SLED DOGS, FIDDLER. IF WE WERE LAPDOGS, THE MEANING OF OUR LIVES WOULD BE OVEREATING UNTIL OUR HIPS FAIL.
WHAT ABOUT A SLED DOG WHO DOESN'T LIKE TO RUN? WHAT'S THE MEANING OF *HIS* LIFE?
THE MEANING OF THAT DOG'S LIFE IS, HE SHOULD BE A CAT.
DON'T EVEN SAY THAT IN JEST.

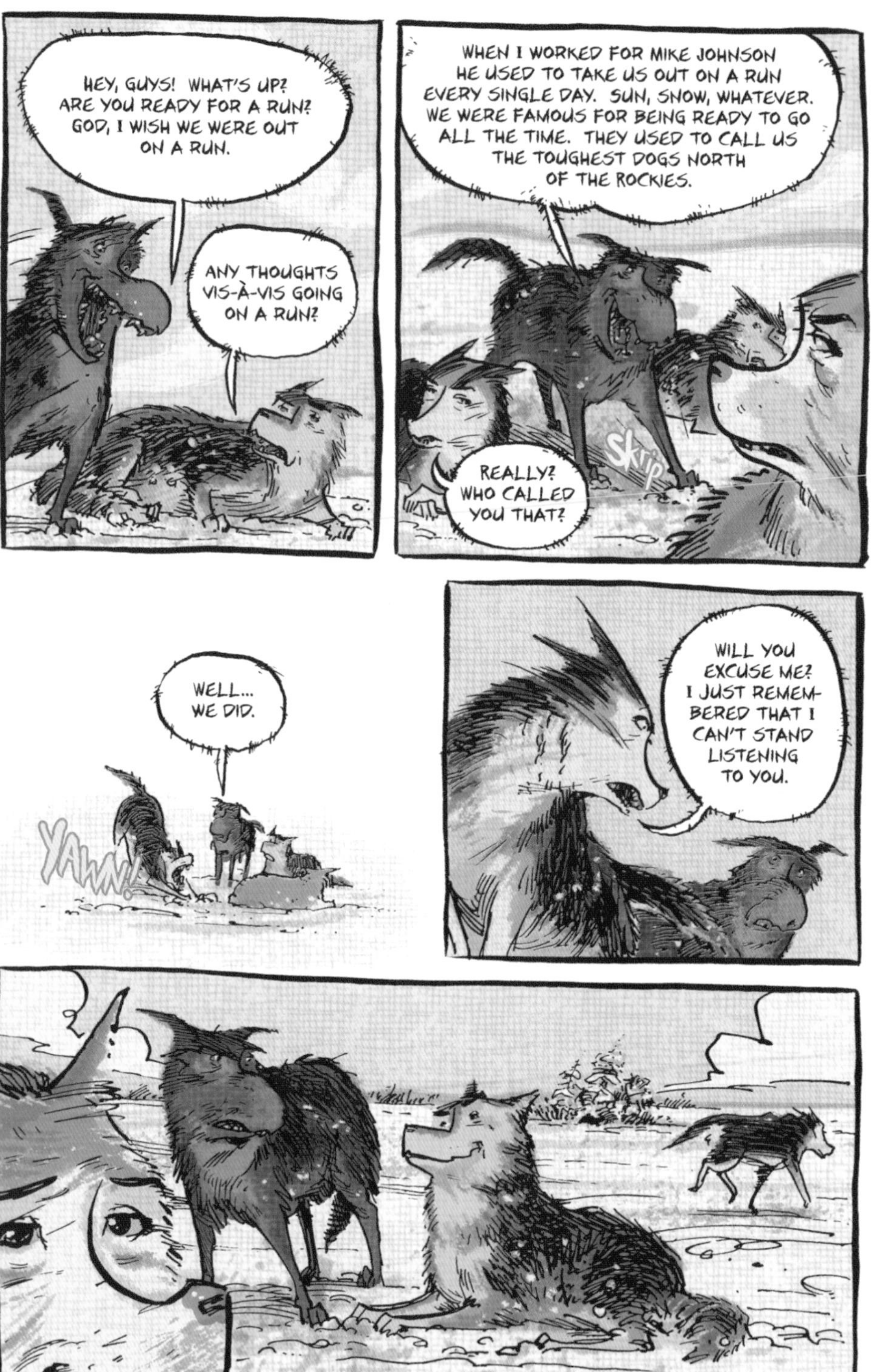
HEY, GUYS! WHAT'S UP? ARE YOU READY FOR A RUN? GOD, I WISH WE WERE OUT ON A RUN.
ANY THOUGHTS VIS-À-VIS GOING ON A RUN?
WHEN I WORKED FOR MIKE JOHNSON HE USED TO TAKE US OUT ON A RUN EVERY SINGLE DAY. SUN, SNOW, WHATEVER. WE WERE FAMOUS FOR BEING READY TO GO ALL THE TIME. THEY USED TO CALL US THE TOUGHEST DOGS NORTH OF THE ROCKIES.
SKRIP
REALLY? WHO CALLED YOU THAT?
WELL... WE DID.
YAWN!
WILL YOU EXCUSE ME? I JUST REMEMBERED THAT I CAN'T STAND LISTENING TO YOU.

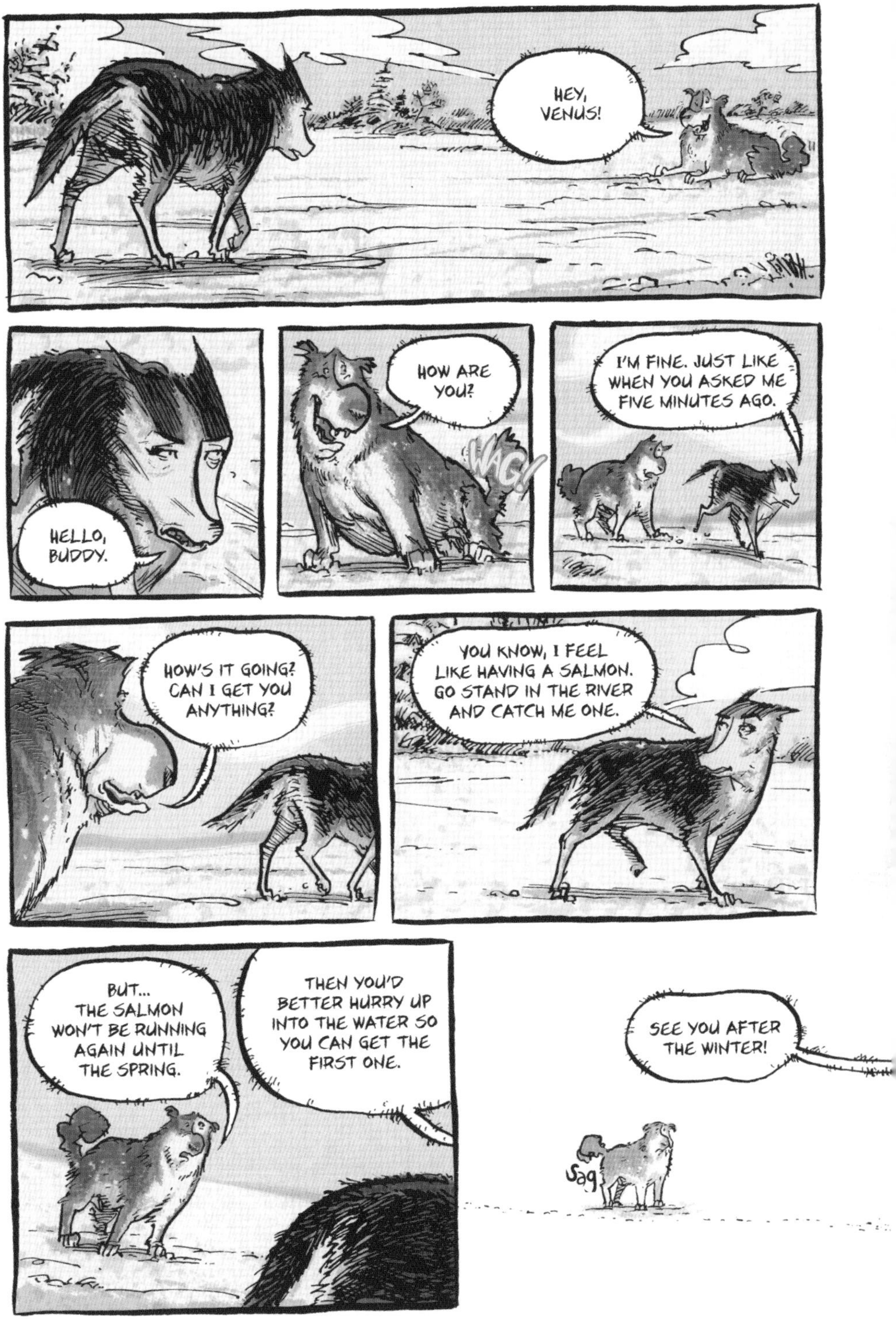
HEY, VENUS!
HELLO, BUDDY.
HOW ARE YOU?
WAG!
I'M FINE. JUST LIKE WHEN YOU ASKED ME FIVE MINUTES AGO.
HOW'S IT GOING? CAN I GET YOU ANYTHING?
YOU KNOW, I FEEL LIKE HAVING A SALMON. GO STAND IN THE RIVER AND CATCH ME ONE.
BUT... THE SALMON WON'T BE RUNNING AGAIN UNTIL THE SPRING.
THEN YOU'D BETTER HURRY UP INTO THE WATER SO YOU CAN GET THE FIRST ONE.
SEE YOU AFTER THE WINTER!
sag

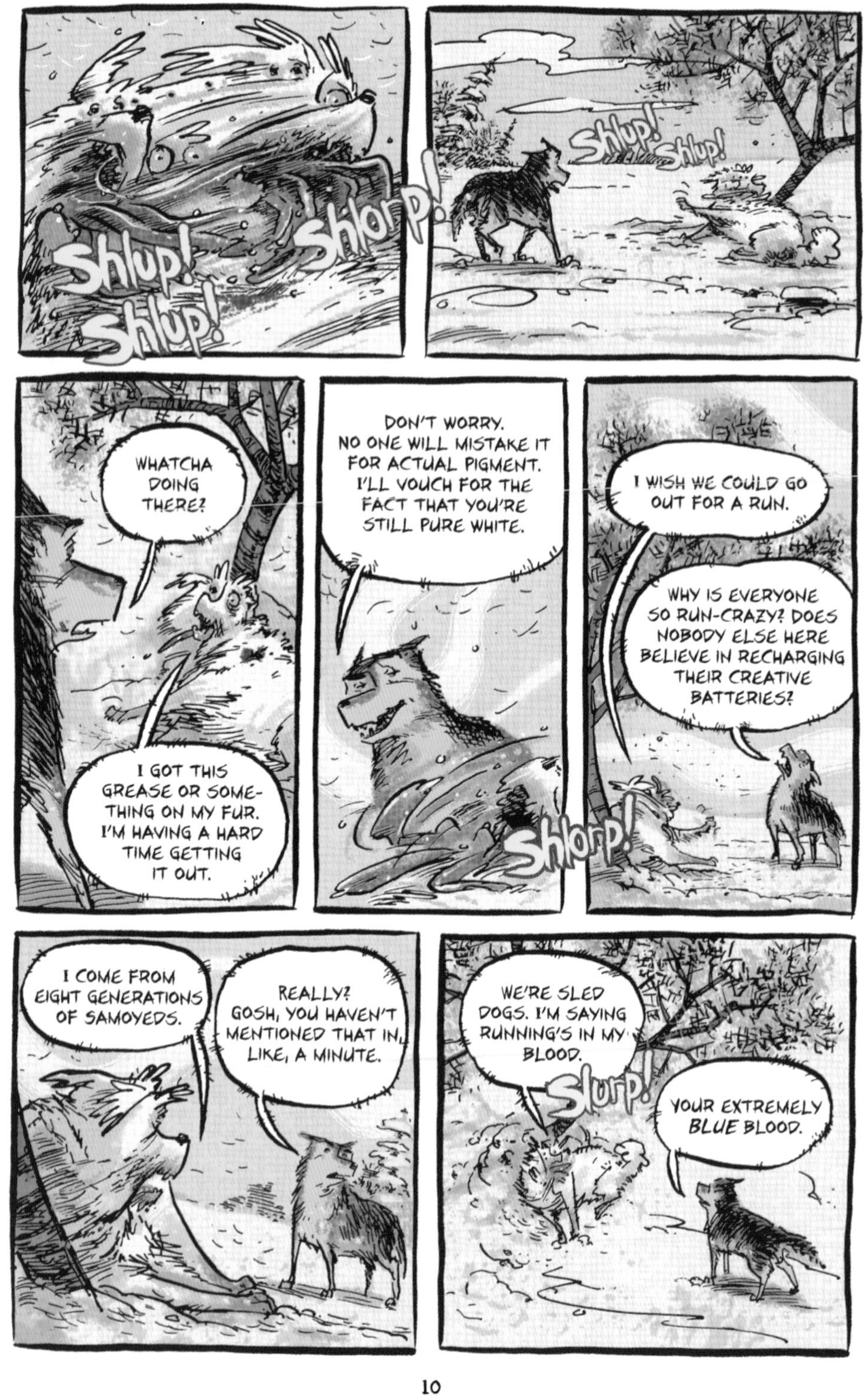
Shlup!
Shlup!
Shlorp!
Shlup!
Shlup!
WHATCHA DOING THERE?
I GOT THIS GREASE OR SOME-THING ON MY FUR. I'M HAVING A HARD TIME GETTING IT OUT.
DON'T WORRY. NO ONE WILL MISTAKE IT FOR ACTUAL PIGMENT. I'LL VOUCH FOR THE FACT THAT YOU'RE STILL PURE WHITE.
Shlorp!
I WISH WE COULD GO OUT FOR A RUN.
WHY IS EVERYONE SO RUN-CRAZY? DOES NOBODY ELSE HERE BELIEVE IN RECHARGING THEIR CREATIVE BATTERIES?
I COME FROM EIGHT GENERATIONS OF SAMOYEDS.
REALLY? GOSH, YOU HAVEN'T MENTIONED THAT IN, LIKE, A MINUTE.
WE'RE SLED DOGS. I'M SAYING RUNNING'S IN MY BLOOD.
Slurp!
YOUR EXTREMELY BLUE BLOOD.

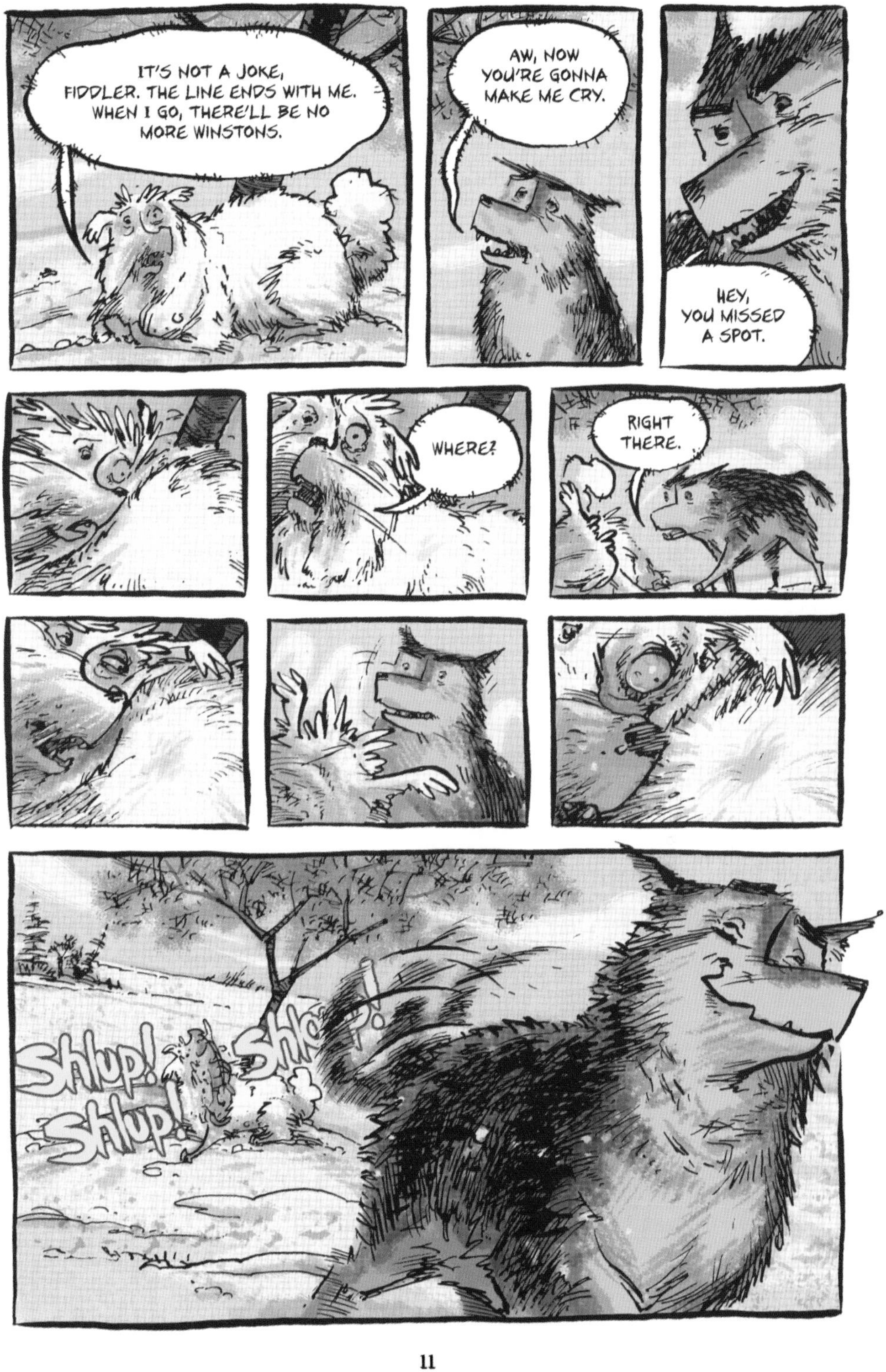
IT'S NOT A JOKE, FIDDLER. THE LINE ENDS WITH ME. WHEN I GO, THERE'LL BE NO MORE WINSTONS.
AW, NOW YOU'RE GONNA MAKE ME CRY.
HEY, YOU MISSED A SPOT.
WHERE?
RIGHT THERE.
Shlup! Shlup!

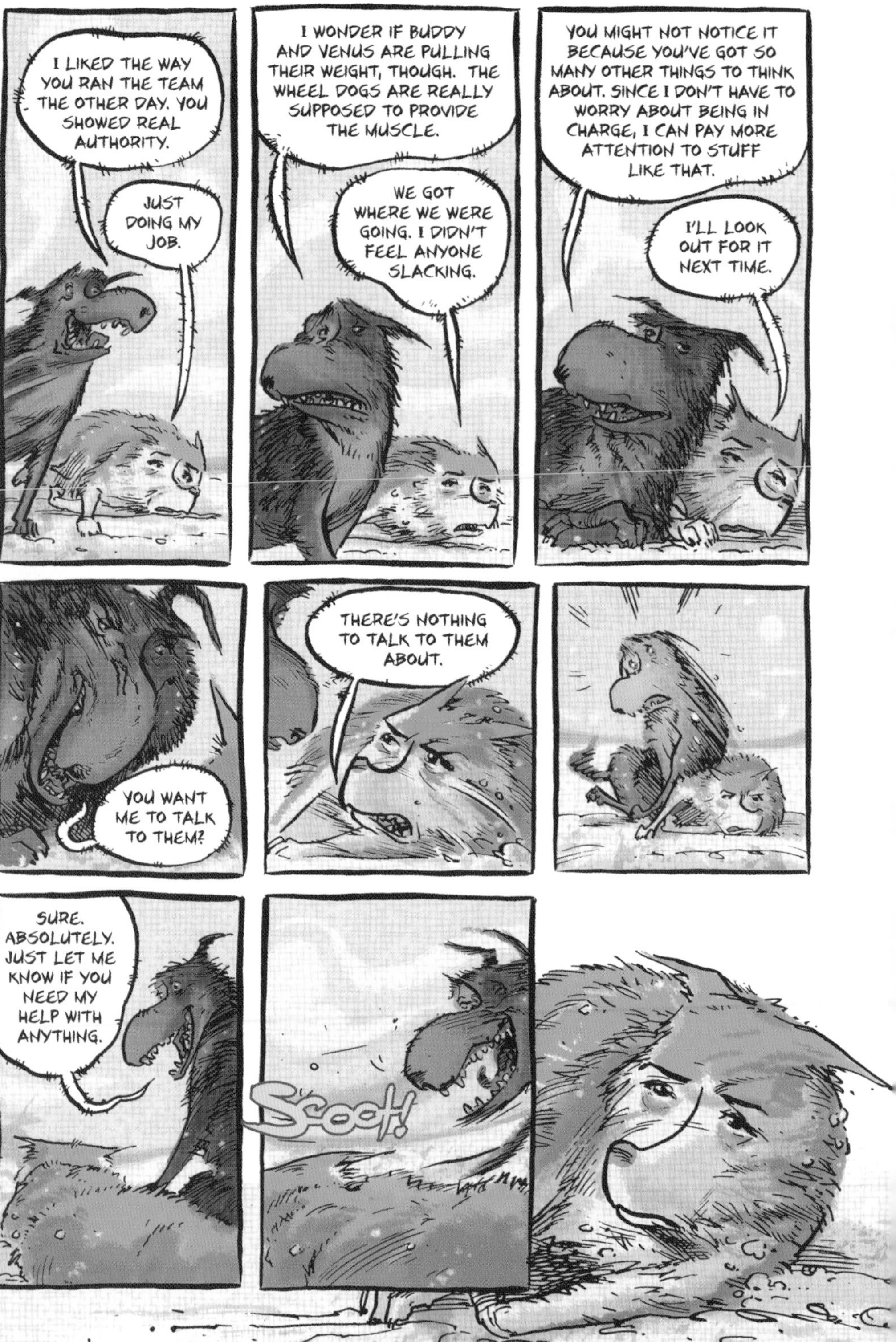
I LIKED THE WAY YOU RAN THE TEAM THE OTHER DAY. YOU SHOWED REAL AUTHORITY.
JUST DOING MY JOB.
I WONDER IF BUDDY AND VENUS ARE PULLING THEIR WEIGHT, THOUGH. THE WHEEL DOGS ARE REALLY SUPPOSED TO PROVIDE THE MUSCLE.
WE GOT WHERE WE WERE GOING. I DIDN'T FEEL ANYONE SLACKING.
YOU MIGHT NOT NOTICE IT BECAUSE YOU'VE GOT SO MANY OTHER THINGS TO THINK ABOUT. SINCE I DON'T HAVE TO WORRY ABOUT BEING IN CHARGE, I CAN PAY MORE ATTENTION TO STUFF LIKE THAT.
I'LL LOOK OUT FOR IT NEXT TIME.
YOU WANT ME TO TALK TO THEM?
THERE'S NOTHING TO TALK TO THEM ABOUT.
SURE. ABSOLUTELY. JUST LET ME KNOW IF YOU NEED MY HELP WITH ANYTHING.
SCOOT!

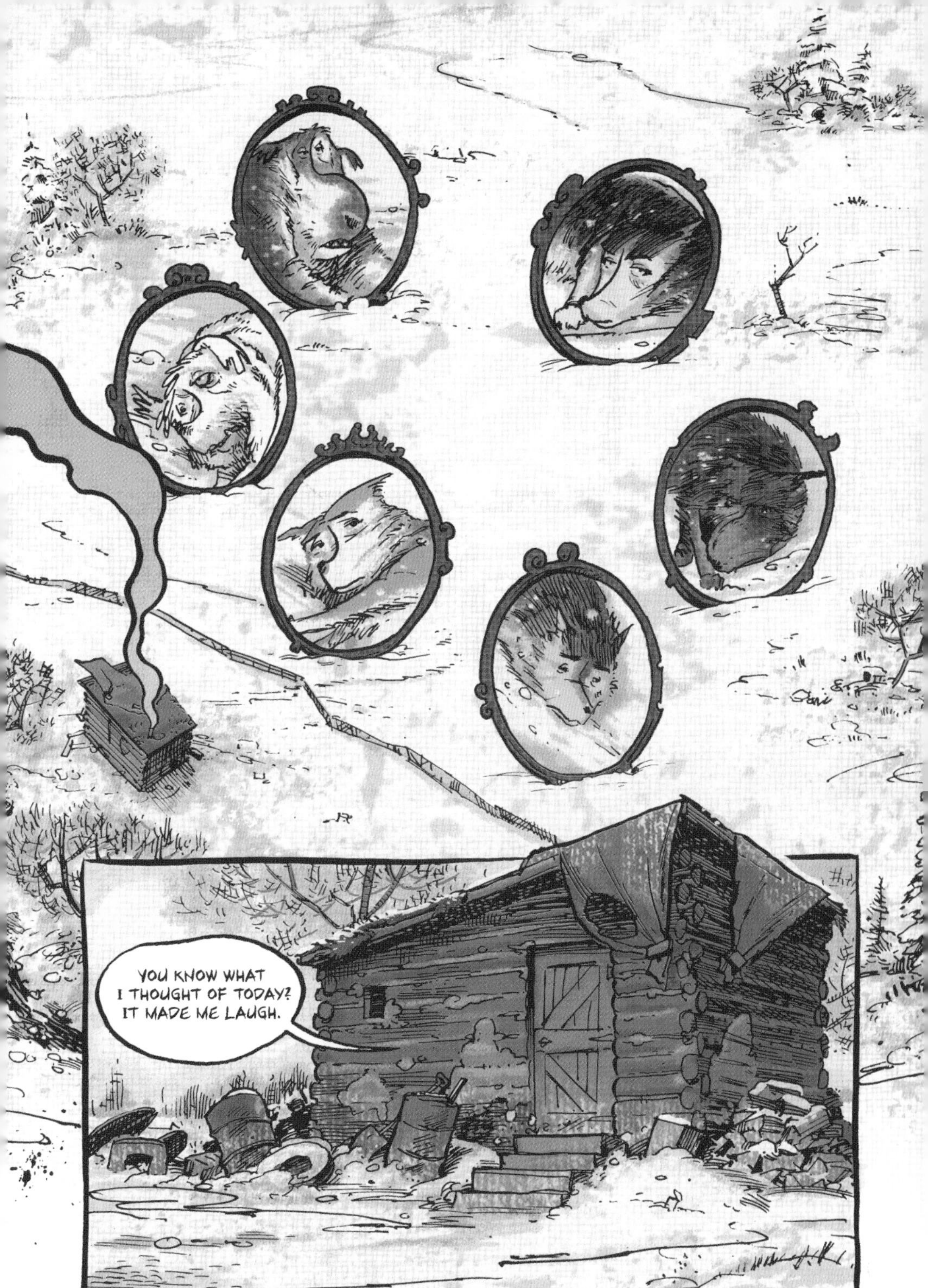
YOU KNOW WHAT I THOUGHT OF TODAY? IT MADE ME LAUGH.

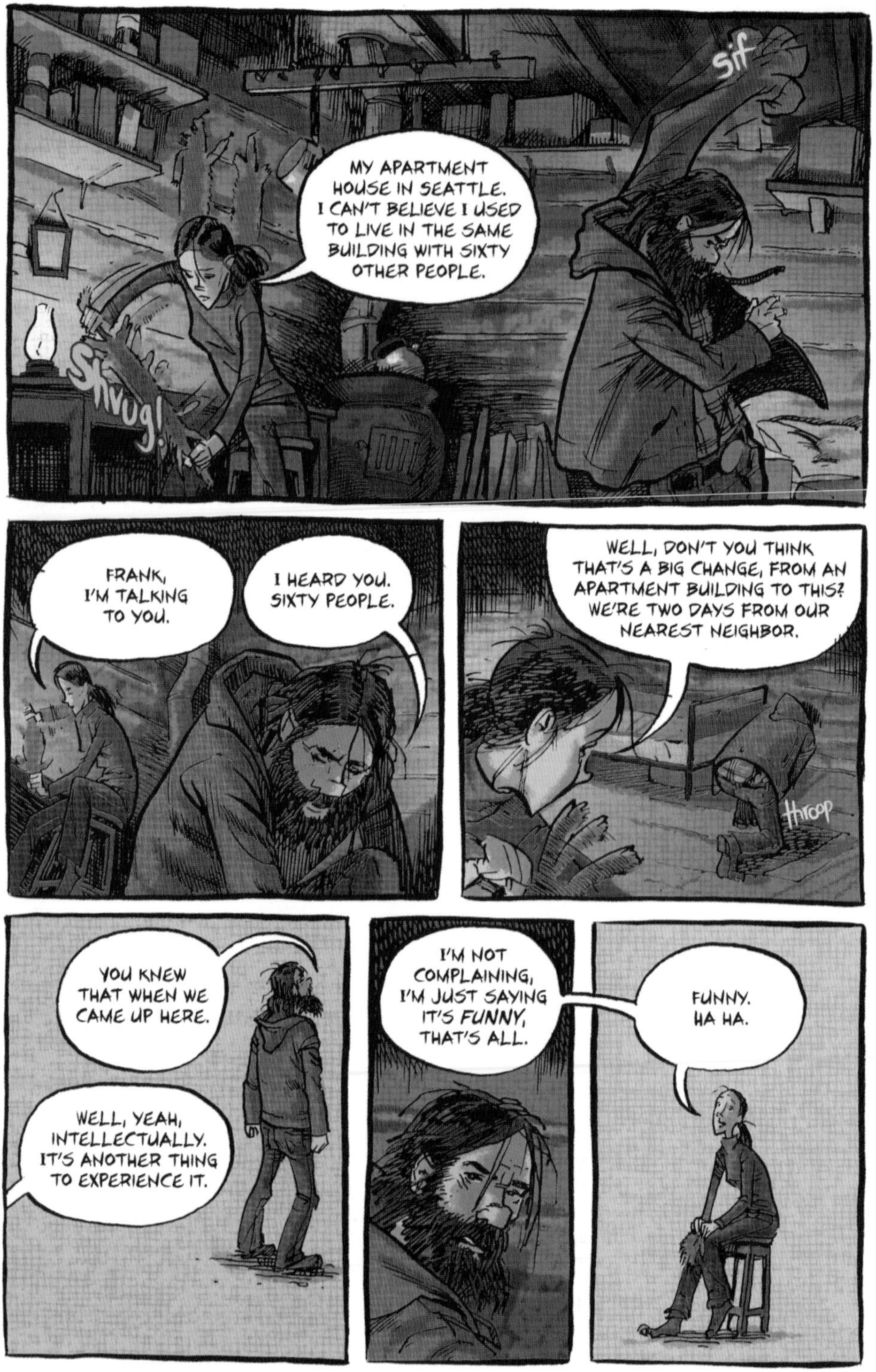
sif
MY APARTMENT HOUSE IN SEATTLE. I CAN'T BELIEVE I USED TO LIVE IN THE SAME BUILDING WITH SIXTY OTHER PEOPLE.
Shvug!
FRANK, I'M TALKING TO YOU.
I HEARD YOU. SIXTY PEOPLE.
WELL, DON'T YOU THINK THAT'S A BIG CHANGE, FROM AN APARTMENT BUILDING TO THIS? WE'RE TWO DAYS FROM OUR NEAREST NEIGHBOR.
Hroop
YOU KNEW THAT WHEN WE CAME UP HERE.
WELL, YEAH, INTELLECTUALLY. IT'S ANOTHER THING TO EXPERIENCE IT.
I'M NOT COMPLAINING, I'M JUST SAYING IT'S FUNNY, THAT'S ALL.
FUNNY. HA HA.

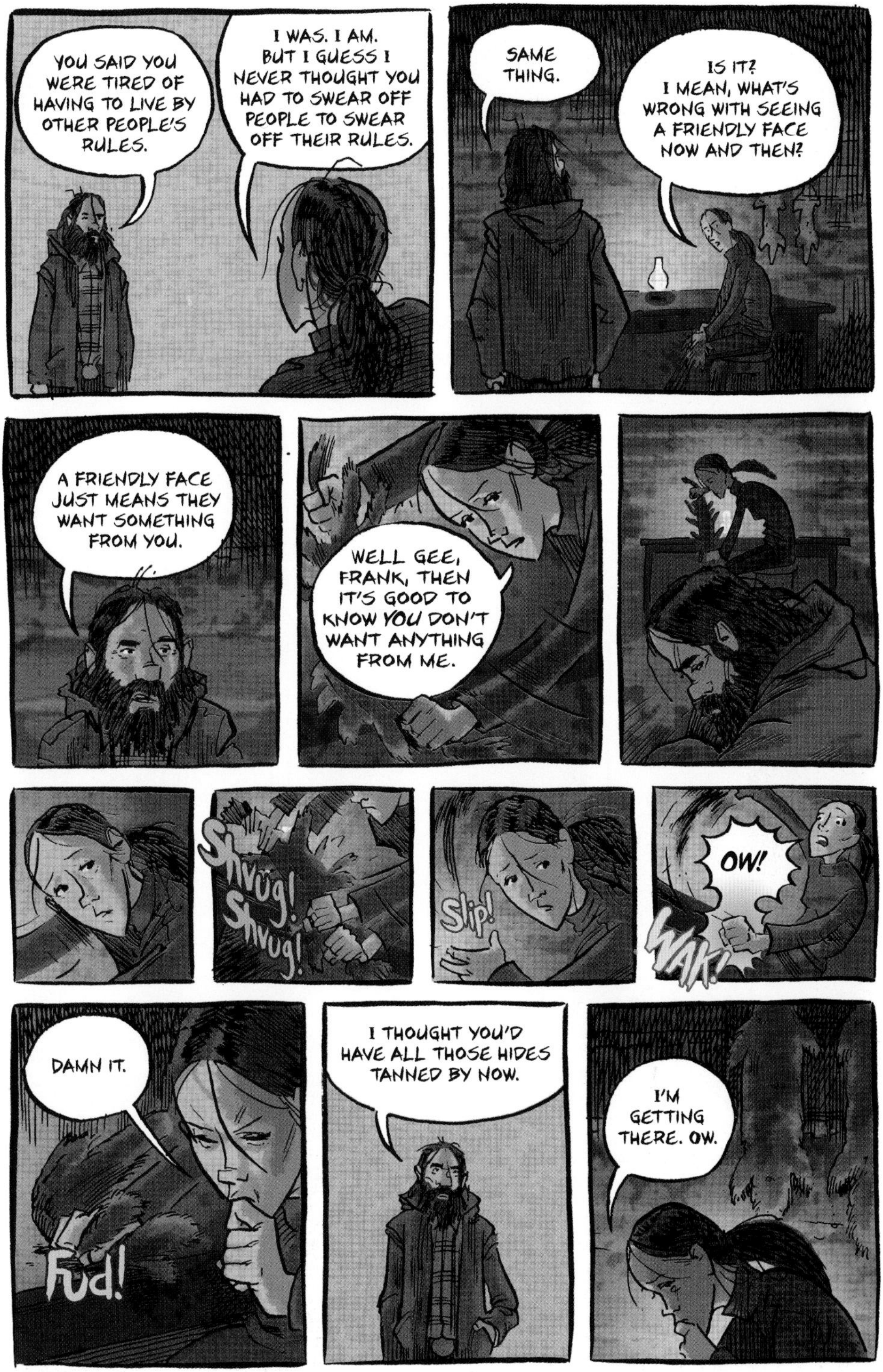
YOU SAID YOU WERE TIRED OF HAVING TO LIVE BY OTHER PEOPLE'S RULES.
I WAS. I AM. BUT I GUESS I NEVER THOUGHT YOU HAD TO SWEAR OFF PEOPLE TO SWEAR OFF THEIR RULES.
SAME THING.
IS IT? I MEAN, WHAT'S WRONG WITH SEEING A FRIENDLY FACE NOW AND THEN?
A FRIENDLY FACE JUST MEANS THEY WANT SOMETHING FROM YOU.
WELL GEE, FRANK, THEN IT'S GOOD TO KNOW YOU DON'T WANT ANYTHING FROM ME.
Shvug! Shvug!
Slip!
OW!
WAK!
DAMN IT.
Fud!
I THOUGHT YOU'D HAVE ALL THOSE HIDES TANNED BY NOW.
I'M GETTING THERE. OW.

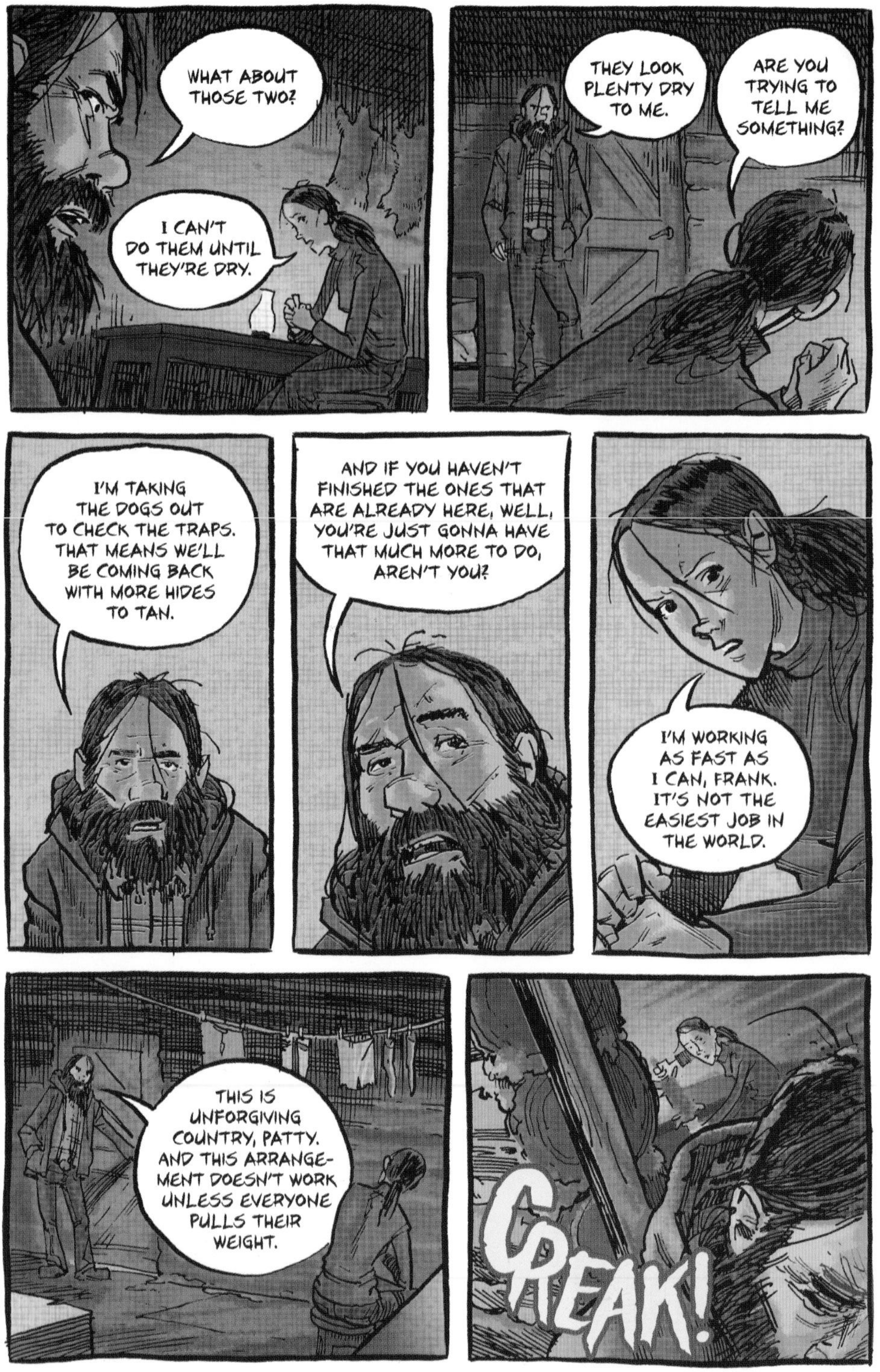
WHAT ABOUT THOSE TWO?
I CAN'T DO THEM UNTIL THEY'RE DRY.
THEY LOOK PLENTY DRY TO ME.
ARE YOU TRYING TO TELL ME SOMETHING?
I'M TAKING THE DOGS OUT TO CHECK THE TRAPS. THAT MEANS WE'LL BE COMING BACK WITH MORE HIDES TO TAN.
AND IF YOU HAVEN'T FINISHED THE ONES THAT ARE ALREADY HERE, WELL, YOU'RE JUST GONNA HAVE THAT MUCH MORE TO DO, AREN'T YOU?
I'M WORKING AS FAST AS I CAN, FRANK. IT'S NOT THE EASIEST JOB IN THE WORLD.
THIS IS UNFORGIVING COUNTRY, PATTY. AND THIS ARRANGEMENT DOESN'T WORK UNLESS EVERYONE PULLS THEIR WEIGHT.
CREAK!

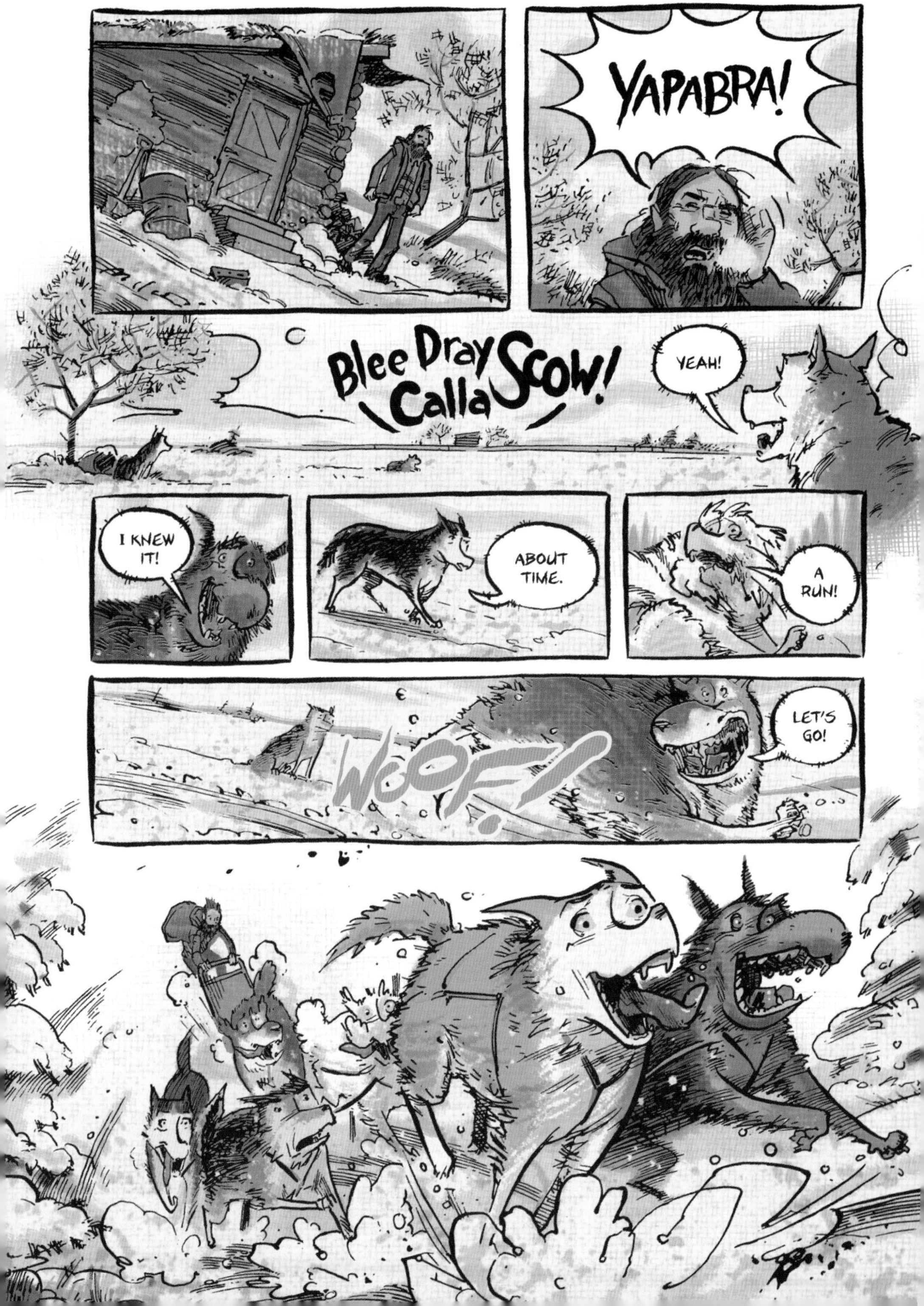
YAPABRA!
Blee Dray Calla Scow!
YEAH!
I KNEW IT!
ABOUT TIME.
A RUN!
WOOF!
LET'S GO!

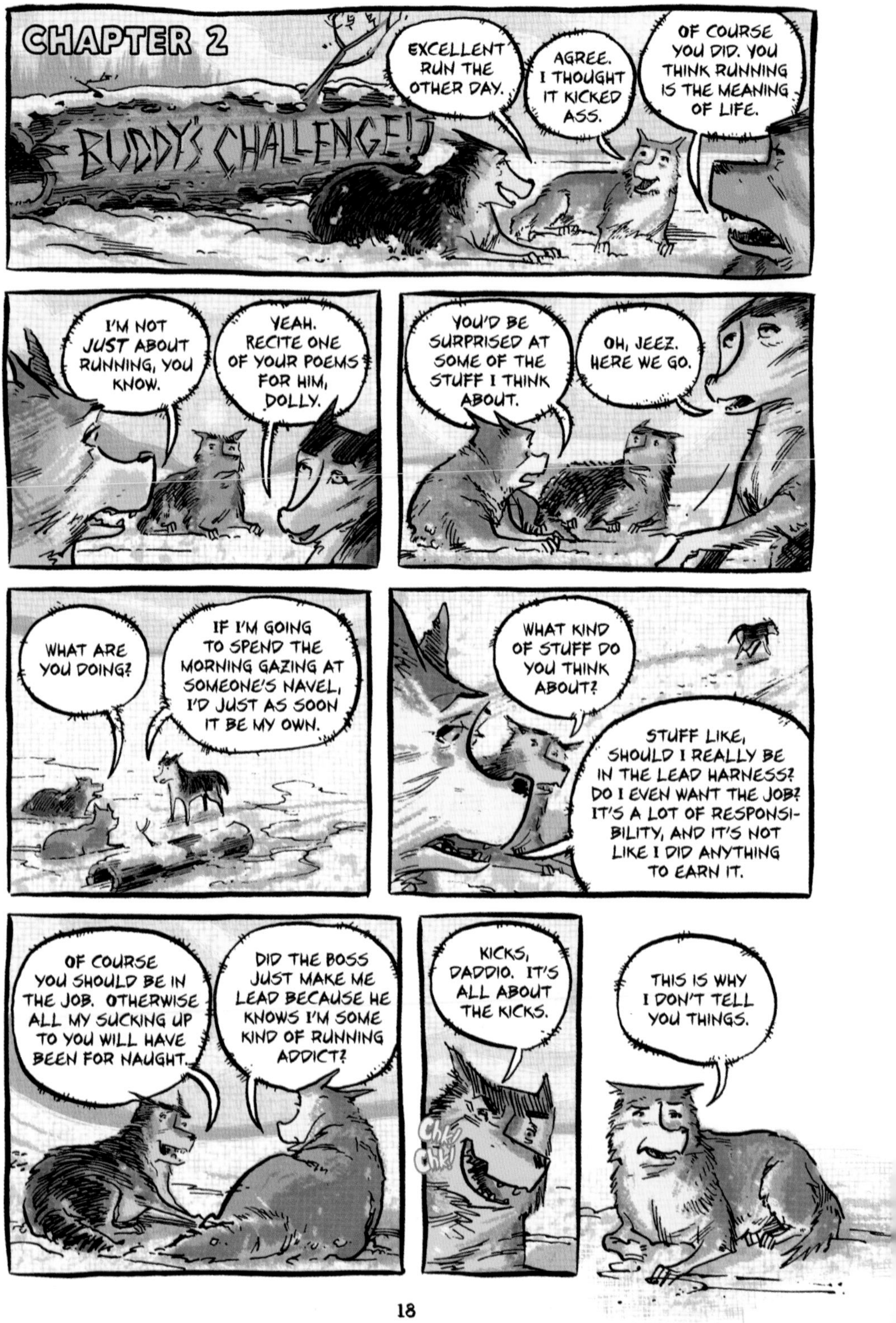
CHAPTER 2
BUDDY'S CHALLENGE!
EXCELLENT RUN THE OTHER DAY.
AGREE. I THOUGHT IT KICKED ASS.
OF COURSE YOU DID. YOU THINK RUNNING IS THE MEANING OF LIFE.
I'M NOT JUST ABOUT RUNNING, YOU KNOW.
YEAH. RECITE ONE OF YOUR POEMS FOR HIM, DOLLY.
YOU'D BE SURPRISED AT SOME OF THE STUFF I THINK ABOUT.
OH, JEEZ. HERE WE GO.
WHAT ARE YOU DOING?
IF I'M GOING TO SPEND THE MORNING GAZING AT SOMEONE'S NAVEL, I'D JUST AS SOON IT BE MY OWN.
WHAT KIND OF STUFF DO YOU THINK ABOUT?
STUFF LIKE, SHOULD I REALLY BE IN THE LEAD HARNESS? DO I EVEN WANT THE JOB? IT'S A LOT OF RESPONSI-BILITY, AND IT'S NOT LIKE I DID ANYTHING TO EARN IT.
OF COURSE YOU SHOULD BE IN THE JOB. OTHERWISE ALL MY SUCKING UP TO YOU WILL HAVE BEEN FOR NAUGHT.
DID THE BOSS JUST MAKE ME LEAD BECAUSE HE KNOWS I'M SOME KIND OF RUNNING ADDICT?
KICKS, DADDIO. IT'S ALL ABOUT THE KICKS.
CHK! CHK!
THIS IS WHY I DON'T TELL YOU THINGS.

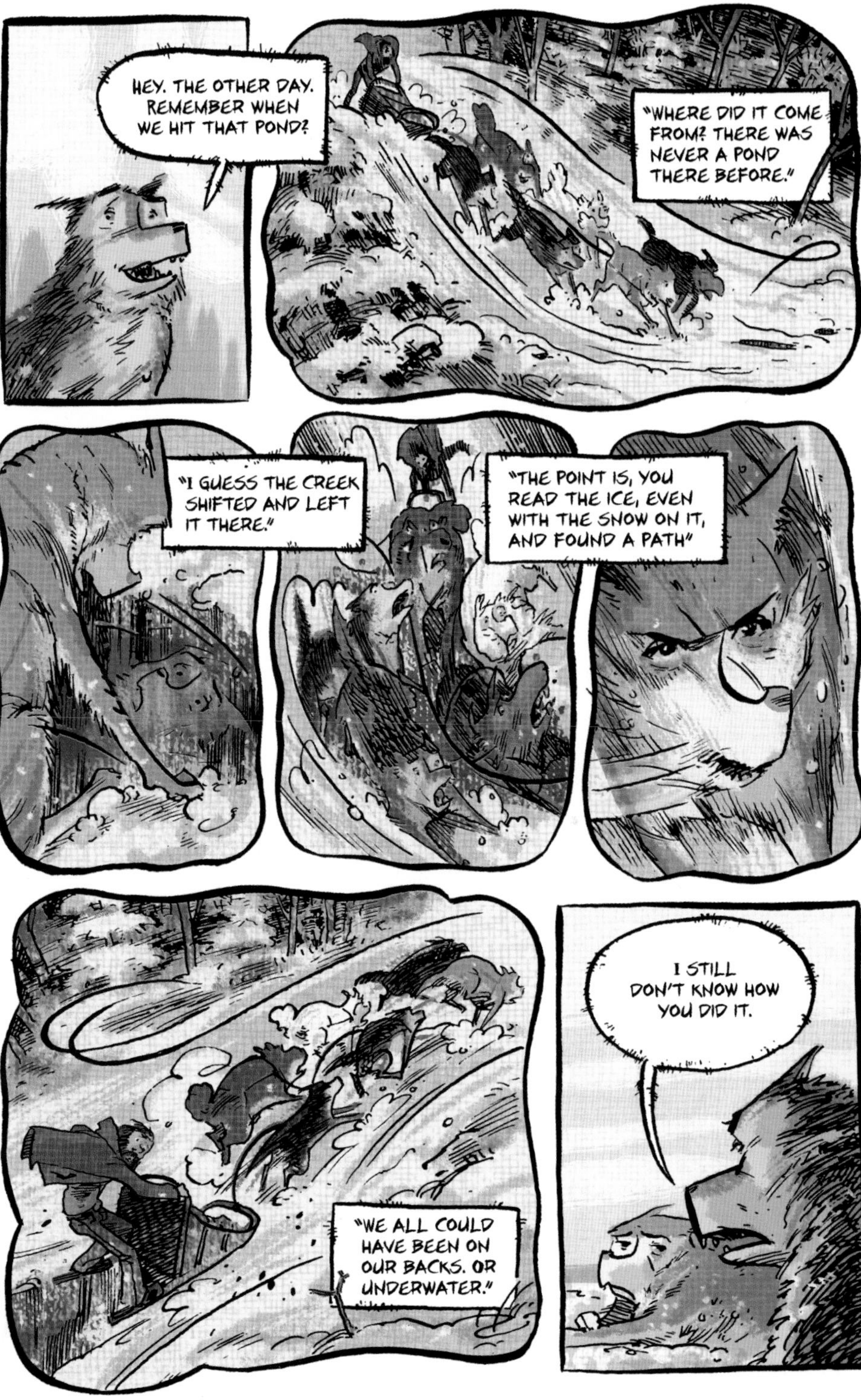
HEY. THE OTHER DAY. REMEMBER WHEN WE HIT THAT POND?
"WHERE DID IT COME FROM? THERE WAS NEVER A POND THERE BEFORE."
"I GUESS THE CREEK SHIFTED AND LEFT IT THERE."
"THE POINT IS, YOU READ THE ICE, EVEN WITH THE SNOW ON IT, AND FOUND A PATH"
"WE ALL COULD HAVE BEEN ON OUR BACKS. OR UNDERWATER."
I STILL DON'T KNOW HOW YOU DID IT.

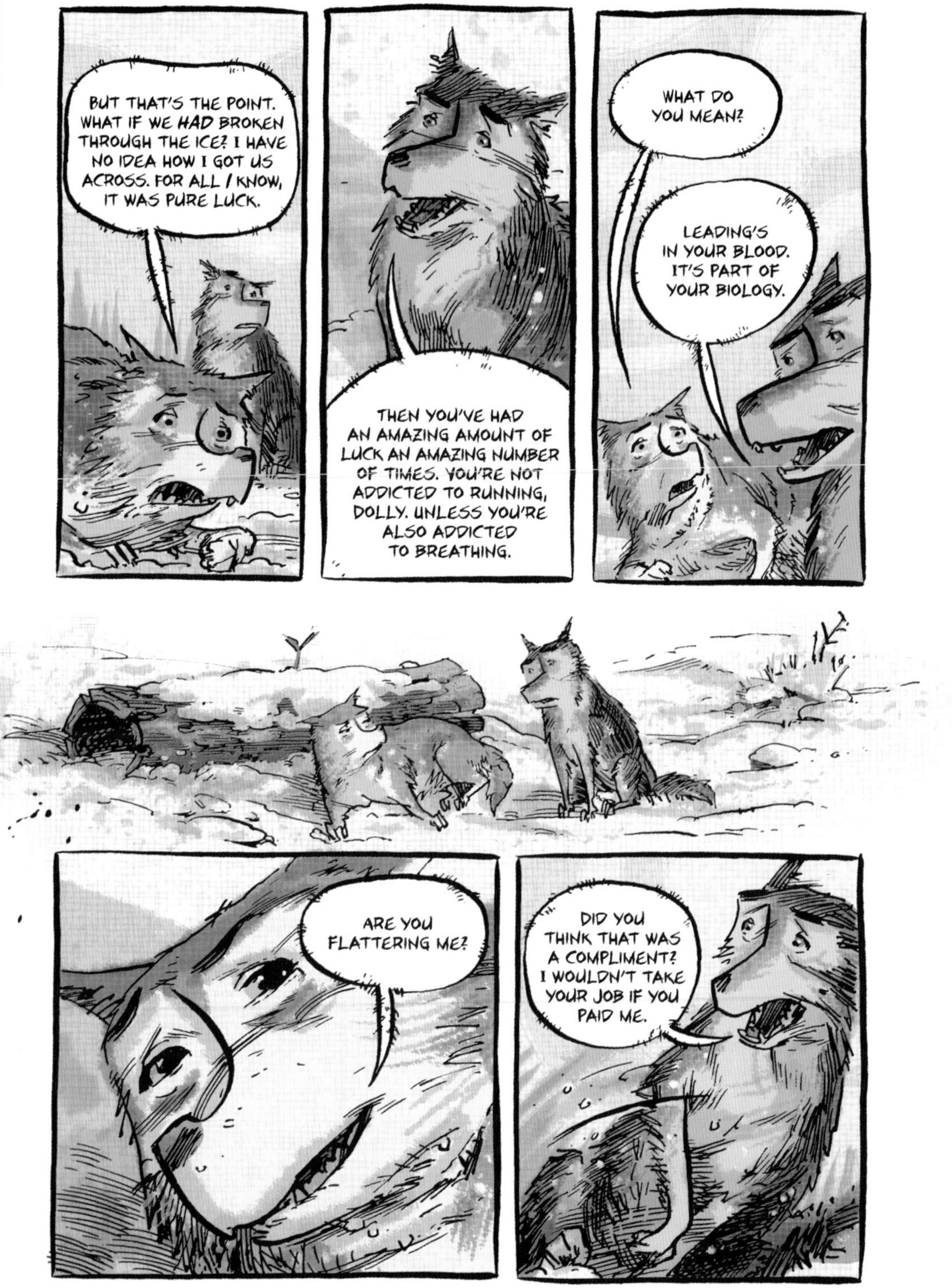
BUT THAT'S THE POINT. WHAT IF WE HAD BROKEN THROUGH THE ICE? I HAVE NO IDEA HOW I GOT US ACROSS. FOR ALL I KNOW, IT WAS PURE LUCK.
THEN YOU'VE HAD AN AMAZING AMOUNT OF LUCK AN AMAZING NUMBER OF TIMES. YOU'RE NOT ADDICTED TO RUNNING, DOLLY. UNLESS YOU'RE ALSO ADDICTED TO BREATHING.
WHAT DO YOU MEAN?
LEADING'S IN YOUR BLOOD. IT'S PART OF YOUR BIOLOGY.
ARE YOU FLATTERING ME?
DID YOU THINK THAT WAS A COMPLIMENT? I WOULDN'T TAKE YOUR JOB IF YOU PAID ME.

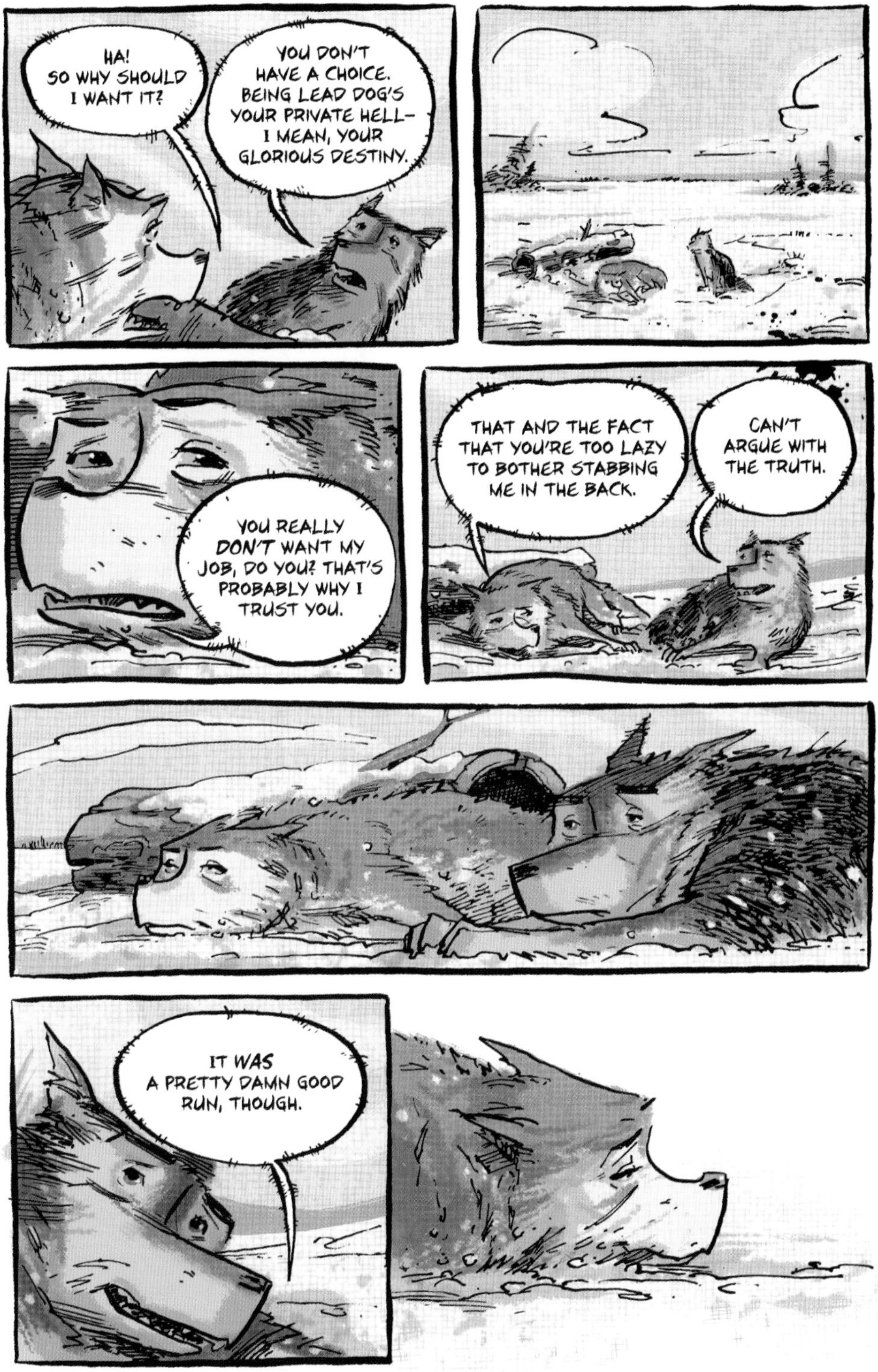
HA! SO WHY SHOULD I WANT IT?
YOU DON'T HAVE A CHOICE. BEING LEAD DOG'S YOUR PRIVATE HELL— I MEAN, YOUR GLORIOUS DESTINY.
YOU REALLY DON'T WANT MY JOB, DO YOU? THAT'S PROBABLY WHY I TRUST YOU.
THAT AND THE FACT THAT YOU'RE TOO LAZY TO BOTHER STABBING ME IN THE BACK.
CAN'T ARGUE WITH THE TRUTH.
IT WAS A PRETTY DAMN GOOD RUN, THOUGH.

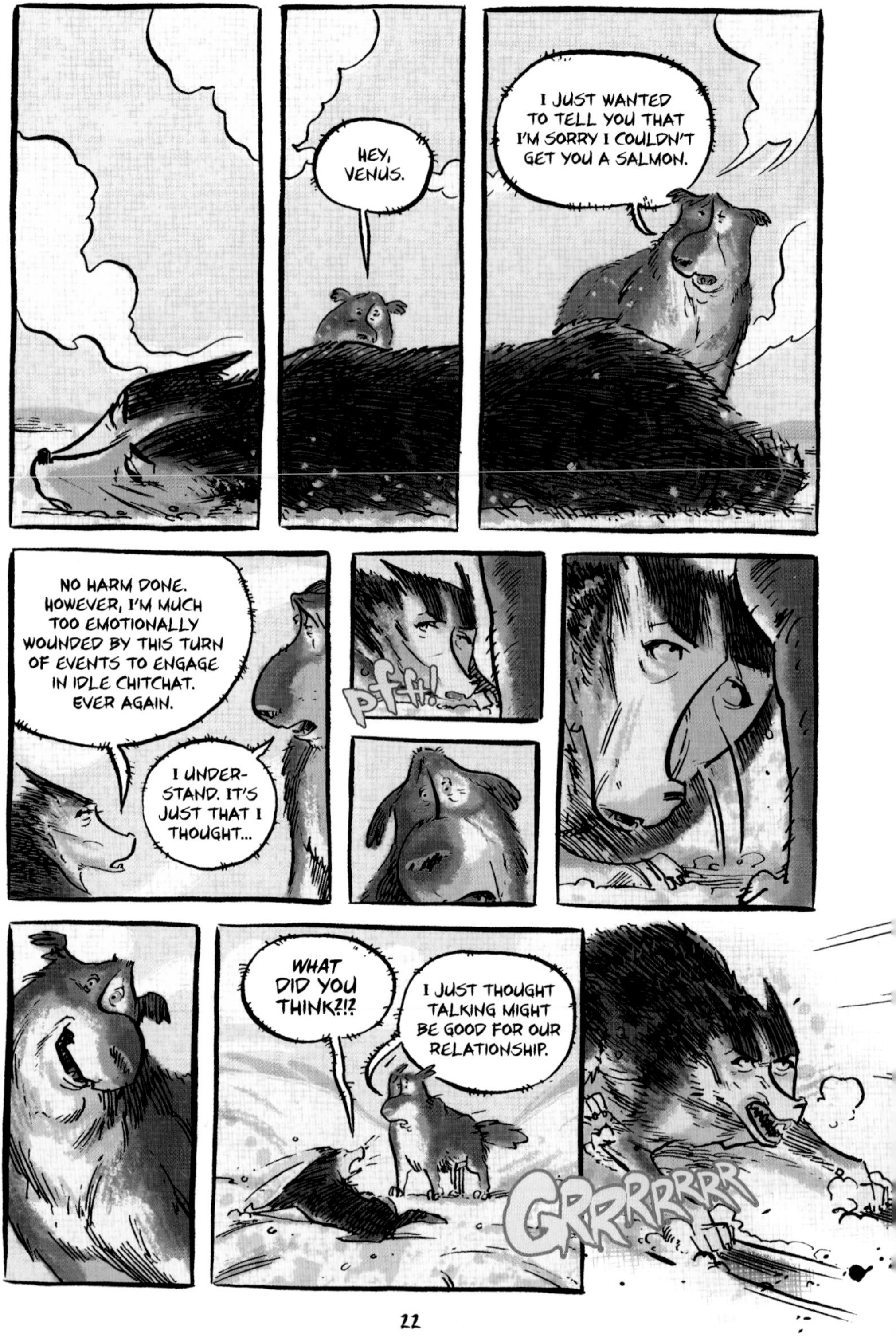

HEY, VENUS.
I JUST WANTED TO TELL YOU THAT I'M SORRY I COULDN'T GET YOU A SALMON.
NO HARM DONE. HOWEVER, I'M MUCH TOO EMOTIONALLY WOUNDED BY THIS TURN OF EVENTS TO ENGAGE IN IDLE CHITCHAT. EVER AGAIN.
I UNDER-STAND. IT'S JUST THAT I THOUGHT...
pfft!
WHAT DID YOU THINK?!?
I JUST THOUGHT TALKING MIGHT BE GOOD FOR OUR RELATIONSHIP.
GRRRRRRR

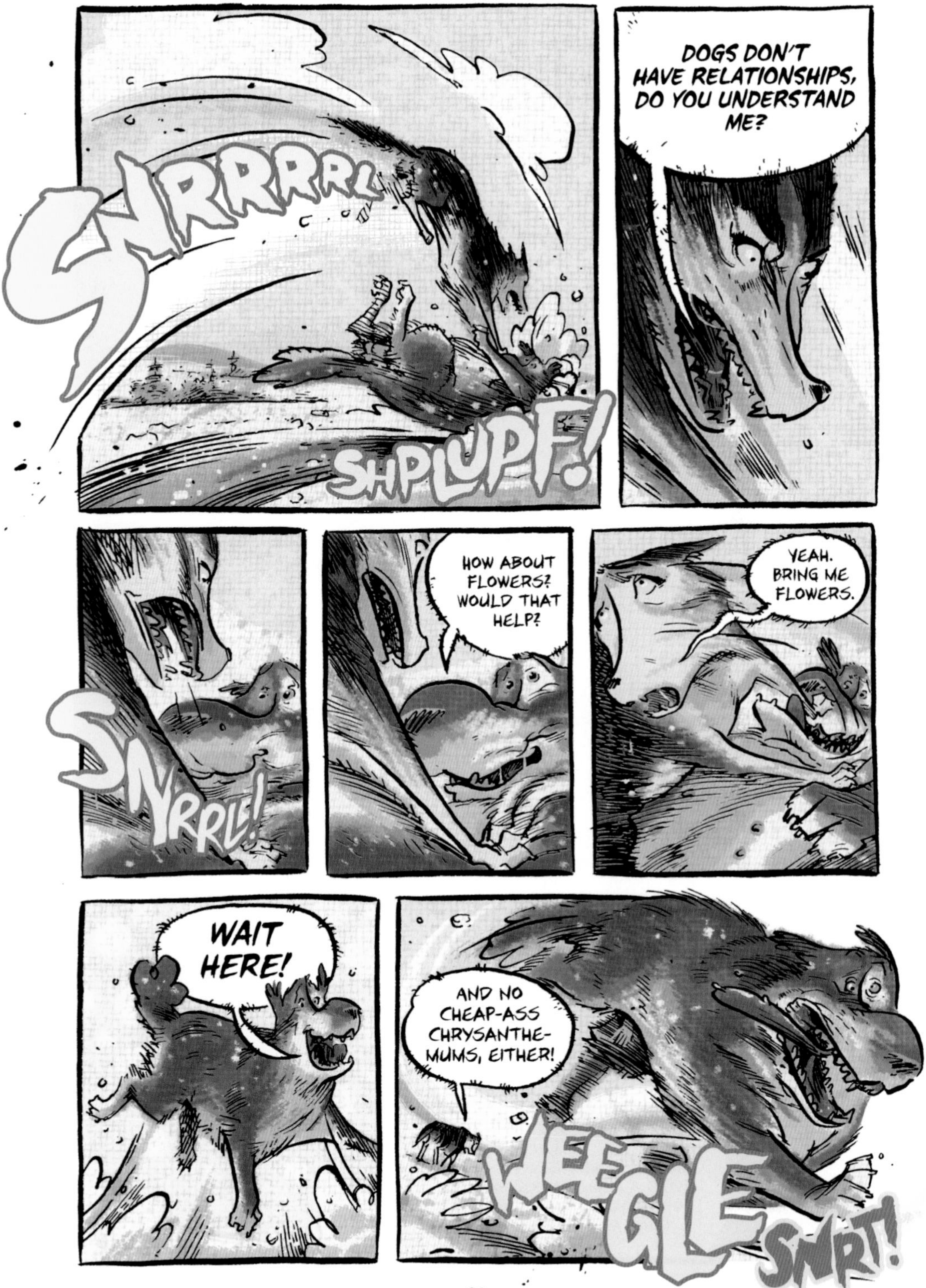
SNRRRRL
SHPLUPF!
DOGS DON'T HAVE RELATIONSHIPS, DO YOU UNDERSTAND ME?
SNYRRLL!
HOW ABOUT FLOWERS? WOULD THAT HELP?
YEAH. BRING ME FLOWERS.
WAIT HERE!
AND NO CHEAP-ASS CHRYSANTHE-MUMS, EITHER!
WEEGLE
SNRT!

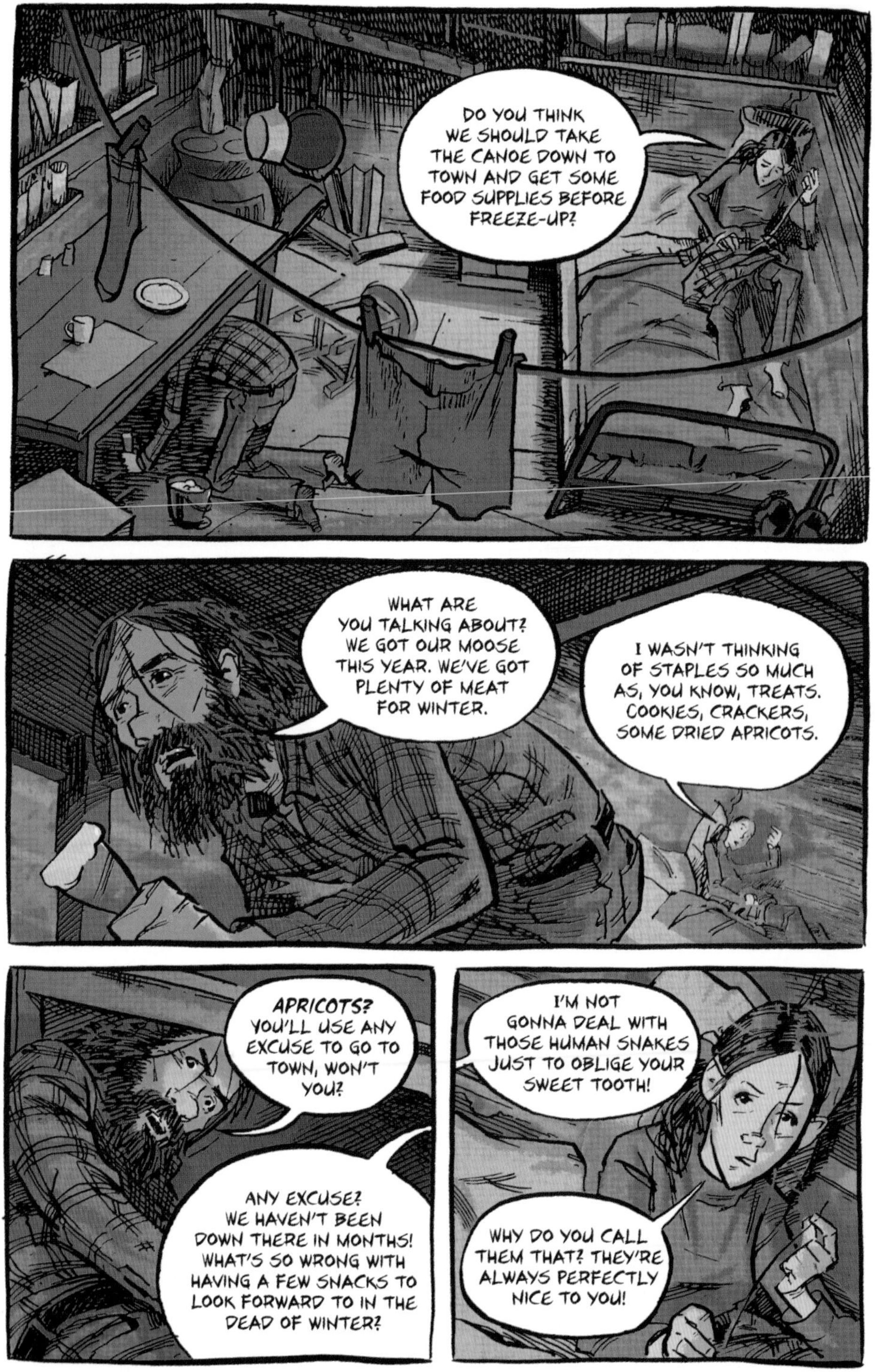

DO YOU THINK WE SHOULD TAKE THE CANOE DOWN TO TOWN AND GET SOME FOOD SUPPLIES BEFORE FREEZE-UP?
WHAT ARE YOU TALKING ABOUT? WE GOT OUR MOOSE THIS YEAR. WE'VE GOT PLENTY OF MEAT FOR WINTER.
I WASN'T THINKING OF STAPLES SO MUCH AS, YOU KNOW, TREATS. COOKIES, CRACKERS, SOME DRIED APRICOTS.
APRICOTS? YOU'LL USE ANY EXCUSE TO GO TO TOWN, WON'T YOU?
ANY EXCUSE? WE HAVEN'T BEEN DOWN THERE IN MONTHS! WHAT'S SO WRONG WITH HAVING A FEW SNACKS TO LOOK FORWARD TO IN THE DEAD OF WINTER?
I'M NOT GONNA DEAL WITH THOSE HUMAN SNAKES JUST TO OBLIGE YOUR SWEET TOOTH!
WHY DO YOU CALL THEM THAT? THEY'RE ALWAYS PERFECTLY NICE TO YOU!

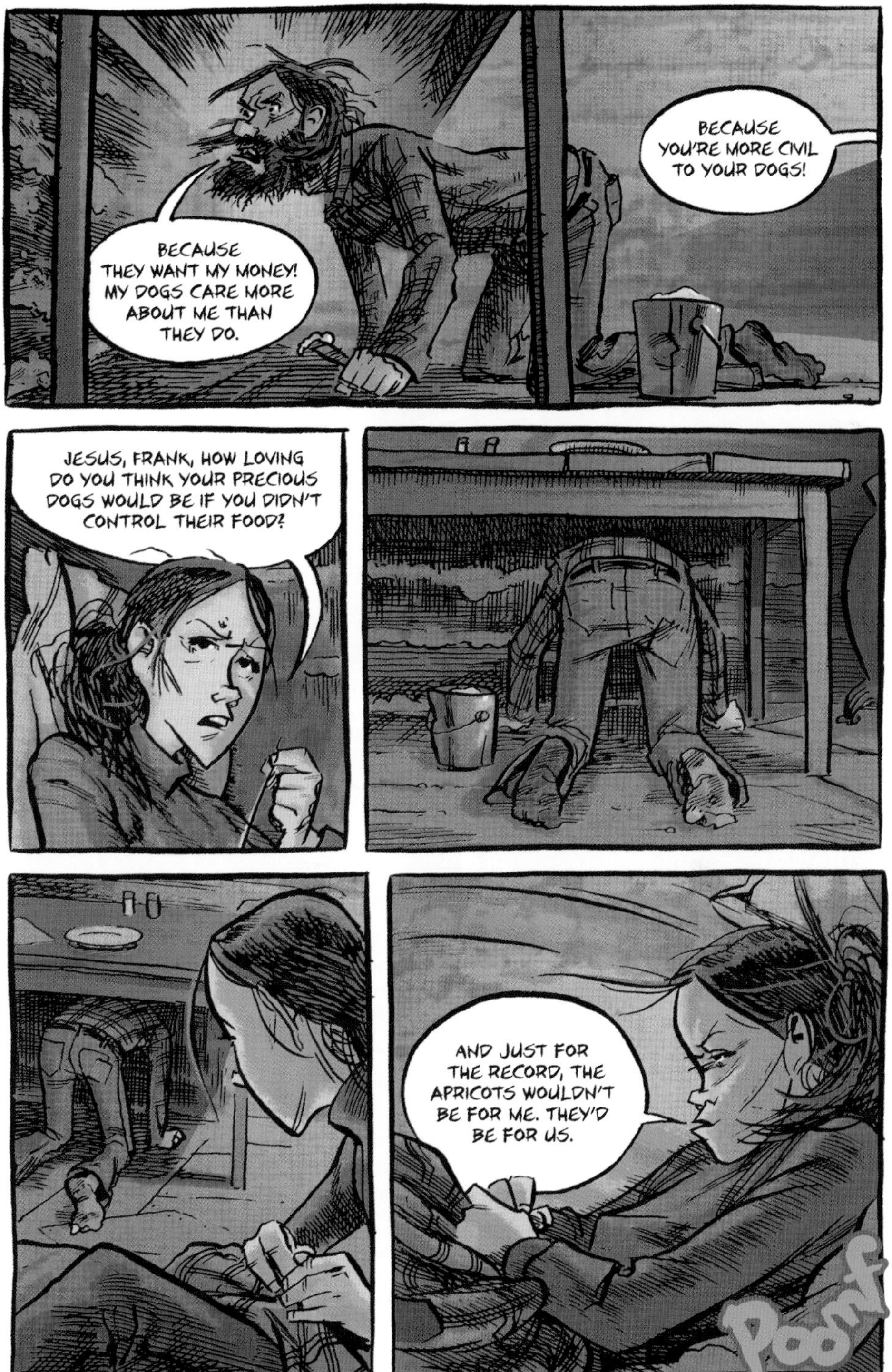
BECAUSE THEY WANT MY MONEY! MY DOGS CARE MORE ABOUT ME THAN THEY DO.
BECAUSE YOU'RE MORE CIVIL TO YOUR DOGS!
JESUS, FRANK, HOW LOVING DO YOU THINK YOUR PRECIOUS DOGS WOULD BE IF YOU DIDN'T CONTROL THEIR FOOD?
AND JUST FOR THE RECORD, THE APRICOTS WOULDN'T BE FOR ME. THEY'D BE FOR US.

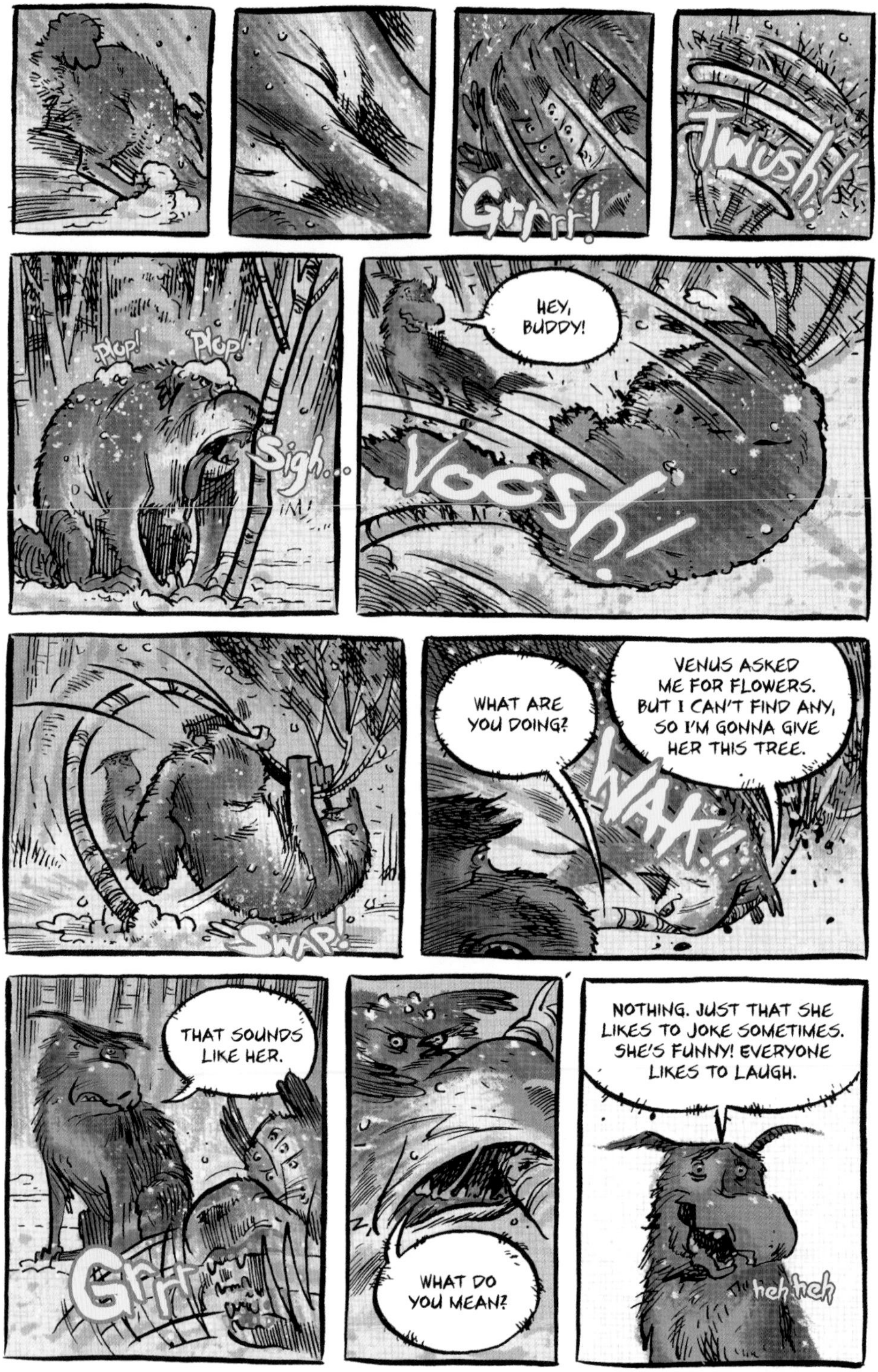
Grrrr!
Twush!
Plop!
Plop!
Sigh...
Hey, buddy!
Voosh!
Swap!
What are you doing?
Venus asked me for flowers. But I can't find any, so I'm gonna give her this tree.
Wak!
That sounds like her.
Grrr
What do you mean?
Nothing. Just that she likes to joke sometimes. She's funny! Everyone likes to laugh.
heh heh

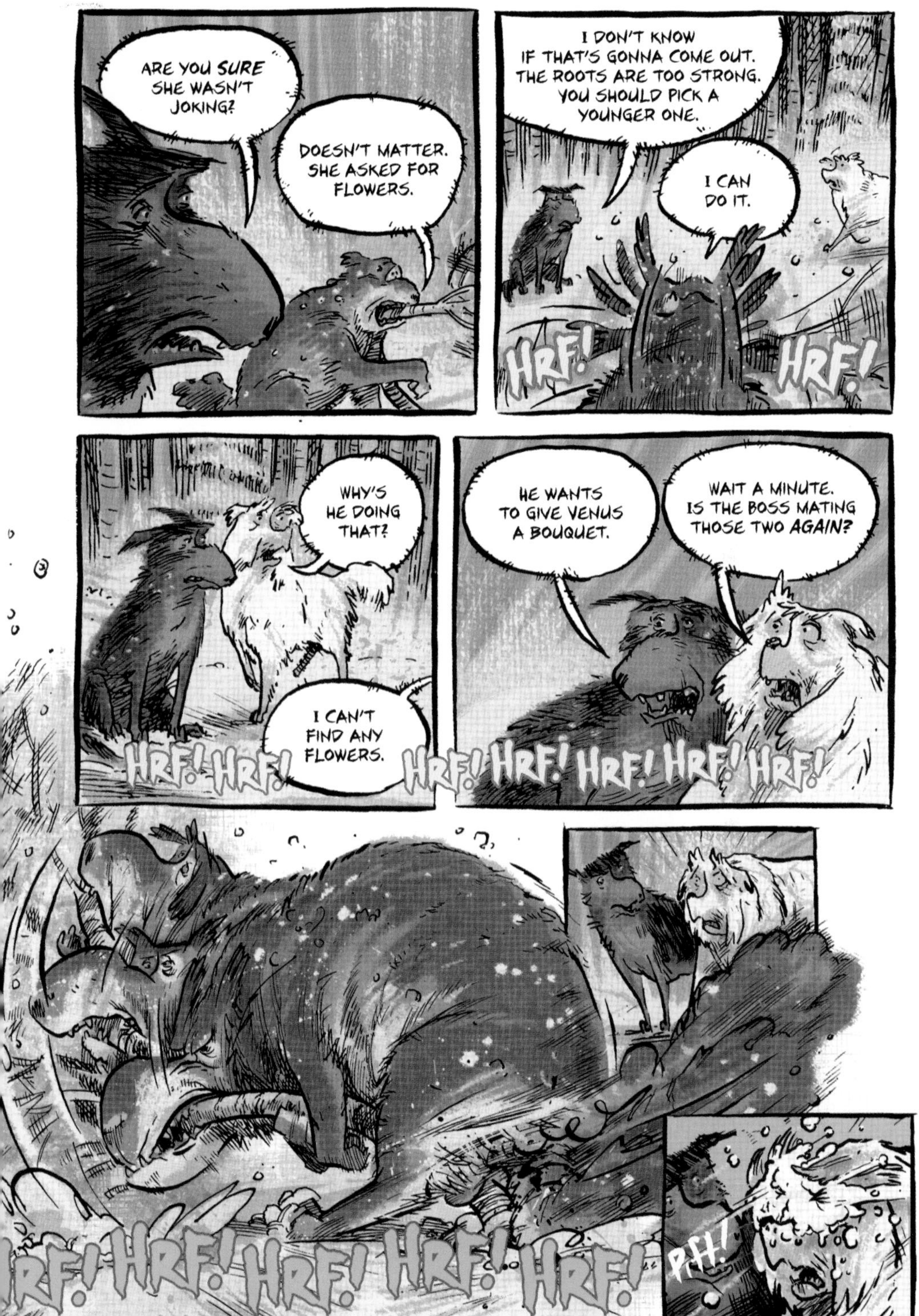
ARE YOU SURE SHE WASN'T JOKING?
DOESN'T MATTER. SHE ASKED FOR FLOWERS.
I DON'T KNOW IF THAT'S GONNA COME OUT. THE ROOTS ARE TOO STRONG. YOU SHOULD PICK A YOUNGER ONE.
I CAN DO IT.
HRF! HRF!
WHY'S HE DOING THAT?
I CAN'T FIND ANY FLOWERS.
HRF! HRF!
HE WANTS TO GIVE VENUS A BOUQUET.
WAIT A MINUTE. IS THE BOSS MATING THOSE TWO AGAIN?
HRF! HRF! HRF! HRF! HRF!
RF! HRF! HRF! HRF! HRF!
P-TH!

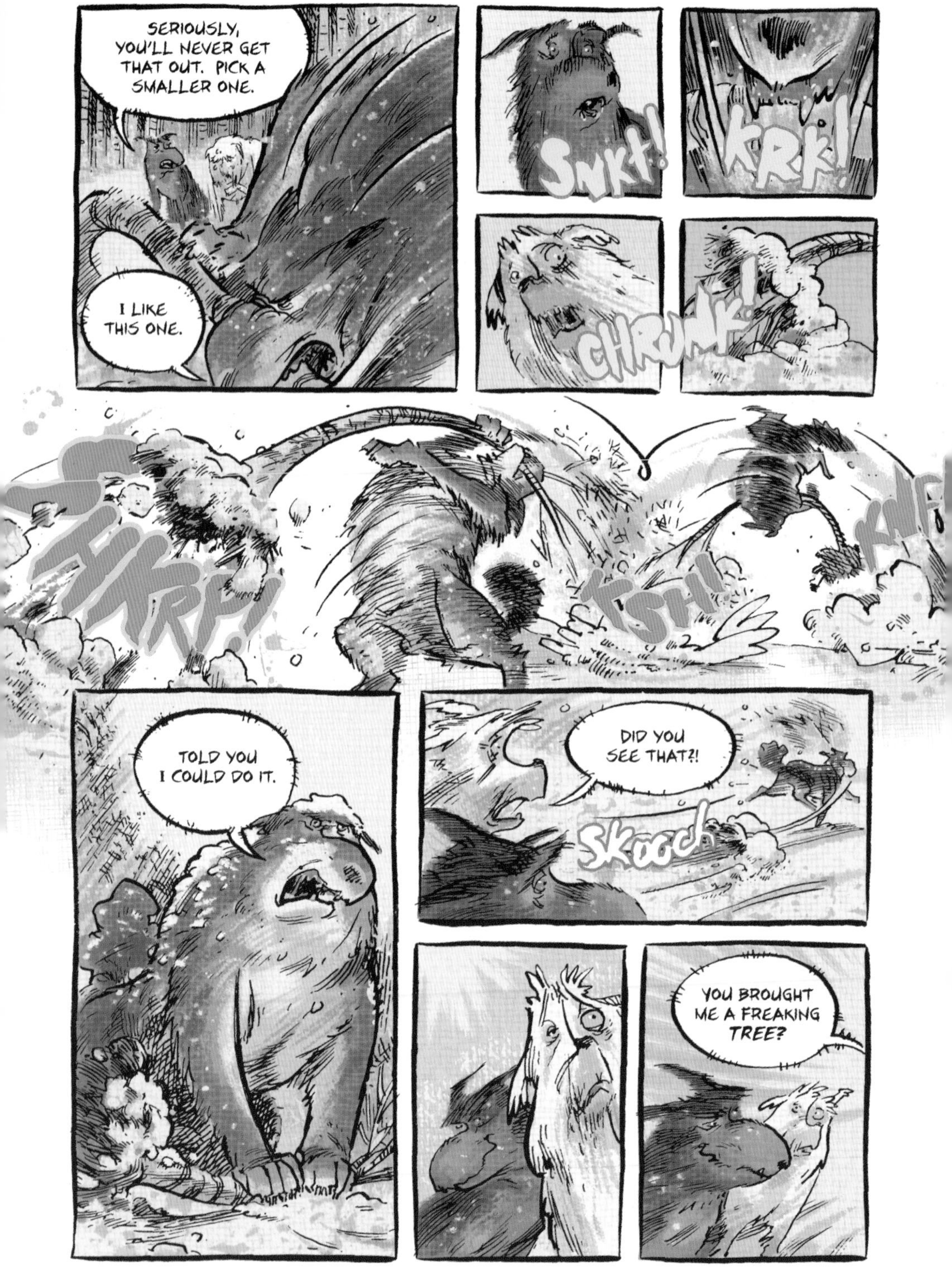
SERIOUSLY, YOU'LL NEVER GET THAT OUT. PICK A SMALLER ONE.
I LIKE THIS ONE.
SNKT!
KRK!
CHRUNK!
TSH!
TOLD YOU I COULD DO IT.
DID YOU SEE THAT?!
SKOOCH
YOU BROUGHT ME A FREAKING TREE?

CHAPTER 3

A LEGACY DENIED

HEY, BUDDY, HOW'S IT GOING? BEAUTIFUL DAY, ISN'T IT? KIND OF DAY THAT MAKES YOU WANT TO GO OUT ON A RUN.

I GUESS.

HEY, HOW DID VENUS LIKE THE TREE?

NOT TOO MUCH. SHE ASKED ME IF I THOUGHT SHE WAS A LUMBERJACK.

FEMALES. WHO CAN EVER FIGURE OUT WHAT THEY'RE THINKING?

NOT ME, THAT'S FOR SURE.

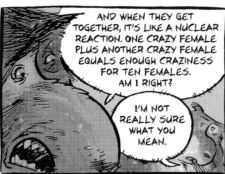

AND WHEN THEY GET TOGETHER, IT'S LIKE A NUCLEAR REACTION. ONE CRAZY FEMALE PLUS ANOTHER CRAZY FEMALE EQUALS ENOUGH CRAZINESS FOR TEN FEMALES. AM I RIGHT?

I'M NOT REALLY SURE WHAT YOU MEAN.

WELL, TAKE VENUS. I'M SURE SHE HAS A FEW LITTLE QUIRKS THAT MAKE HER SPECIAL. MANAGE-ABLE STUFF, NOTHING YOU CAN'T HANDLE.

Blink Blink

BUT GET HER TALKING TO HER PAL DOLLY, AND ALL BETS ARE OFF. IT'S CUCKOO TIME.

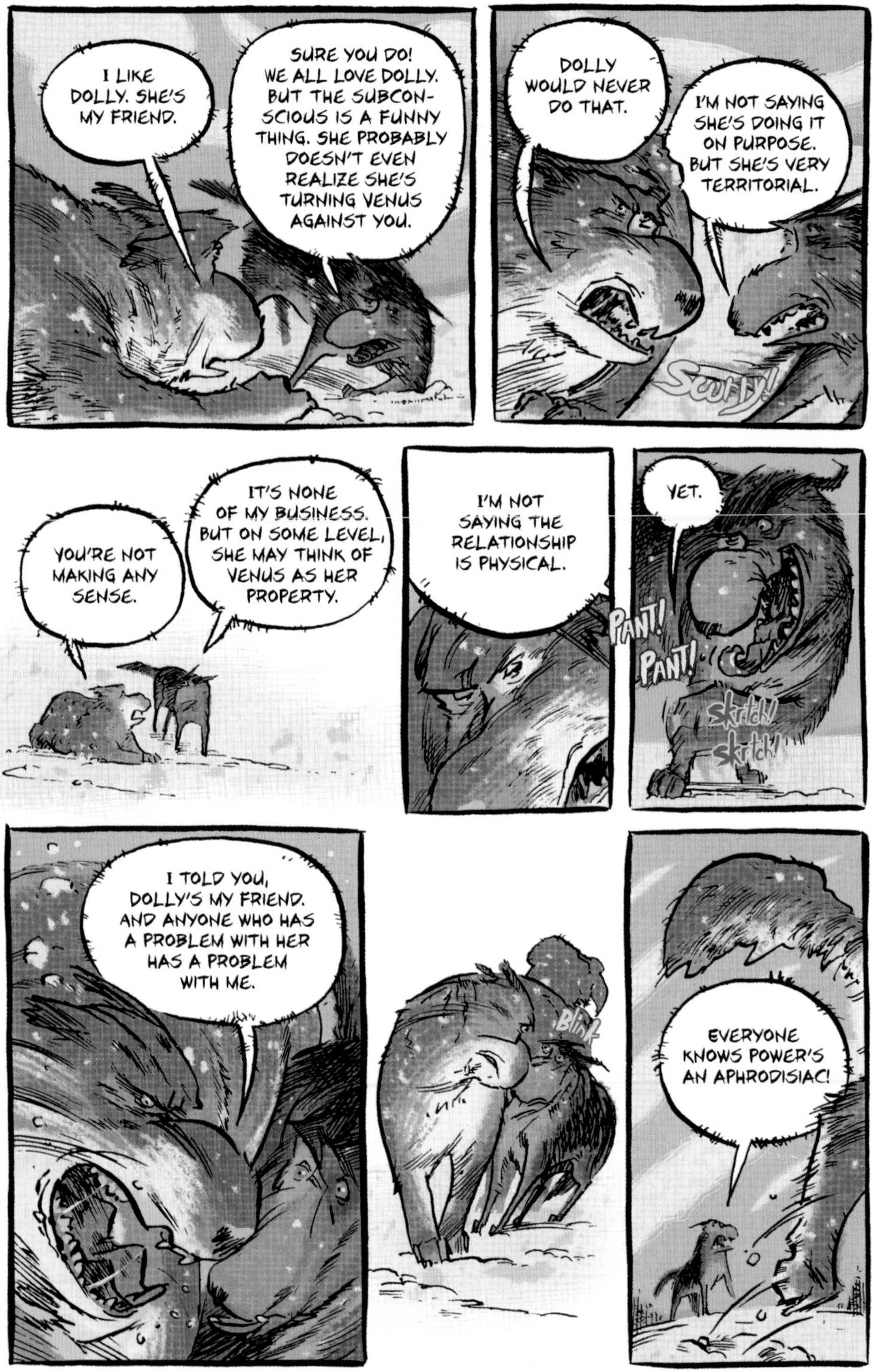
I LIKE DOLLY. SHE'S MY FRIEND.
SURE YOU DO! WE ALL LOVE DOLLY. BUT THE SUBCON-SCIOUS IS A FUNNY THING. SHE PROBABLY DOESN'T EVEN REALIZE SHE'S TURNING VENUS AGAINST YOU.
DOLLY WOULD NEVER DO THAT.
I'M NOT SAYING SHE'S DOING IT ON PURPOSE. BUT SHE'S VERY TERRITORIAL.
Scurry!
YOU'RE NOT MAKING ANY SENSE.
IT'S NONE OF MY BUSINESS. BUT ON SOME LEVEL, SHE MAY THINK OF VENUS AS HER PROPERTY.
I'M NOT SAYING THE RELATIONSHIP IS PHYSICAL.
YET.
PANT! PANT!
skritch! skritch!
I TOLD YOU, DOLLY'S MY FRIEND. AND ANYONE WHO HAS A PROBLEM WITH HER HAS A PROBLEM WITH ME.
Blink
EVERYONE KNOWS POWER'S AN APHRODISIAC!

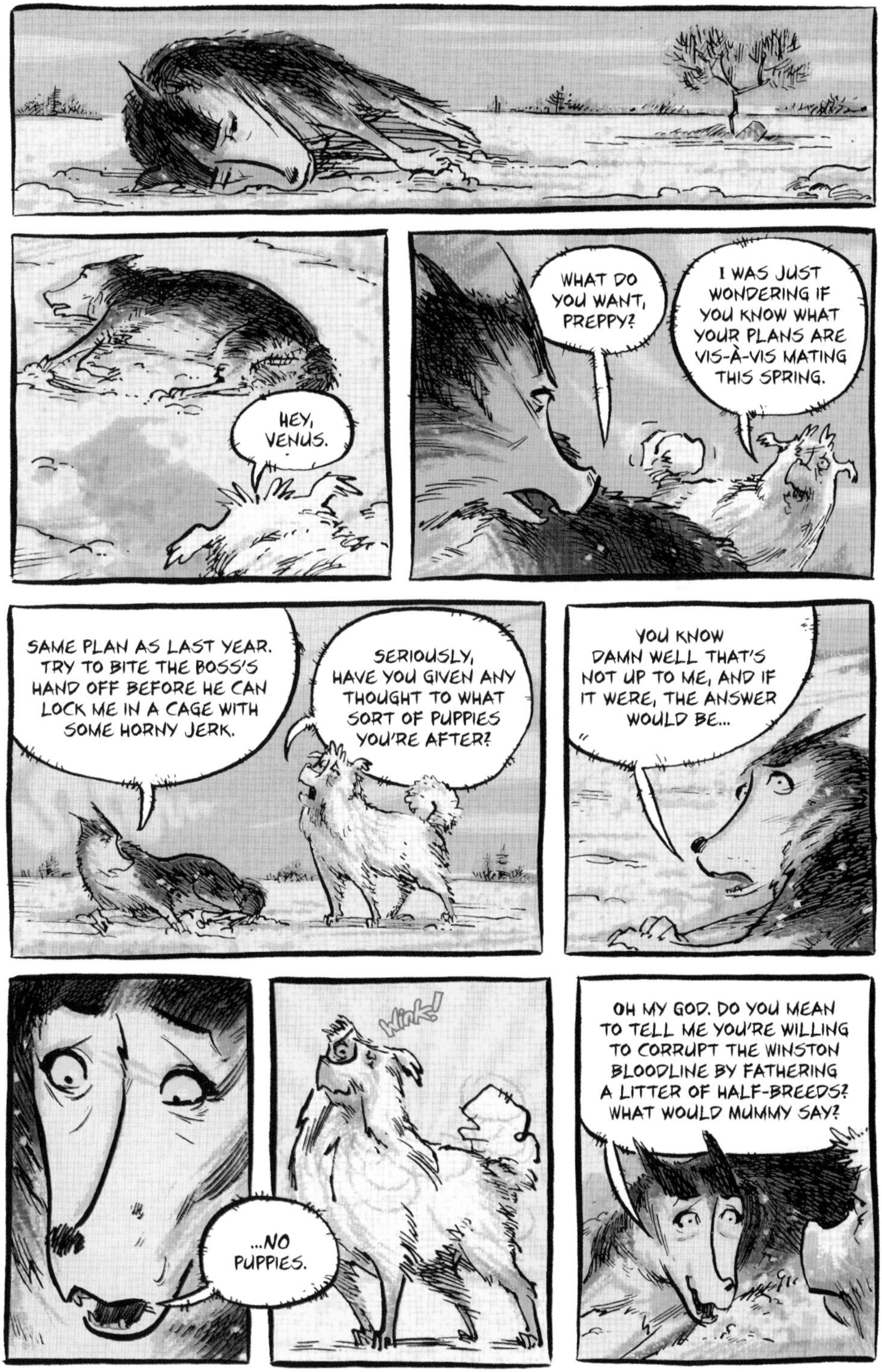
HEY, VENUS.
WHAT DO YOU WANT, PREPPY?
I WAS JUST WONDERING IF YOU KNOW WHAT YOUR PLANS ARE VIS-À-VIS MATING THIS SPRING.
SAME PLAN AS LAST YEAR. TRY TO BITE THE BOSS'S HAND OFF BEFORE HE CAN LOCK ME IN A CAGE WITH SOME HORNY JERK.
SERIOUSLY, HAVE YOU GIVEN ANY THOUGHT TO WHAT SORT OF PUPPIES YOU'RE AFTER?
YOU KNOW DAMN WELL THAT'S NOT UP TO ME, AND IF IT WERE, THE ANSWER WOULD BE...
...NO PUPPIES.
WINK!
OH MY GOD. DO YOU MEAN TO TELL ME YOU'RE WILLING TO CORRUPT THE WINSTON BLOODLINE BY FATHERING A LITTER OF HALF-BREEDS? WHAT WOULD MUMMY SAY?

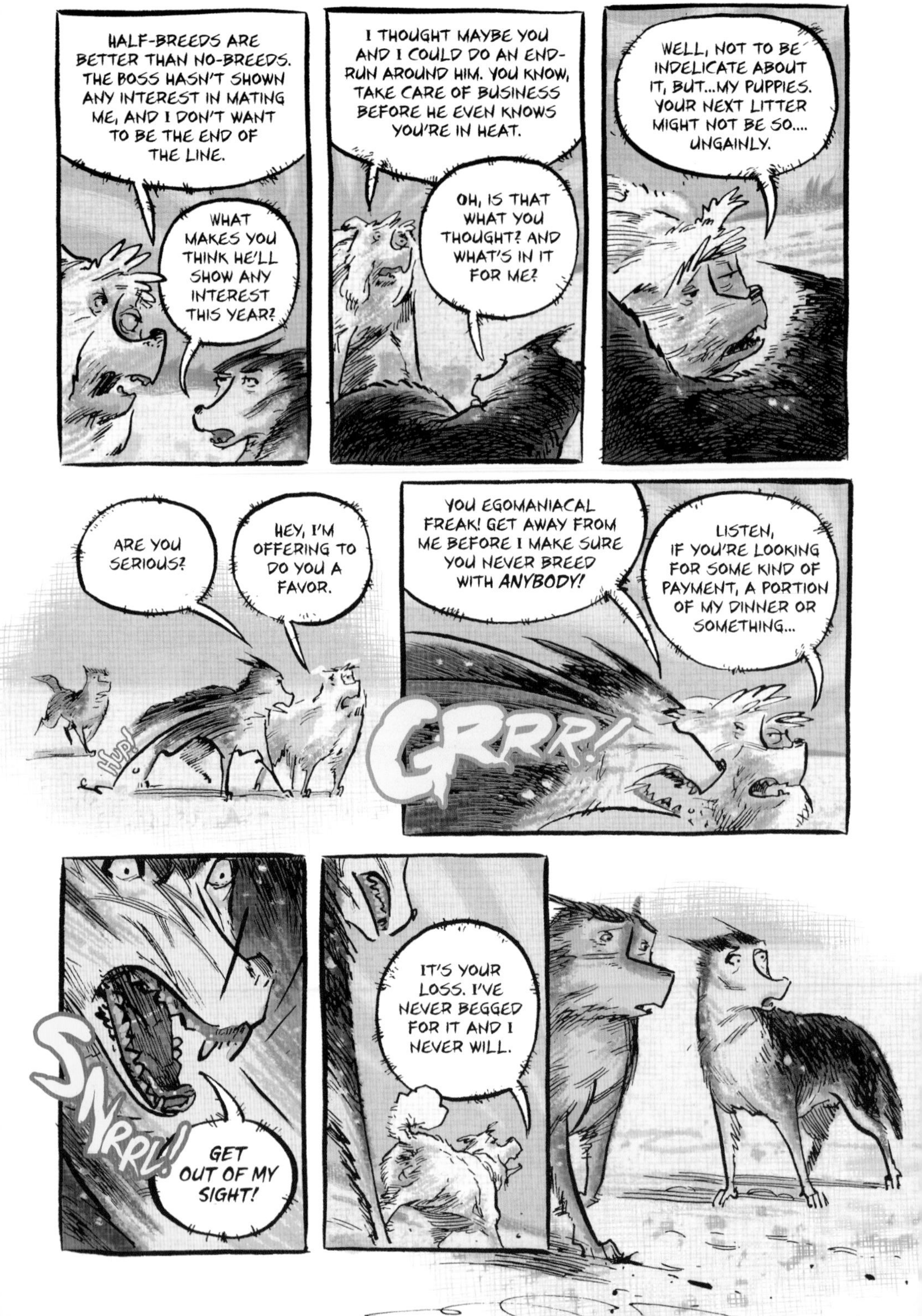
HALF-BREEDS ARE BETTER THAN NO-BREEDS. THE BOSS HASN'T SHOWN ANY INTEREST IN MATING ME, AND I DON'T WANT TO BE THE END OF THE LINE.
WHAT MAKES YOU THINK HE'LL SHOW ANY INTEREST THIS YEAR?
I THOUGHT MAYBE YOU AND I COULD DO AN END-RUN AROUND HIM. YOU KNOW, TAKE CARE OF BUSINESS BEFORE HE EVEN KNOWS YOU'RE IN HEAT.
OH, IS THAT WHAT YOU THOUGHT? AND WHAT'S IN IT FOR ME?
WELL, NOT TO BE INDELICATE ABOUT IT, BUT...MY PUPPIES. YOUR NEXT LITTER MIGHT NOT BE SO.... UNGAINLY.
ARE YOU SERIOUS?
HEY, I'M OFFERING TO DO YOU A FAVOR.
HUP!
YOU EGOMANIACAL FREAK! GET AWAY FROM ME BEFORE I MAKE SURE YOU NEVER BREED WITH *ANYBODY!*
LISTEN, IF YOU'RE LOOKING FOR SOME KIND OF PAYMENT, A PORTION OF MY DINNER OR SOMETHING...
GRRR!
SNRRL!
GET OUT OF MY SIGHT!
IT'S YOUR LOSS. I'VE NEVER BEGGED FOR IT AND I NEVER WILL.

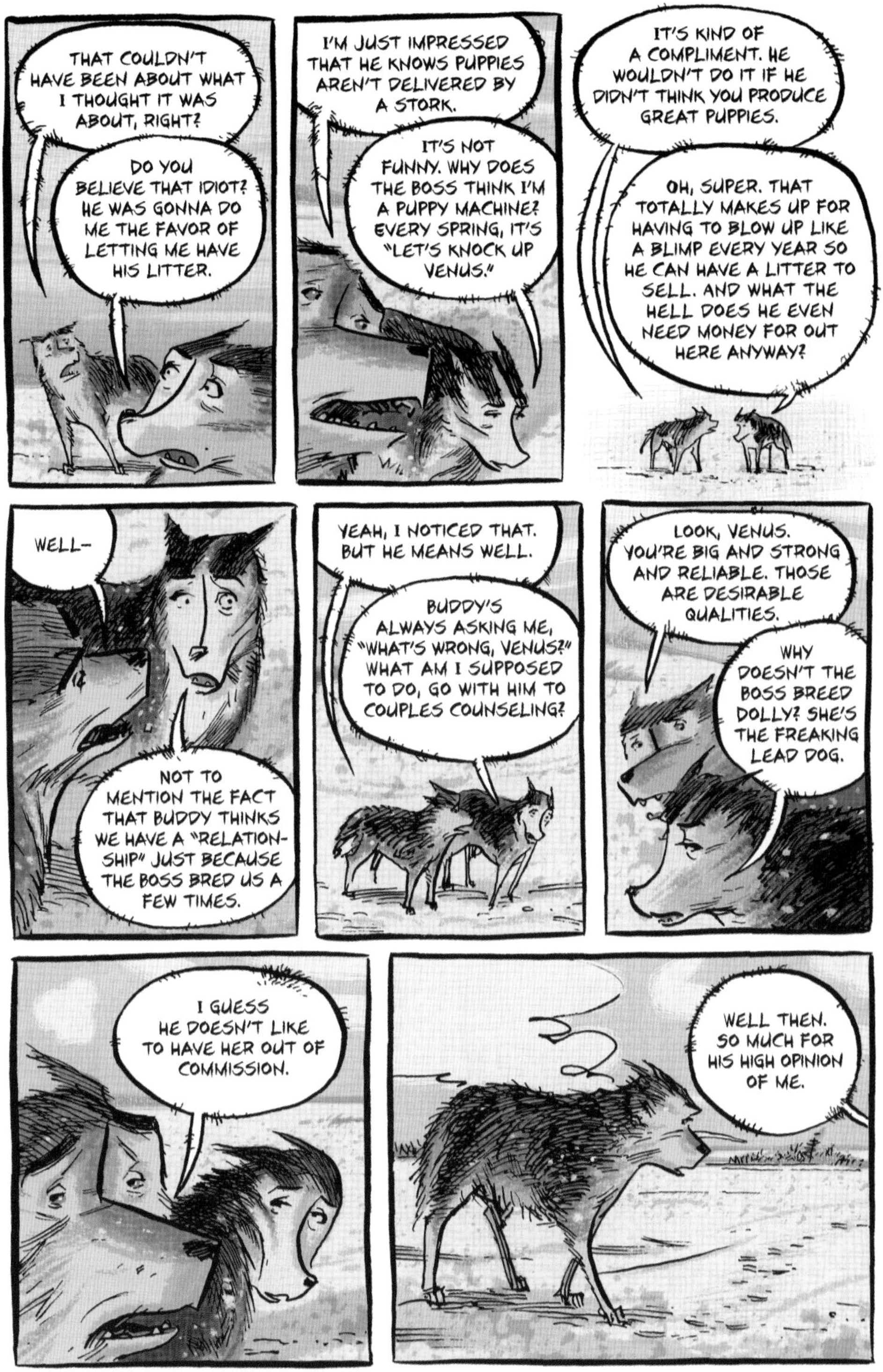
THAT COULDN'T HAVE BEEN ABOUT WHAT I THOUGHT IT WAS ABOUT, RIGHT?
DO YOU BELIEVE THAT IDIOT? HE WAS GONNA DO ME THE FAVOR OF LETTING ME HAVE HIS LITTER.
I'M JUST IMPRESSED THAT HE KNOWS PUPPIES AREN'T DELIVERED BY A STORK.
IT'S NOT FUNNY. WHY DOES THE BOSS THINK I'M A PUPPY MACHINE? EVERY SPRING, IT'S "LET'S KNOCK UP VENUS."
IT'S KIND OF A COMPLIMENT. HE WOULDN'T DO IT IF HE DIDN'T THINK YOU PRODUCE GREAT PUPPIES.
OH, SUPER. THAT TOTALLY MAKES UP FOR HAVING TO BLOW UP LIKE A BLIMP EVERY YEAR SO HE CAN HAVE A LITTER TO SELL. AND WHAT THE HELL DOES HE EVEN NEED MONEY FOR OUT HERE ANYWAY?
WELL-
NOT TO MENTION THE FACT THAT BUDDY THINKS WE HAVE A "RELATION-SHIP" JUST BECAUSE THE BOSS BRED US A FEW TIMES.
YEAH, I NOTICED THAT. BUT HE MEANS WELL.
BUDDY'S ALWAYS ASKING ME, "WHAT'S WRONG, VENUS?" WHAT AM I SUPPOSED TO DO, GO WITH HIM TO COUPLES COUNSELING?
LOOK, VENUS. YOU'RE BIG AND STRONG AND RELIABLE. THOSE ARE DESIRABLE QUALITIES.
WHY DOESN'T THE BOSS BREED DOLLY? SHE'S THE FREAKING LEAD DOG.
I GUESS HE DOESN'T LIKE TO HAVE HER OUT OF COMMISSION.
WELL THEN. SO MUCH FOR HIS HIGH OPINION OF ME.

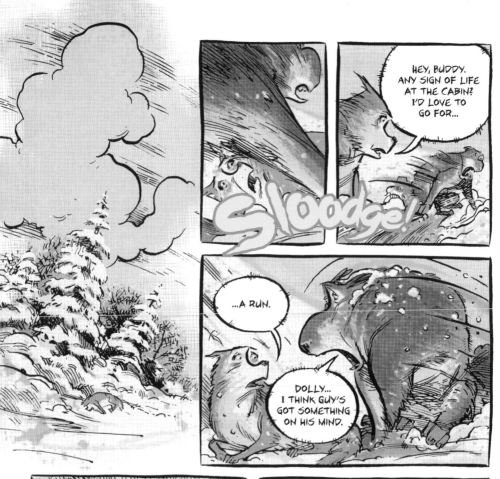

SLOODGE!

HEY, BUDDY. ANY SIGN OF LIFE AT THE CABIN? I'D LOVE TO GO FOR...

...A RUN.

DOLLY... I THINK GUY'S GOT SOMETHING ON HIS MIND.

SOMETHING BESIDES HOW HE CAN SABOTAGE ME AND TAKE MY JOB?

GUY'S ABOUT AS SUBTLE AS AN AVALANCHE.

Buh!

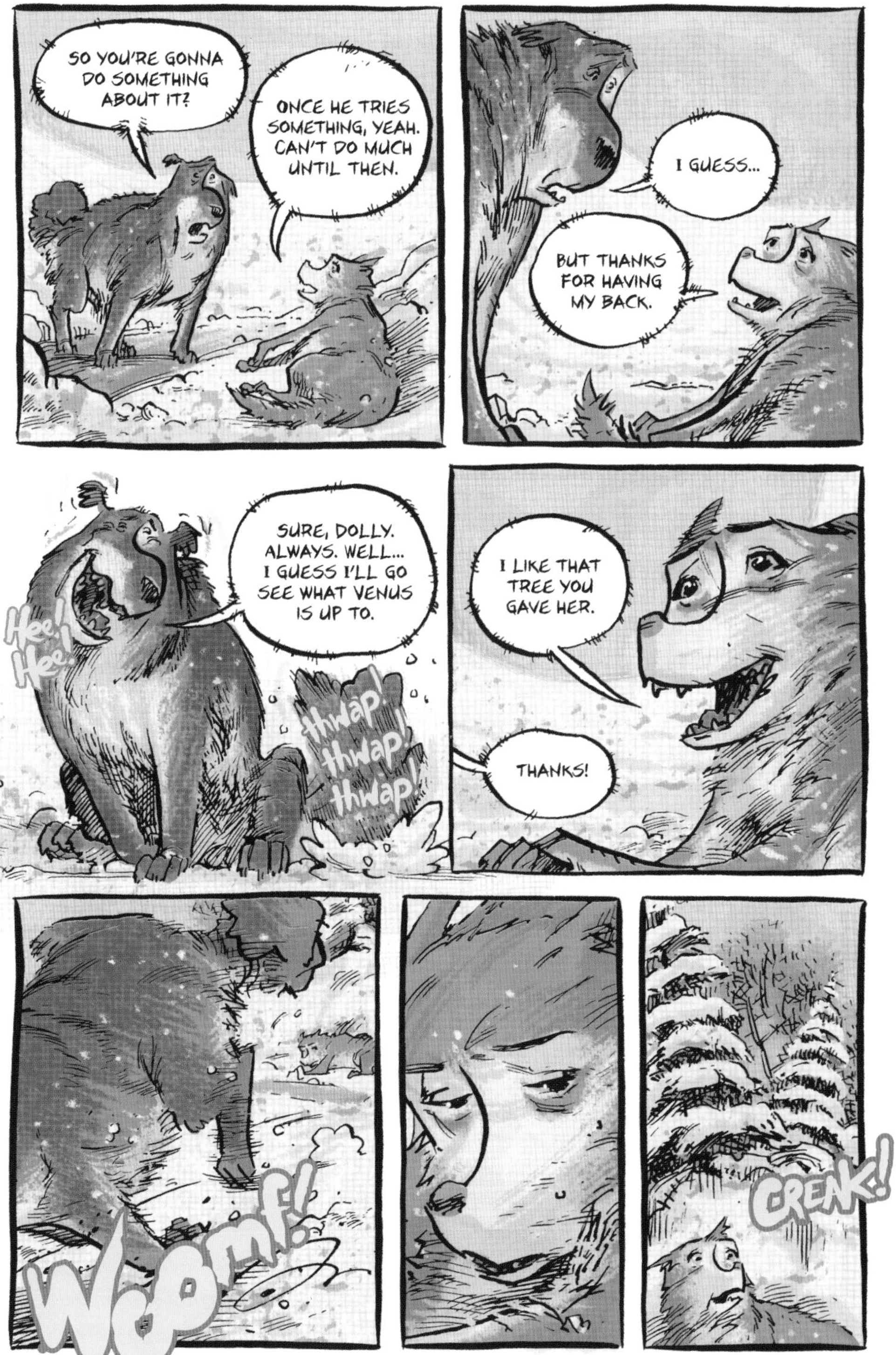
SO YOU'RE GONNA DO SOMETHING ABOUT IT?
ONCE HE TRIES SOMETHING, YEAH. CAN'T DO MUCH UNTIL THEN.
I GUESS...
BUT THANKS FOR HAVING MY BACK.
SURE, DOLLY. ALWAYS. WELL... I GUESS I'LL GO SEE WHAT VENUS IS UP TO.
Hee! Hee!
thwap! thwap! thwap!
I LIKE THAT TREE YOU GAVE HER.
THANKS!
WOOMF!
CREAK!

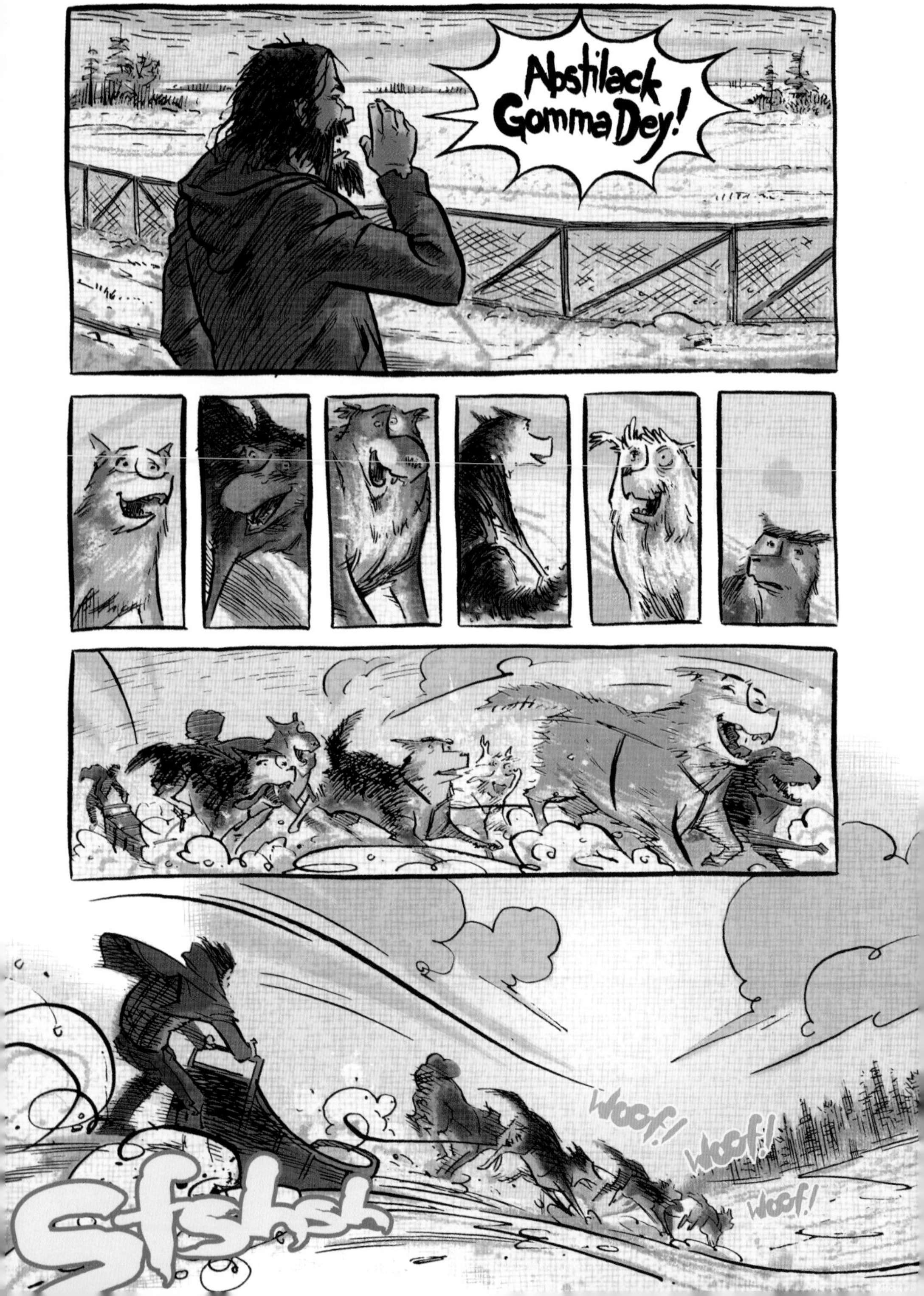
Abstilack Gomma Dey!
Woof!
Woof!
Woof!
Sfshsh

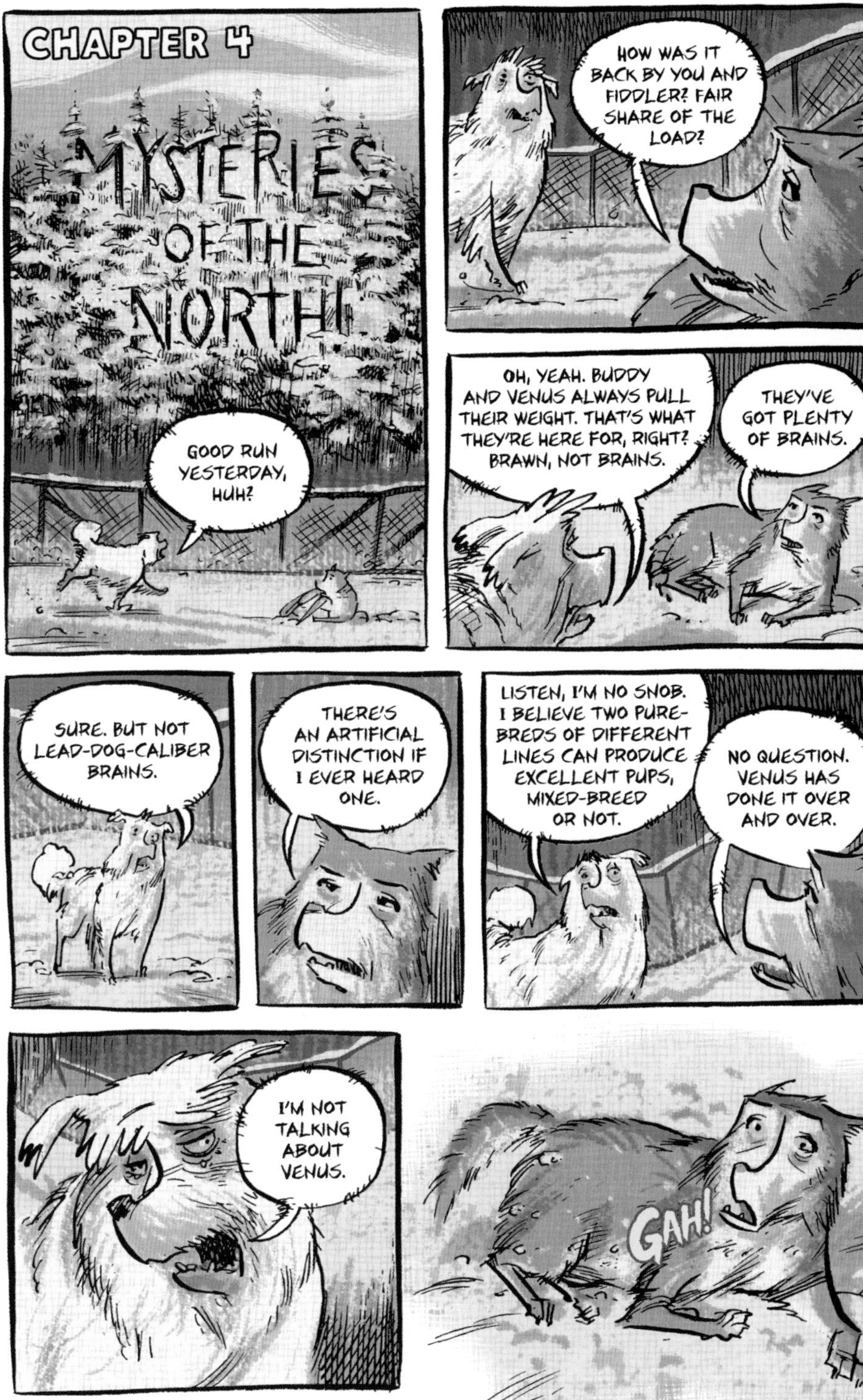
CHAPTER 4
MYSTERIES OF THE NORTH!
GOOD RUN YESTERDAY, HUH?
HOW WAS IT BACK BY YOU AND FIDDLER? FAIR SHARE OF THE LOAD?
OH, YEAH. BUDDY AND VENUS ALWAYS PULL THEIR WEIGHT. THAT'S WHAT THEY'RE HERE FOR, RIGHT? BRAWN, NOT BRAINS.
THEY'VE GOT PLENTY OF BRAINS.
SURE. BUT NOT LEAD-DOG-CALIBER BRAINS.
THERE'S AN ARTIFICIAL DISTINCTION IF I EVER HEARD ONE.
LISTEN, I'M NO SNOB. I BELIEVE TWO PURE-BREDS OF DIFFERENT LINES CAN PRODUCE EXCELLENT PUPS, MIXED-BREED OR NOT.
NO QUESTION. VENUS HAS DONE IT OVER AND OVER.
I'M NOT TALKING ABOUT VENUS.
GAH!

WAIT A MINUTE. YOU KNOW THE BOSS ISN'T BREEDING EITHER ONE OF US.

YEAH. BUT WE DON'T REALLY NEED HIM TO DO IT.

UM, I'M FLATTERED, I GUESS. BUT IF I'M NOT BEING BRED, WHY WOULD I EVER WANT TO GET PREGNANT?

WHAT ABOUT POSTERITY? WHAT ABOUT EXTENDING YOUR LINE? WHAT ABOUT THE JOYS OF MOTHERHOOD?

*Scooch*

THAT ONE'S A MYSTERY TO ME. I'VE NEVER FELT ANY BIG URGE TO EAT AFTERBIRTH.

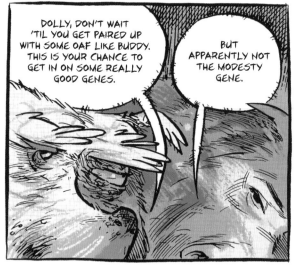

DOLLY, DON'T WAIT 'TIL YOU GET PAIRED UP WITH SOME OAF LIKE BUDDY. THIS IS YOUR CHANCE TO GET IN ON SOME REALLY GOOD GENES.

BUT APPARENTLY NOT THE MODESTY GENE.

YOU'VE GOT A WINDOW HERE.

A WINSTON WINDOW.

38

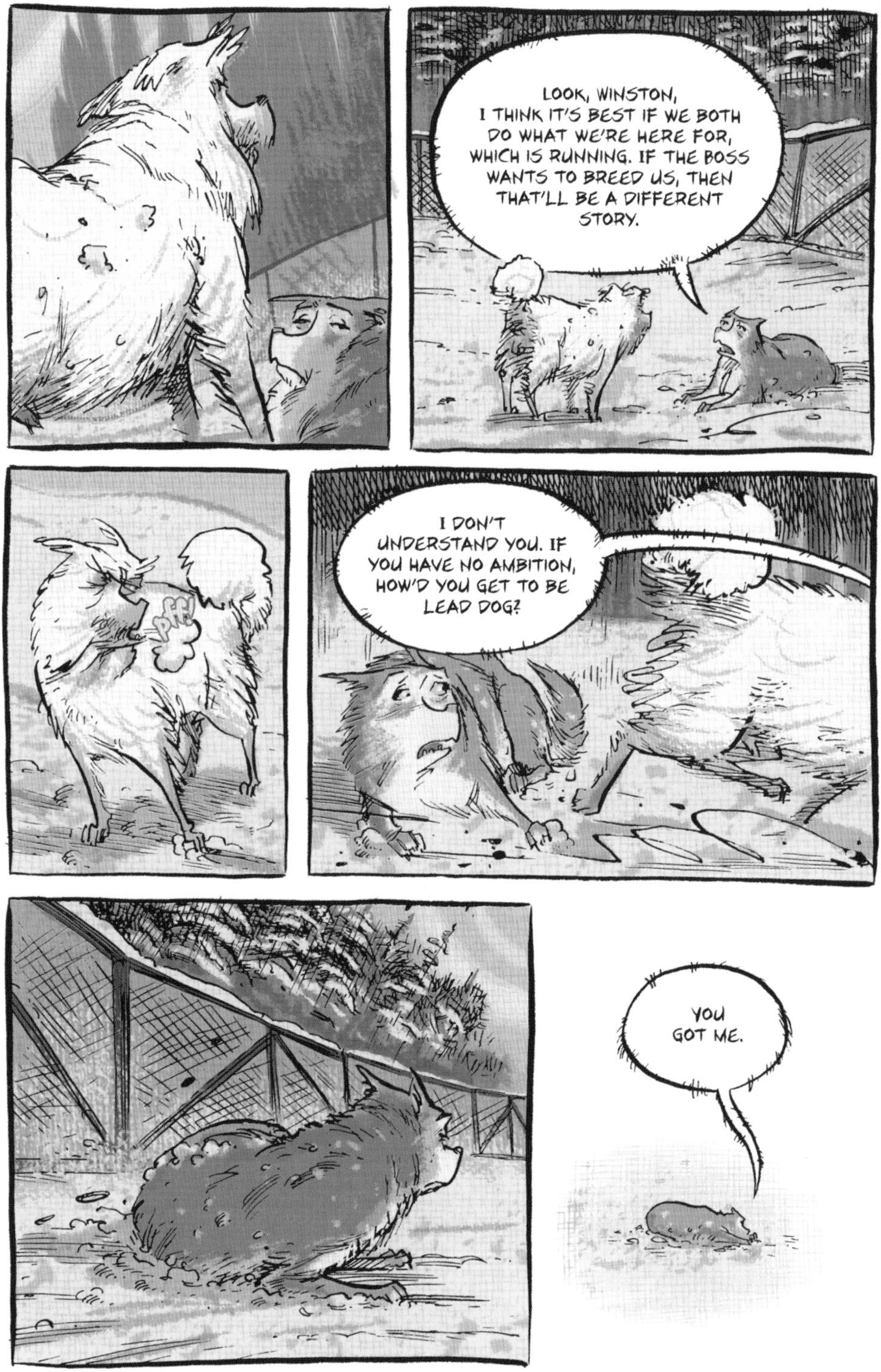
LOOK, WINSTON, I THINK IT'S BEST IF WE BOTH DO WHAT WE'RE HERE FOR, WHICH IS RUNNING. IF THE BOSS WANTS TO BREED US, THEN THAT'LL BE A DIFFERENT STORY.
pff!
I DON'T UNDERSTAND YOU. IF YOU HAVE NO AMBITION, HOW'D YOU GET TO BE LEAD DOG?
YOU GOT ME.

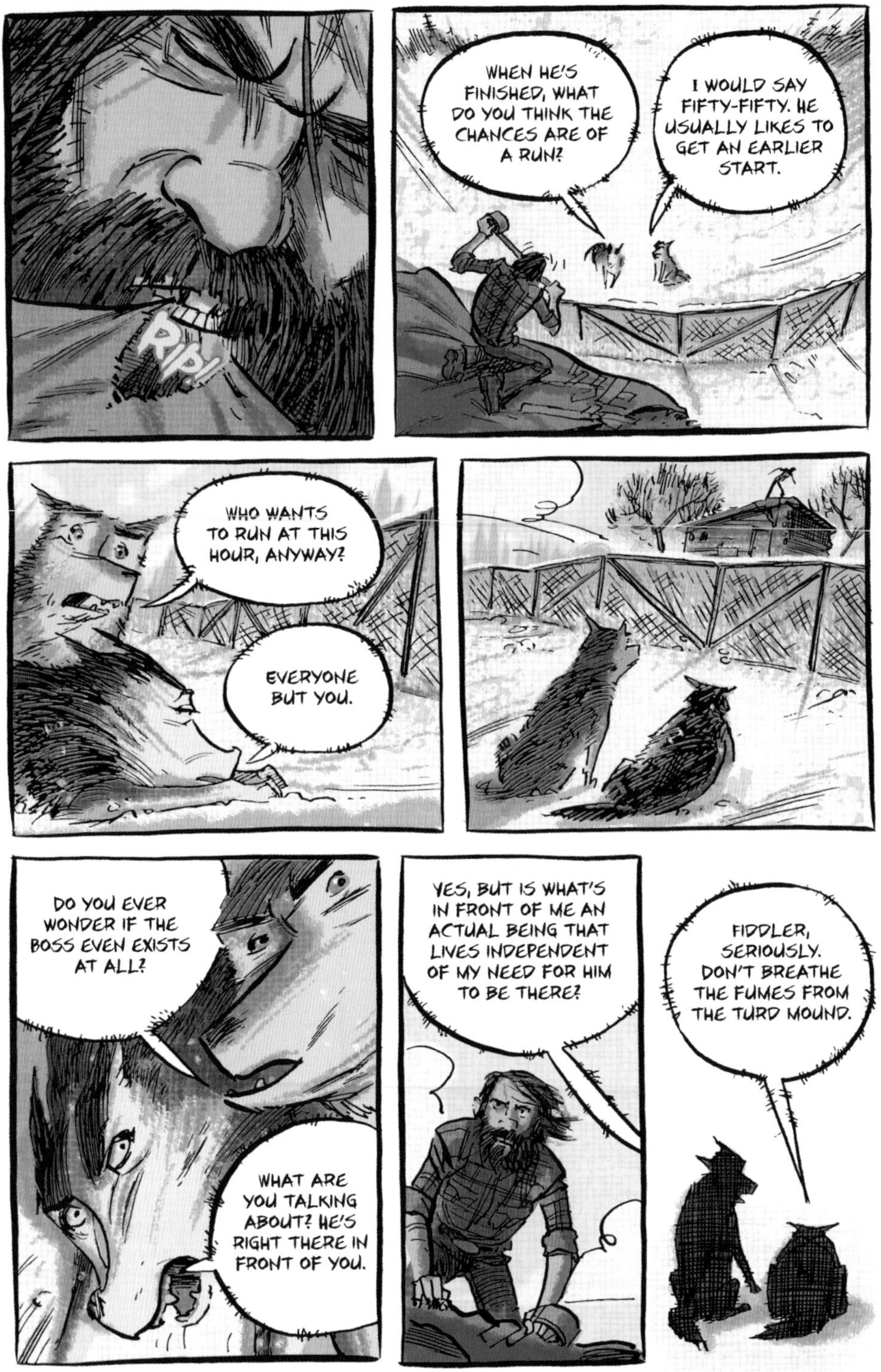
RIP!
WHEN HE'S FINISHED, WHAT DO YOU THINK THE CHANCES ARE OF A RUN?
I WOULD SAY FIFTY-FIFTY. HE USUALLY LIKES TO GET AN EARLIER START.
WHO WANTS TO RUN AT THIS HOUR, ANYWAY?
EVERYONE BUT YOU.
DO YOU EVER WONDER IF THE BOSS EVEN EXISTS AT ALL?
WHAT ARE YOU TALKING ABOUT? HE'S RIGHT THERE IN FRONT OF YOU.
YES, BUT IS WHAT'S IN FRONT OF ME AN ACTUAL BEING THAT LIVES INDEPENDENT OF MY NEED FOR HIM TO BE THERE?
FIDDLER, SERIOUSLY. DON'T BREATHE THE FUMES FROM THE TURD MOUND.

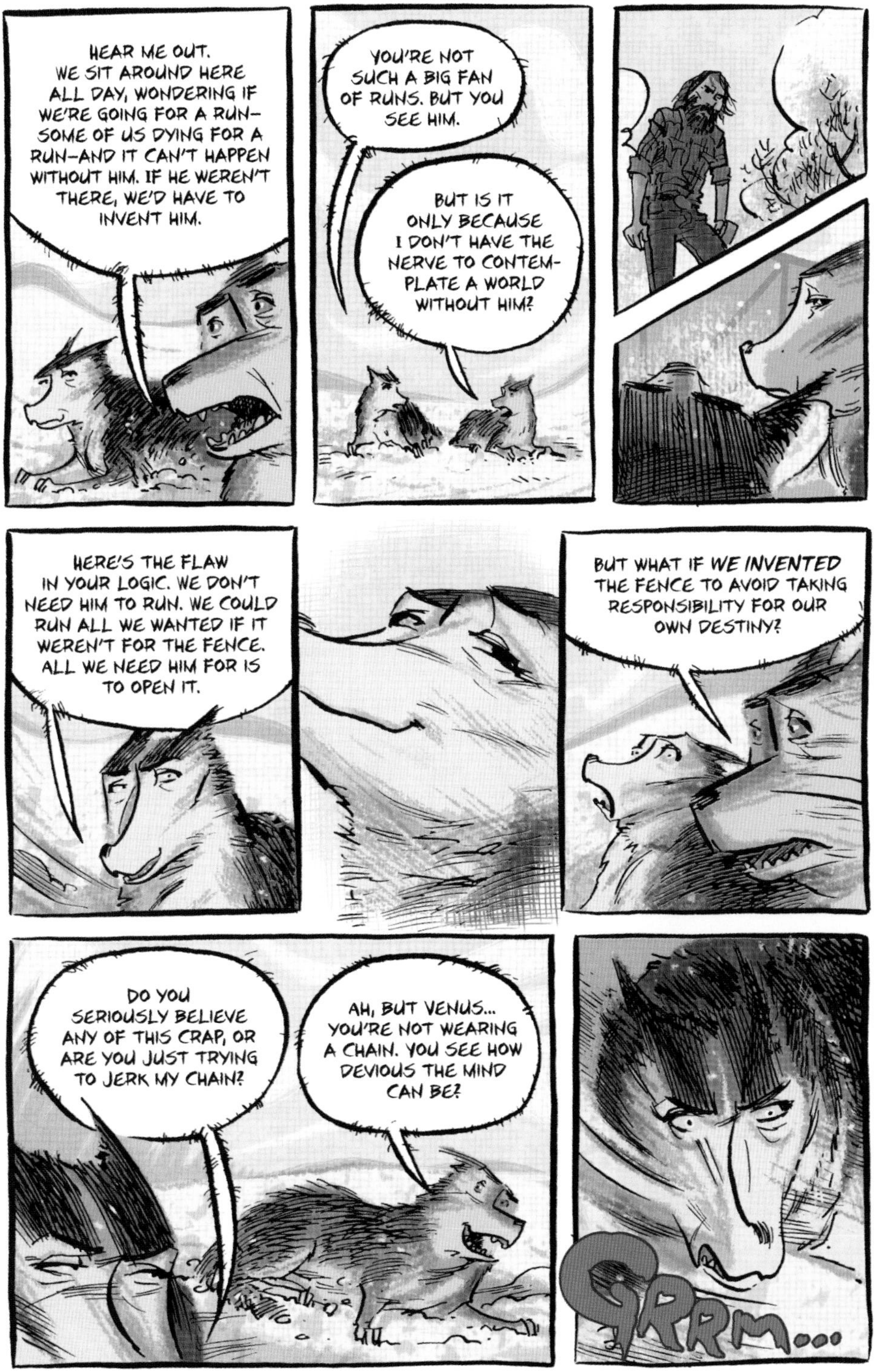
HEAR ME OUT. WE SIT AROUND HERE ALL DAY, WONDERING IF WE'RE GOING FOR A RUN– SOME OF US DYING FOR A RUN–AND IT CAN'T HAPPEN WITHOUT HIM. IF HE WEREN'T THERE, WE'D HAVE TO INVENT HIM.
YOU'RE NOT SUCH A BIG FAN OF RUNS. BUT YOU SEE HIM.
BUT IS IT ONLY BECAUSE I DON'T HAVE THE NERVE TO CONTEMPLATE A WORLD WITHOUT HIM?
HERE'S THE FLAW IN YOUR LOGIC. WE DON'T NEED HIM TO RUN. WE COULD RUN ALL WE WANTED IF IT WEREN'T FOR THE FENCE. ALL WE NEED HIM FOR IS TO OPEN IT.
BUT WHAT IF *WE INVENTED* THE FENCE TO AVOID TAKING RESPONSIBILITY FOR OUR OWN DESTINY?
DO YOU SERIOUSLY BELIEVE ANY OF THIS CRAP, OR ARE YOU JUST TRYING TO JERK MY CHAIN?
AH, BUT VENUS... YOU'RE NOT WEARING A CHAIN. YOU SEE HOW DEVIOUS THE MIND CAN BE?
GRRM...

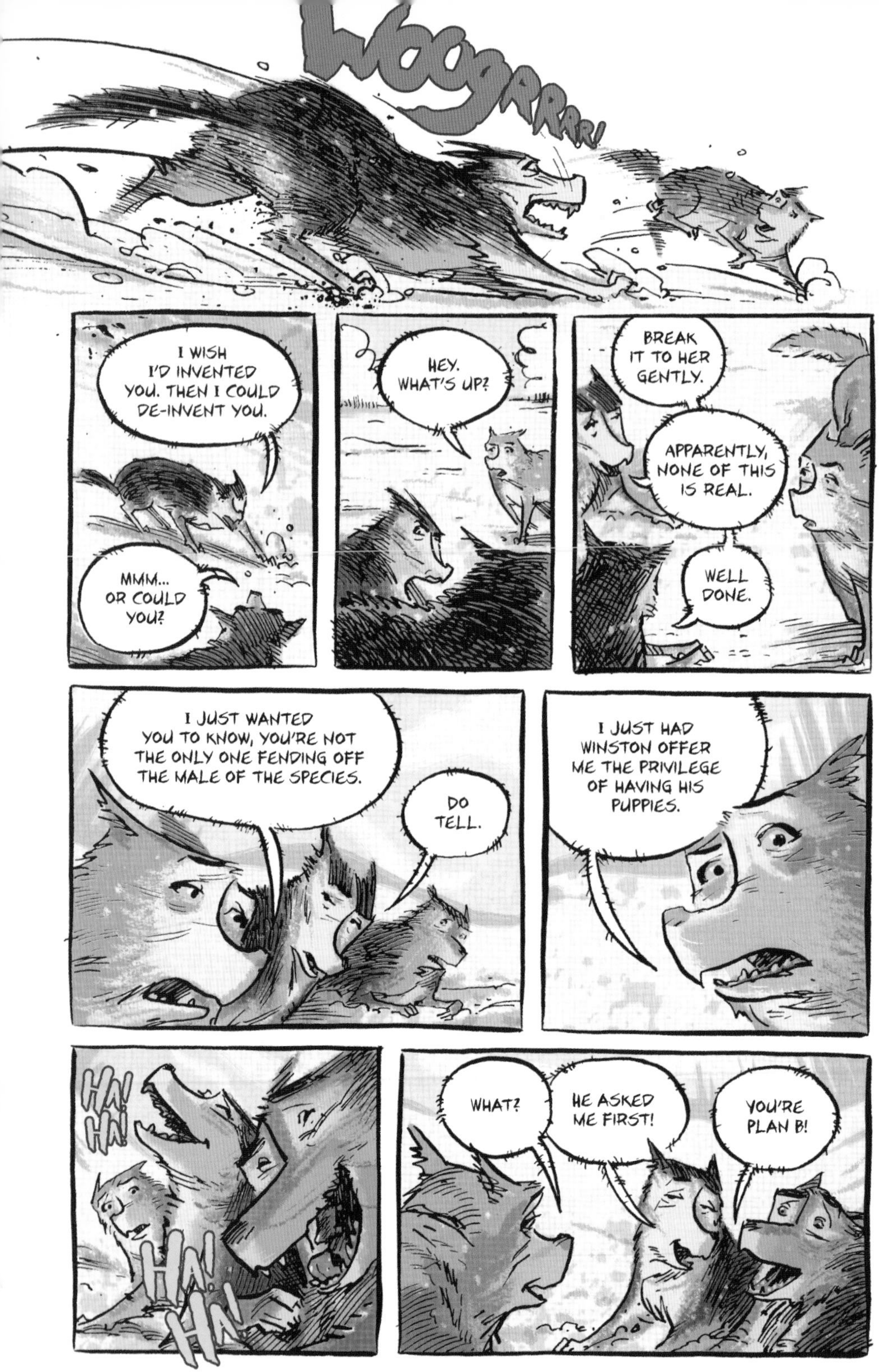
WOOGRRAR!
I WISH I'D INVENTED YOU. THEN I COULD DE-INVENT YOU.
MMM... OR COULD YOU?
HEY. WHAT'S UP?
BREAK IT TO HER GENTLY.
APPARENTLY, NONE OF THIS IS REAL.
WELL DONE.
I JUST WANTED YOU TO KNOW, YOU'RE NOT THE ONLY ONE FENDING OFF THE MALE OF THE SPECIES.
DO TELL.
I JUST HAD WINSTON OFFER ME THE PRIVILEGE OF HAVING HIS PUPPIES.
HA! HA!
HA! HA!
WHAT?
HE ASKED ME FIRST!
YOU'RE PLAN B!

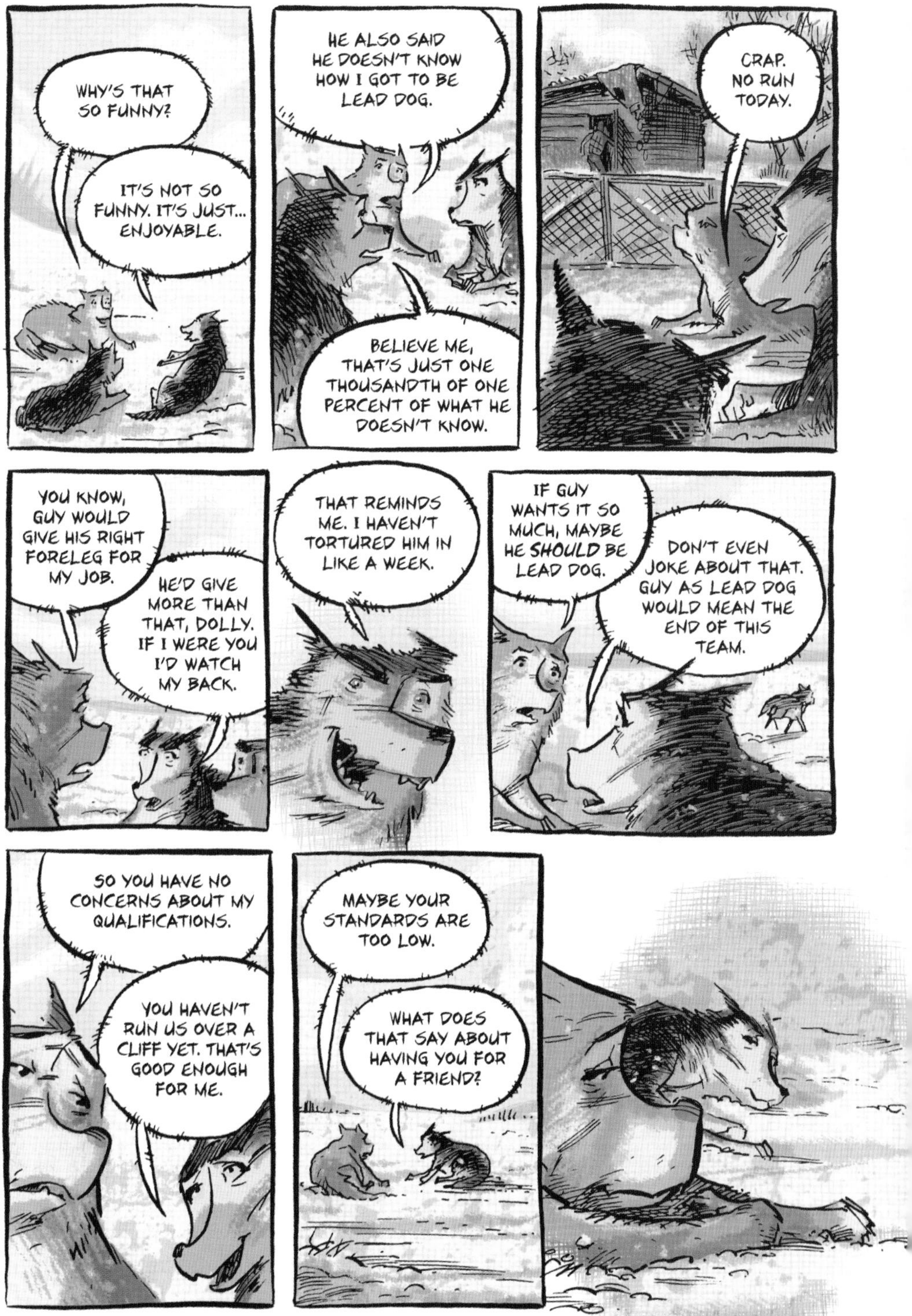
WHY'S THAT SO FUNNY?
IT'S NOT SO FUNNY. IT'S JUST... ENJOYABLE.
HE ALSO SAID HE DOESN'T KNOW HOW I GOT TO BE LEAD DOG.
BELIEVE ME, THAT'S JUST ONE THOUSANDTH OF ONE PERCENT OF WHAT HE DOESN'T KNOW.
CRAP. NO RUN TODAY.
YOU KNOW, GUY WOULD GIVE HIS RIGHT FORELEG FOR MY JOB.
HE'D GIVE MORE THAN THAT, DOLLY. IF I WERE YOU I'D WATCH MY BACK.
THAT REMINDS ME. I HAVEN'T TORTURED HIM IN LIKE A WEEK.
IF GUY WANTS IT SO MUCH, MAYBE HE *SHOULD* BE LEAD DOG.
DON'T EVEN JOKE ABOUT THAT. GUY AS LEAD DOG WOULD MEAN THE END OF THIS TEAM.
SO YOU HAVE NO CONCERNS ABOUT MY QUALIFICATIONS.
YOU HAVEN'T RUN US OVER A CLIFF YET. THAT'S GOOD ENOUGH FOR ME.
MAYBE YOUR STANDARDS ARE TOO LOW.
WHAT DOES THAT SAY ABOUT HAVING YOU FOR A FRIEND?

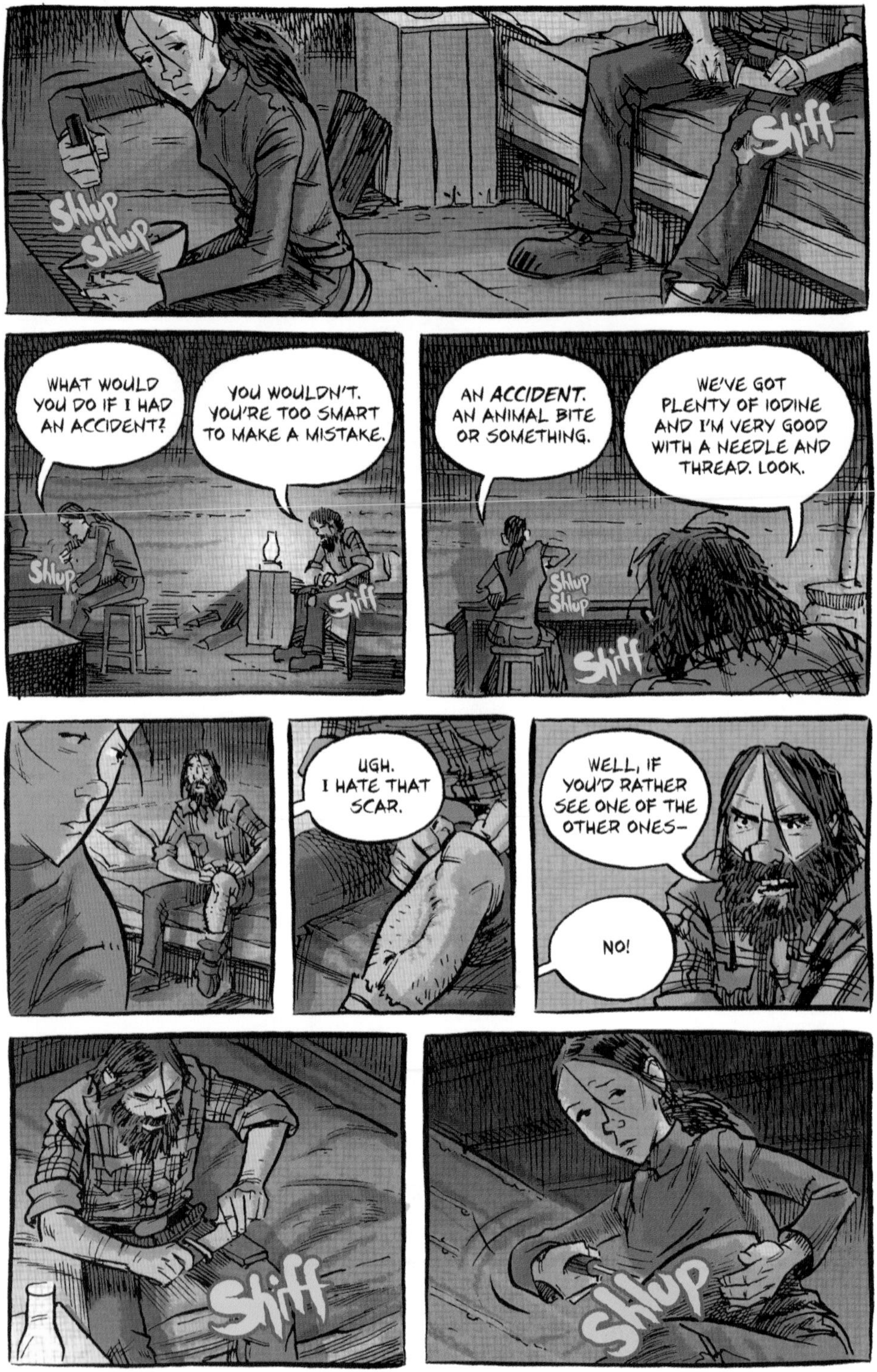
Shlup
Shlup
Shiff
WHAT WOULD YOU DO IF I HAD AN ACCIDENT?
Shlup
YOU WOULDN'T. YOU'RE TOO SMART TO MAKE A MISTAKE.
Shiff
AN *ACCIDENT*. AN ANIMAL BITE OR SOMETHING.
Shlup
Shlup
WE'VE GOT PLENTY OF IODINE AND I'M VERY GOOD WITH A NEEDLE AND THREAD. LOOK.
Shiff
UGH. I HATE THAT SCAR.
WELL, IF YOU'D RATHER SEE ONE OF THE OTHER ONES—
NO!
Shiff
Shlup

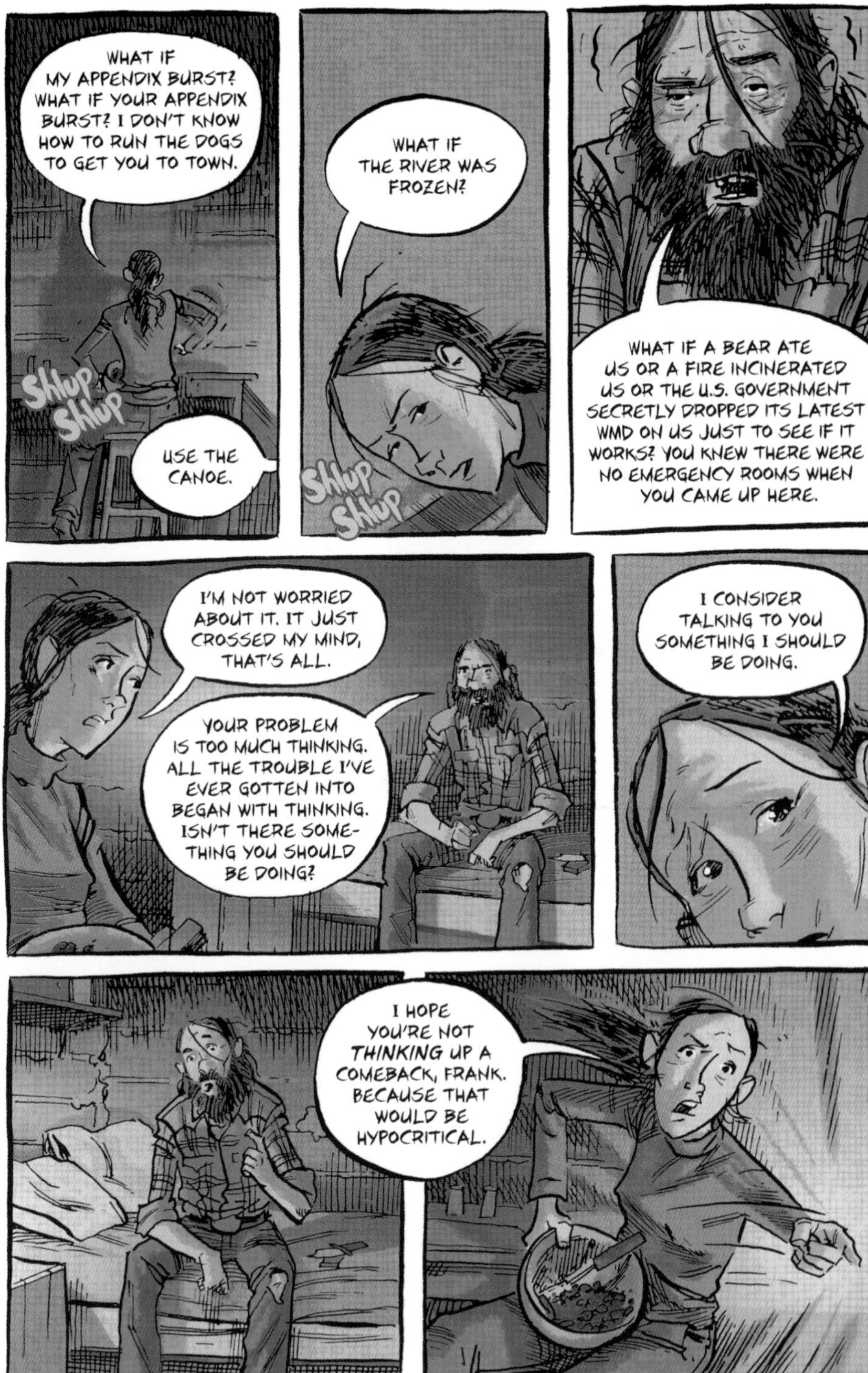
WHAT IF MY APPENDIX BURST? WHAT IF YOUR APPENDIX BURST? I DON'T KNOW HOW TO RUN THE DOGS TO GET YOU TO TOWN.
Shlup Shlup
USE THE CANOE.
WHAT IF THE RIVER WAS FROZEN?
Shlup Shlup
WHAT IF A BEAR ATE US OR A FIRE INCINERATED US OR THE U.S. GOVERNMENT SECRETLY DROPPED ITS LATEST WMD ON US JUST TO SEE IF IT WORKS? YOU KNEW THERE WERE NO EMERGENCY ROOMS WHEN YOU CAME UP HERE.
I'M NOT WORRIED ABOUT IT. IT JUST CROSSED MY MIND, THAT'S ALL.
YOUR PROBLEM IS TOO MUCH THINKING. ALL THE TROUBLE I'VE EVER GOTTEN INTO BEGAN WITH THINKING. ISN'T THERE SOME-THING YOU SHOULD BE DOING?
I CONSIDER TALKING TO YOU SOMETHING I SHOULD BE DOING.
I HOPE YOU'RE NOT *THINKING* UP A COMEBACK, FRANK. BECAUSE THAT WOULD BE HYPOCRITICAL.

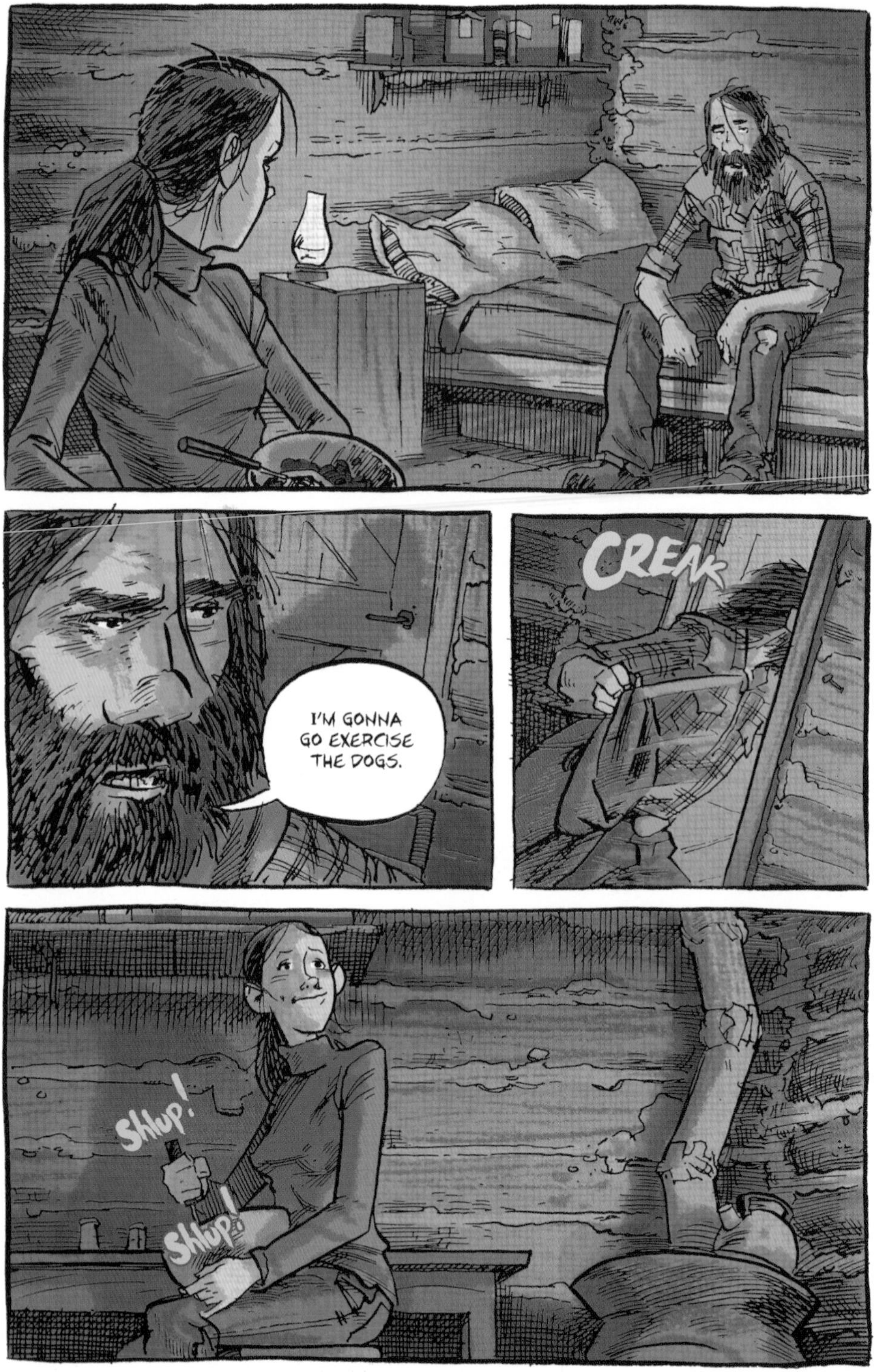
I'M GONNA GO EXERCISE THE DOGS.
CREAK
SHLUP!
SHLUP!

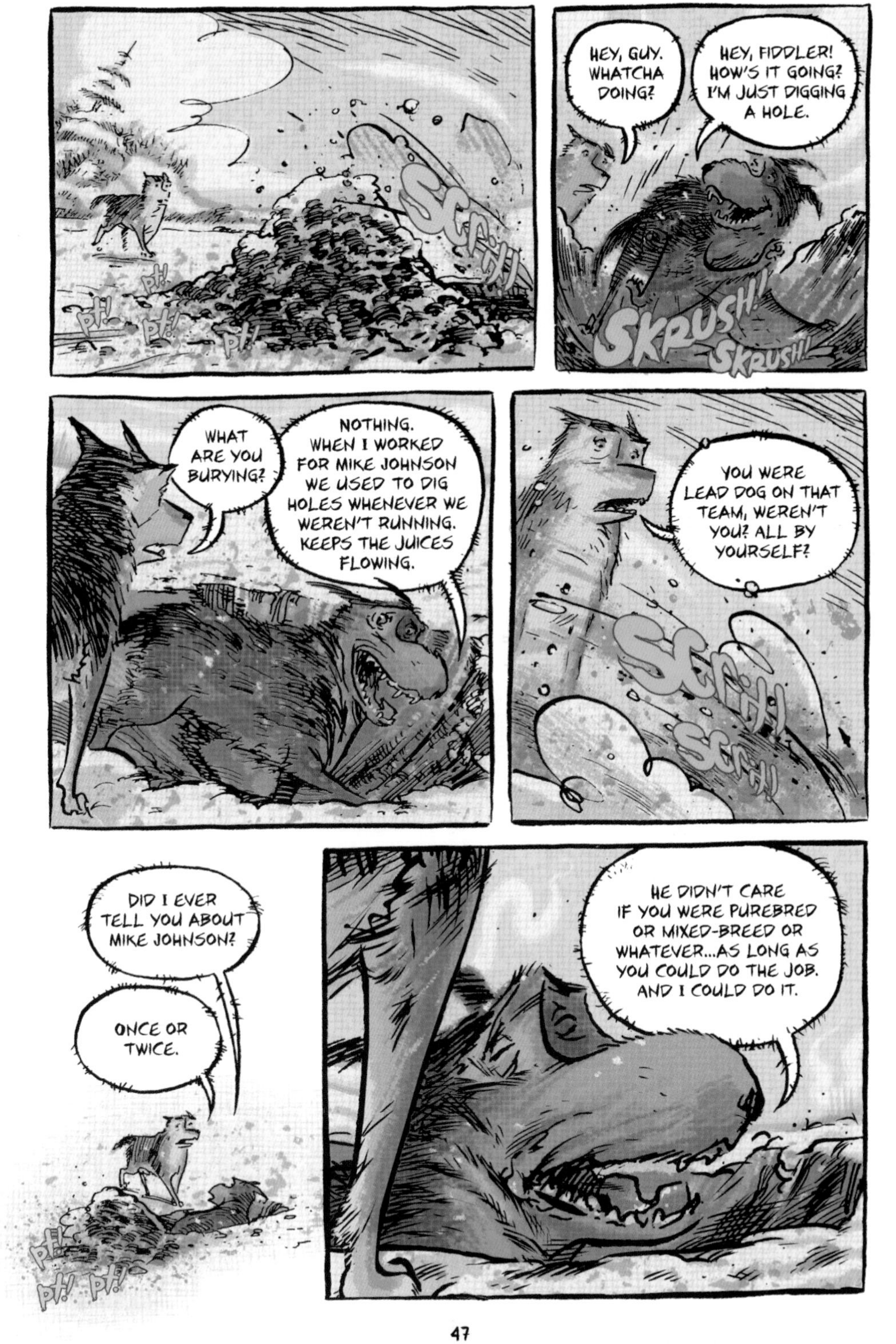
pt! pt! pt! pt!
SCRITI!
HEY, GUY. WHATCHA DOING?
HEY, FIDDLER! HOW'S IT GOING? I'M JUST DIGGING A HOLE.
SKRUSH! SKRUSH!
WHAT ARE YOU BURYING?
NOTHING. WHEN I WORKED FOR MIKE JOHNSON WE USED TO DIG HOLES WHENEVER WE WEREN'T RUNNING. KEEPS THE JUICES FLOWING.
YOU WERE LEAD DOG ON THAT TEAM, WEREN'T YOU? ALL BY YOURSELF?
SCRITI! SCRITI!
DID I EVER TELL YOU ABOUT MIKE JOHNSON?
ONCE OR TWICE.
HE DIDN'T CARE IF YOU WERE PUREBRED OR MIXED-BREED OR WHATEVER...AS LONG AS YOU COULD DO THE JOB. AND I COULD DO IT.
pt! pt! pt!

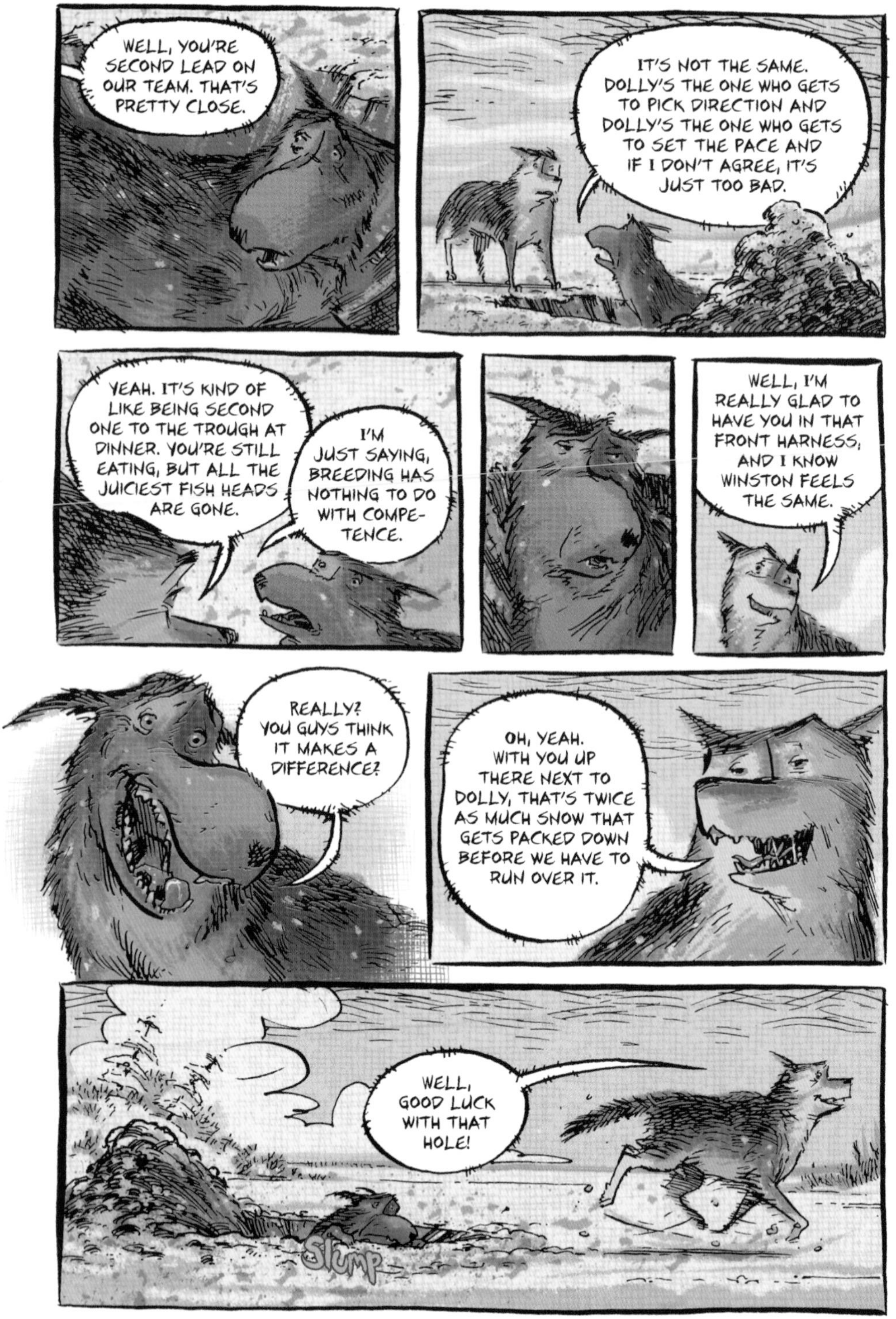
WELL, YOU'RE SECOND LEAD ON OUR TEAM. THAT'S PRETTY CLOSE.
IT'S NOT THE SAME. DOLLY'S THE ONE WHO GETS TO PICK DIRECTION AND DOLLY'S THE ONE WHO GETS TO SET THE PACE AND IF I DON'T AGREE, IT'S JUST TOO BAD.
YEAH. IT'S KIND OF LIKE BEING SECOND ONE TO THE TROUGH AT DINNER. YOU'RE STILL EATING, BUT ALL THE JUICIEST FISH HEADS ARE GONE.
I'M JUST SAYING, BREEDING HAS NOTHING TO DO WITH COMPE-TENCE.
WELL, I'M REALLY GLAD TO HAVE YOU IN THAT FRONT HARNESS, AND I KNOW WINSTON FEELS THE SAME.
REALLY? YOU GUYS THINK IT MAKES A DIFFERENCE?
OH, YEAH. WITH YOU UP THERE NEXT TO DOLLY, THAT'S TWICE AS MUCH SNOW THAT GETS PACKED DOWN BEFORE WE HAVE TO RUN OVER IT.
WELL, GOOD LUCK WITH THAT HOLE!
SLUMP

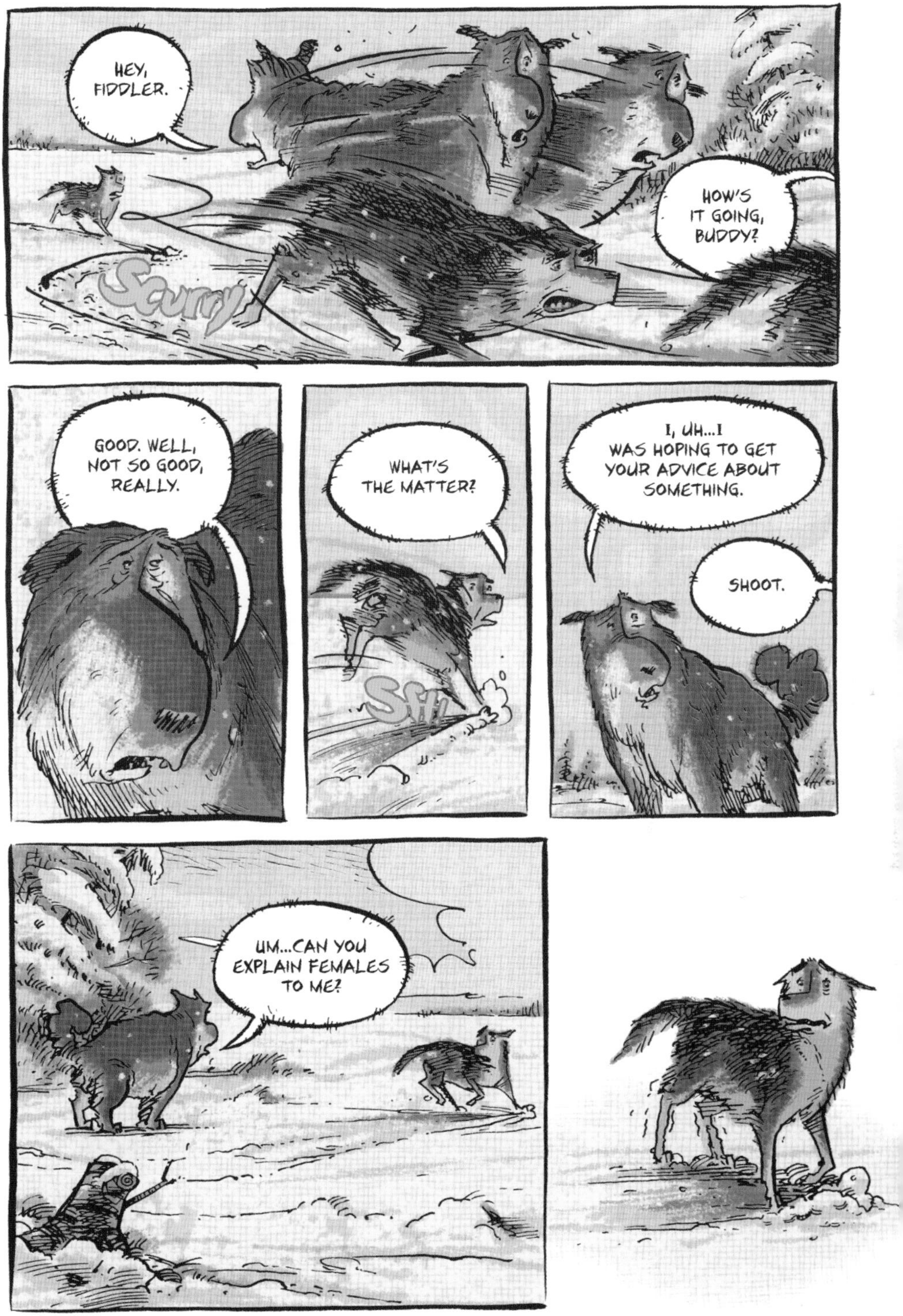
HEY, FIDDLER.
Scurry
HOW'S IT GOING, BUDDY?
GOOD. WELL, NOT SO GOOD, REALLY.
WHAT'S THE MATTER?
Sfft
I, UH...I WAS HOPING TO GET YOUR ADVICE ABOUT SOMETHING.
SHOOT.
UM...CAN YOU EXPLAIN FEMALES TO ME?

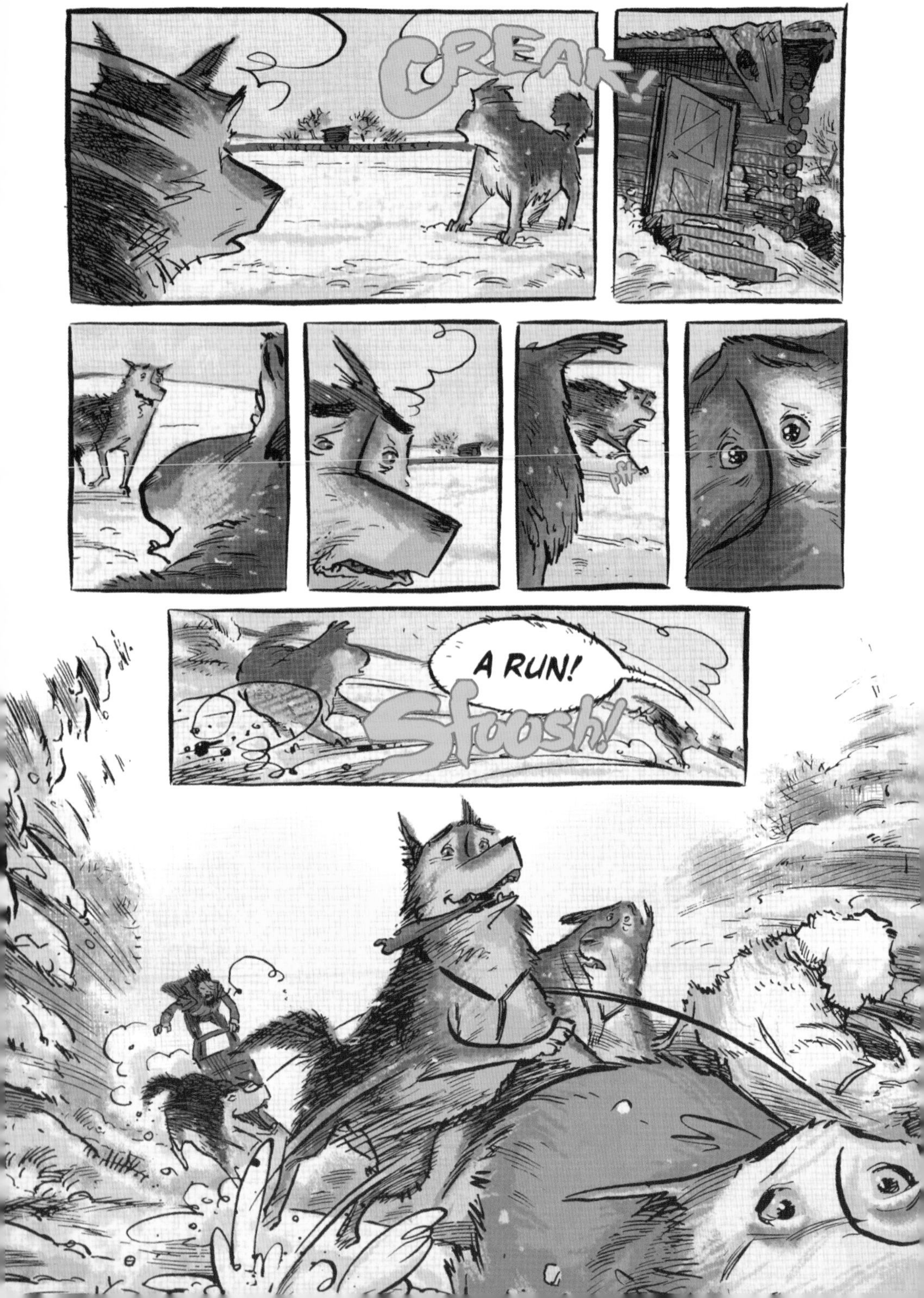
CREAK!
pft
A RUN!
Sfoosh!

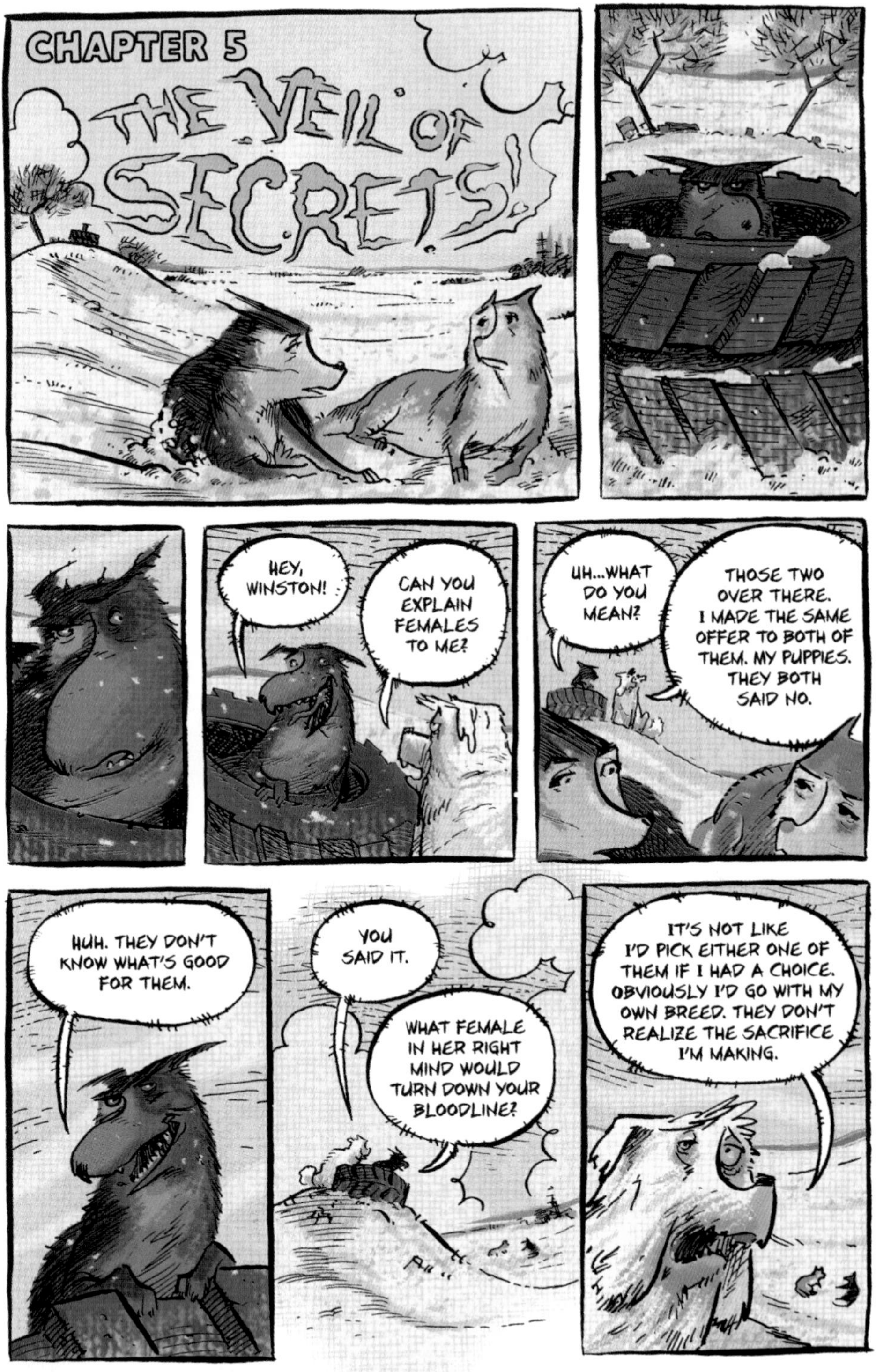
CHAPTER 5
THE VEIL OF SECRETS!
HEY, WINSTON!
CAN YOU EXPLAIN FEMALES TO ME?
UH...WHAT DO YOU MEAN?
THOSE TWO OVER THERE. I MADE THE SAME OFFER TO BOTH OF THEM. MY PUPPIES. THEY BOTH SAID NO.
HUH. THEY DON'T KNOW WHAT'S GOOD FOR THEM.
YOU SAID IT.
WHAT FEMALE IN HER RIGHT MIND WOULD TURN DOWN YOUR BLOODLINE?
IT'S NOT LIKE I'D PICK EITHER ONE OF THEM IF I HAD A CHOICE. OBVIOUSLY I'D GO WITH MY OWN BREED. THEY DON'T REALIZE THE SACRIFICE I'M MAKING.

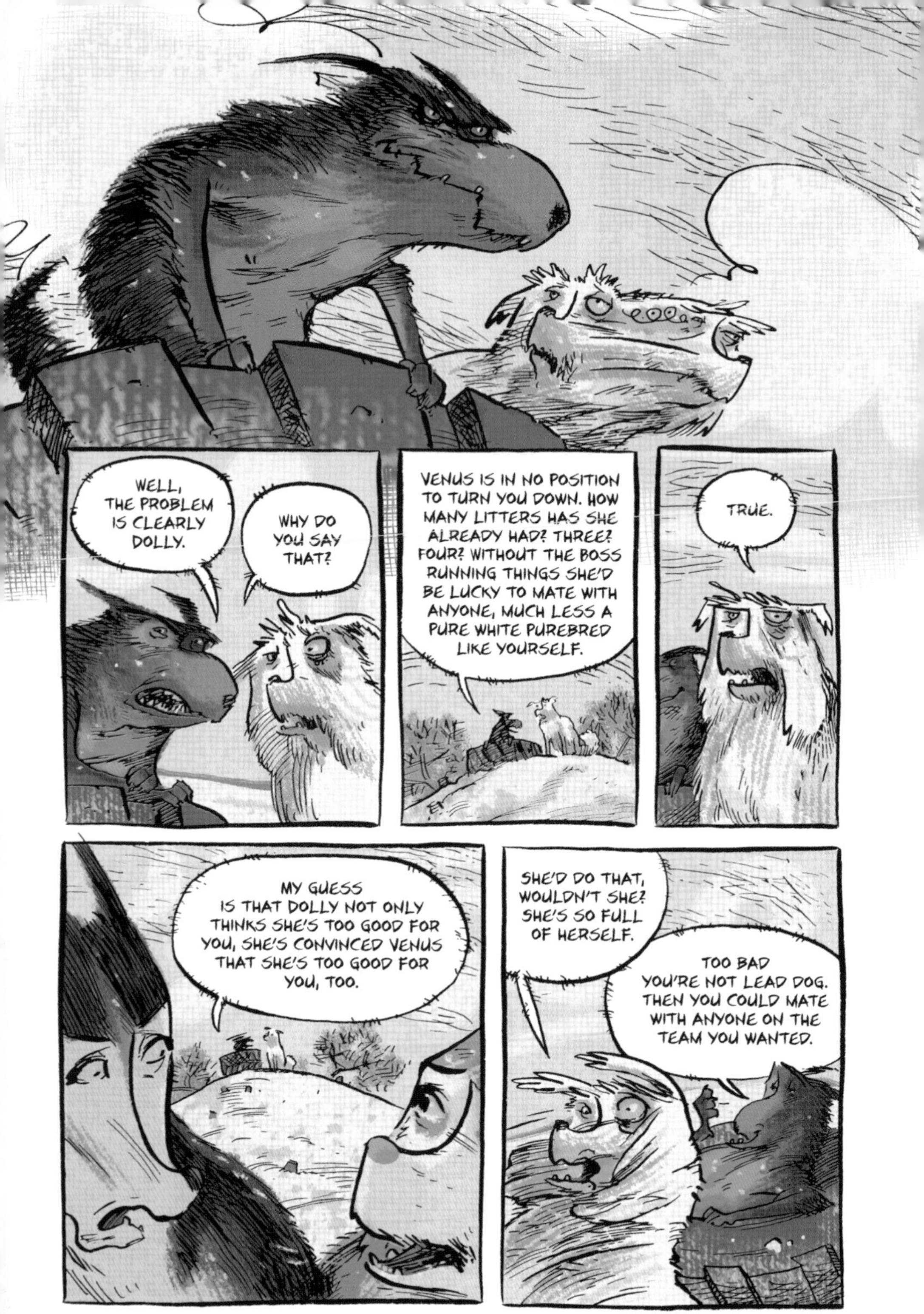
WELL, THE PROBLEM IS CLEARLY DOLLY.
WHY DO YOU SAY THAT?
VENUS IS IN NO POSITION TO TURN YOU DOWN. HOW MANY LITTERS HAS SHE ALREADY HAD? THREE? FOUR? WITHOUT THE BOSS RUNNING THINGS SHE'D BE LUCKY TO MATE WITH ANYONE, MUCH LESS A PURE WHITE PUREBRED LIKE YOURSELF.
TRUE.
MY GUESS IS THAT DOLLY NOT ONLY THINKS SHE'S TOO GOOD FOR YOU, SHE'S CONVINCED VENUS THAT SHE'S TOO GOOD FOR YOU, TOO.
SHE'D DO THAT, WOULDN'T SHE? SHE'S SO FULL OF HERSELF.
TOO BAD YOU'RE NOT LEAD DOG. THEN YOU COULD MATE WITH ANYONE ON THE TEAM YOU WANTED.

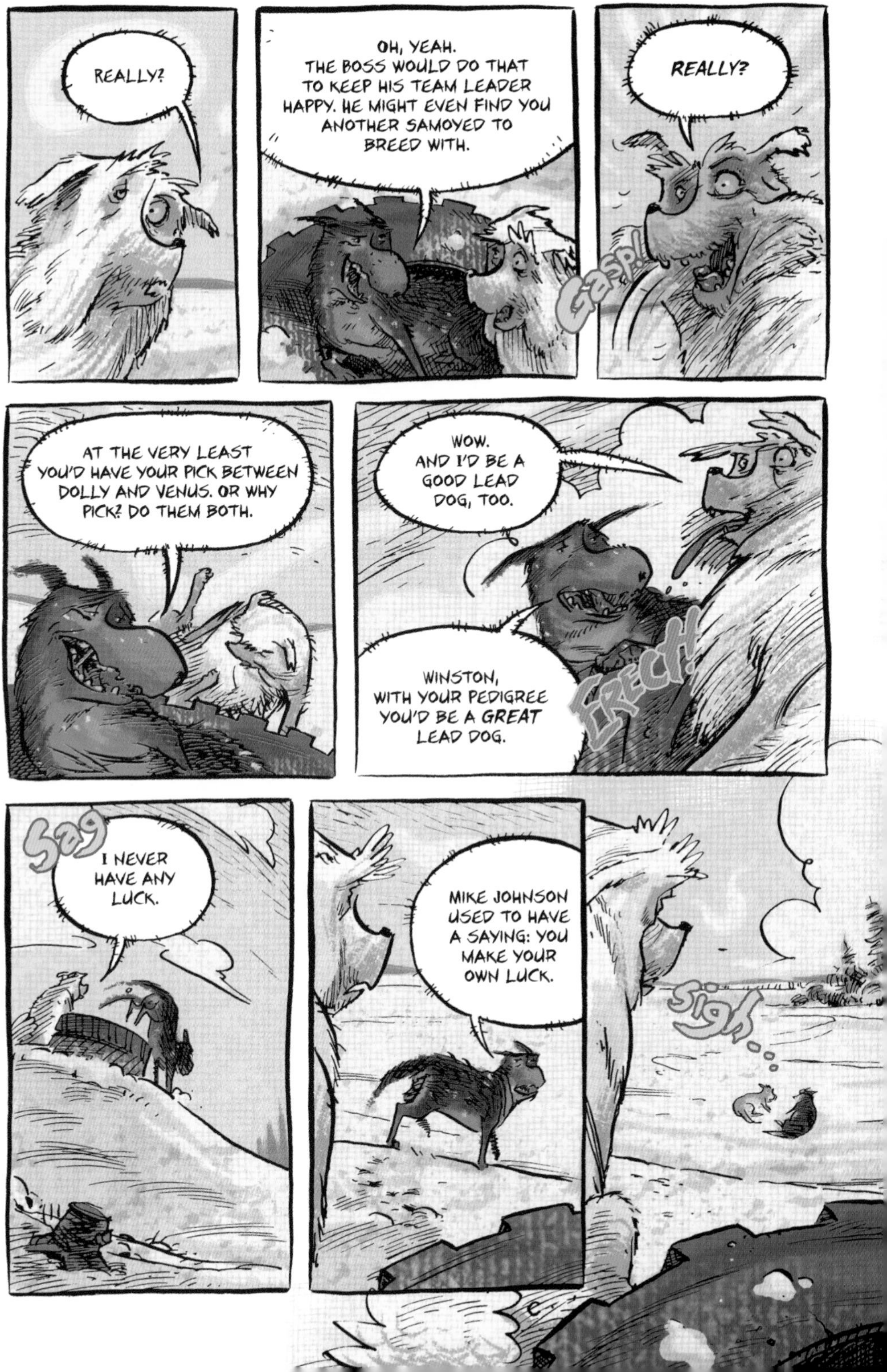

REALLY?
OH, YEAH. THE BOSS WOULD DO THAT TO KEEP HIS TEAM LEADER HAPPY. HE MIGHT EVEN FIND YOU ANOTHER SAMOYED TO BREED WITH.
REALLY?
Gasp!
AT THE VERY LEAST YOU'D HAVE YOUR PICK BETWEEN DOLLY AND VENUS. OR WHY PICK? DO THEM BOTH.
WOW. AND I'D BE A GOOD LEAD DOG, TOO.
WINSTON, WITH YOUR PEDIGREE YOU'D BE A GREAT LEAD DOG.
FRECH!
Sag
I NEVER HAVE ANY LUCK.
MIKE JOHNSON USED TO HAVE A SAYING: YOU MAKE YOUR OWN LUCK.
Sigh...

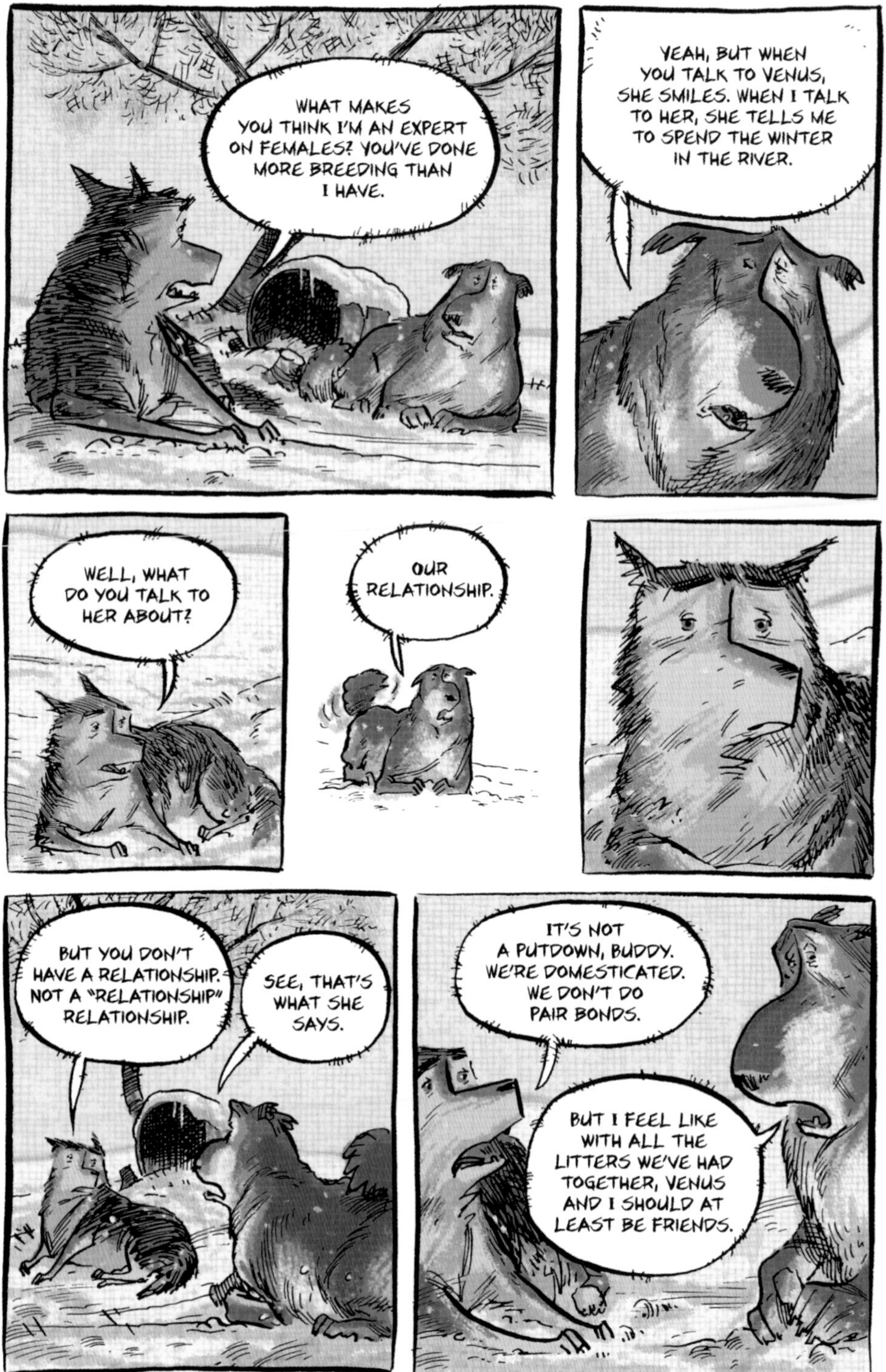
WHAT MAKES YOU THINK I'M AN EXPERT ON FEMALES? YOU'VE DONE MORE BREEDING THAN I HAVE.
YEAH, BUT WHEN YOU TALK TO VENUS, SHE SMILES. WHEN I TALK TO HER, SHE TELLS ME TO SPEND THE WINTER IN THE RIVER.
WELL, WHAT DO YOU TALK TO HER ABOUT?
OUR RELATIONSHIP.
BUT YOU DON'T HAVE A RELATIONSHIP. NOT A "RELATIONSHIP" RELATIONSHIP.
SEE, THAT'S WHAT SHE SAYS.
IT'S NOT A PUTDOWN, BUDDY. WE'RE DOMESTICATED. WE DON'T DO PAIR BONDS.
BUT I FEEL LIKE WITH ALL THE LITTERS WE'VE HAD TOGETHER, VENUS AND I SHOULD AT LEAST BE FRIENDS.

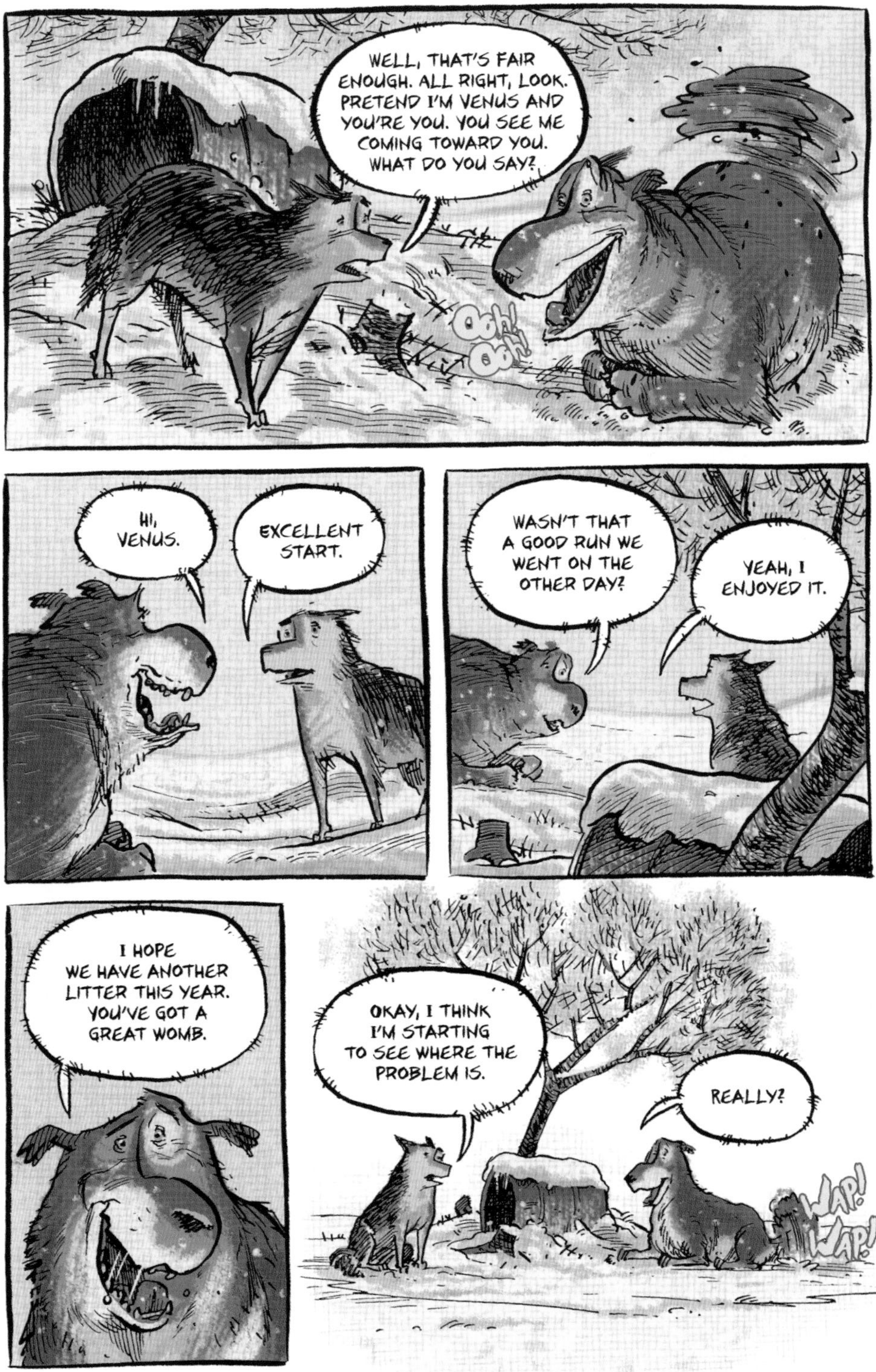
WELL, THAT'S FAIR ENOUGH. ALL RIGHT, LOOK. PRETEND I'M VENUS AND YOU'RE YOU. YOU SEE ME COMING TOWARD YOU. WHAT DO YOU SAY?
OOH! OOH!
HI, VENUS.
EXCELLENT START.
WASN'T THAT A GOOD RUN WE WENT ON THE OTHER DAY?
YEAH, I ENJOYED IT.
I HOPE WE HAVE ANOTHER LITTER THIS YEAR. YOU'VE GOT A GREAT WOMB.
OKAY, I THINK I'M STARTING TO SEE WHERE THE PROBLEM IS.
REALLY?
WAP! WAP!

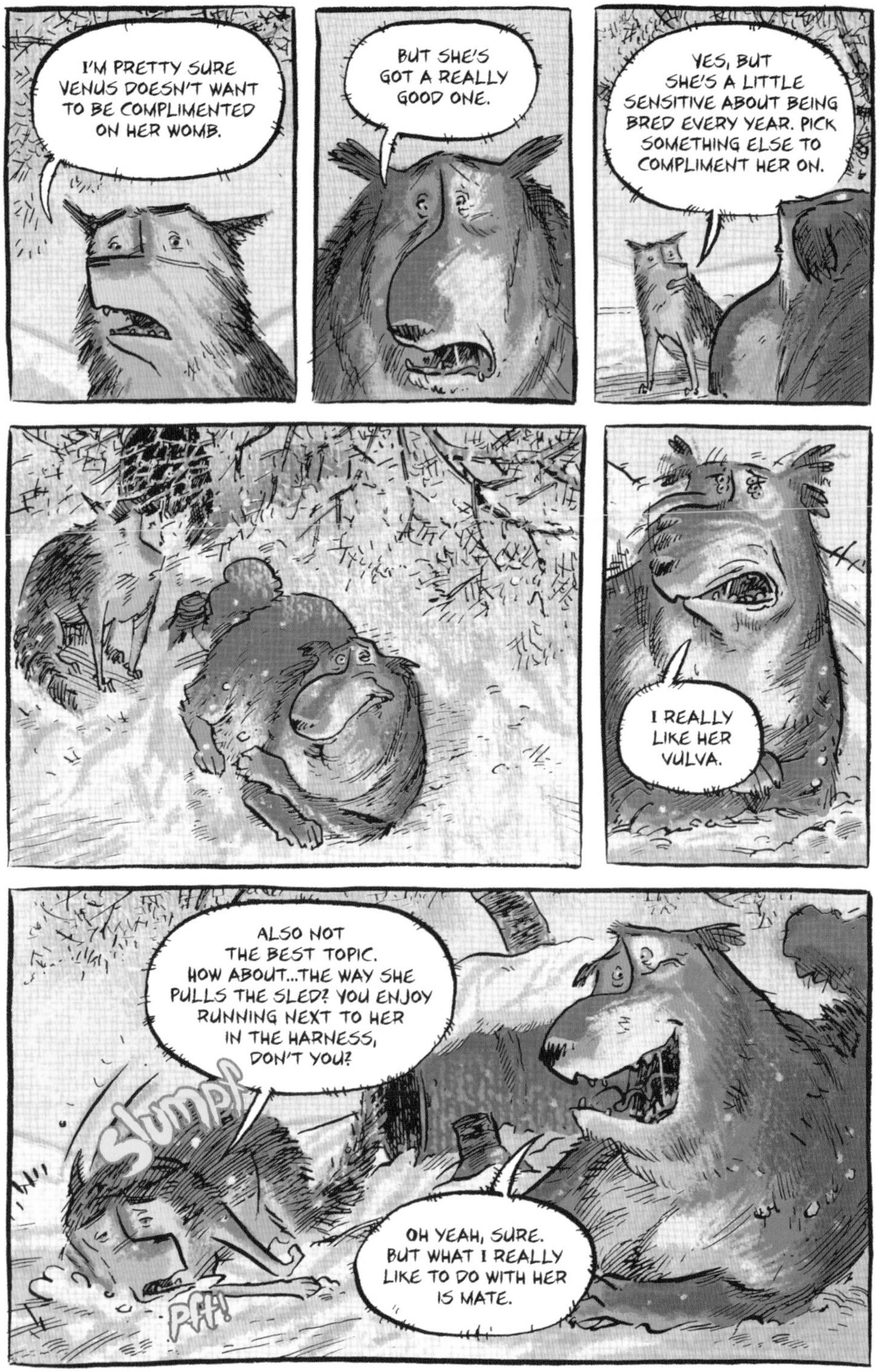
I'M PRETTY SURE VENUS DOESN'T WANT TO BE COMPLIMENTED ON HER WOMB.
BUT SHE'S GOT A REALLY GOOD ONE.
YES, BUT SHE'S A LITTLE SENSITIVE ABOUT BEING BRED EVERY YEAR. PICK SOMETHING ELSE TO COMPLIMENT HER ON.
I REALLY LIKE HER VULVA.
ALSO NOT THE BEST TOPIC. HOW ABOUT...THE WAY SHE PULLS THE SLED? YOU ENJOY RUNNING NEXT TO HER IN THE HARNESS, DON'T YOU?
slumpf
OH YEAH, SURE. BUT WHAT I REALLY LIKE TO DO WITH HER IS MATE.
pft!

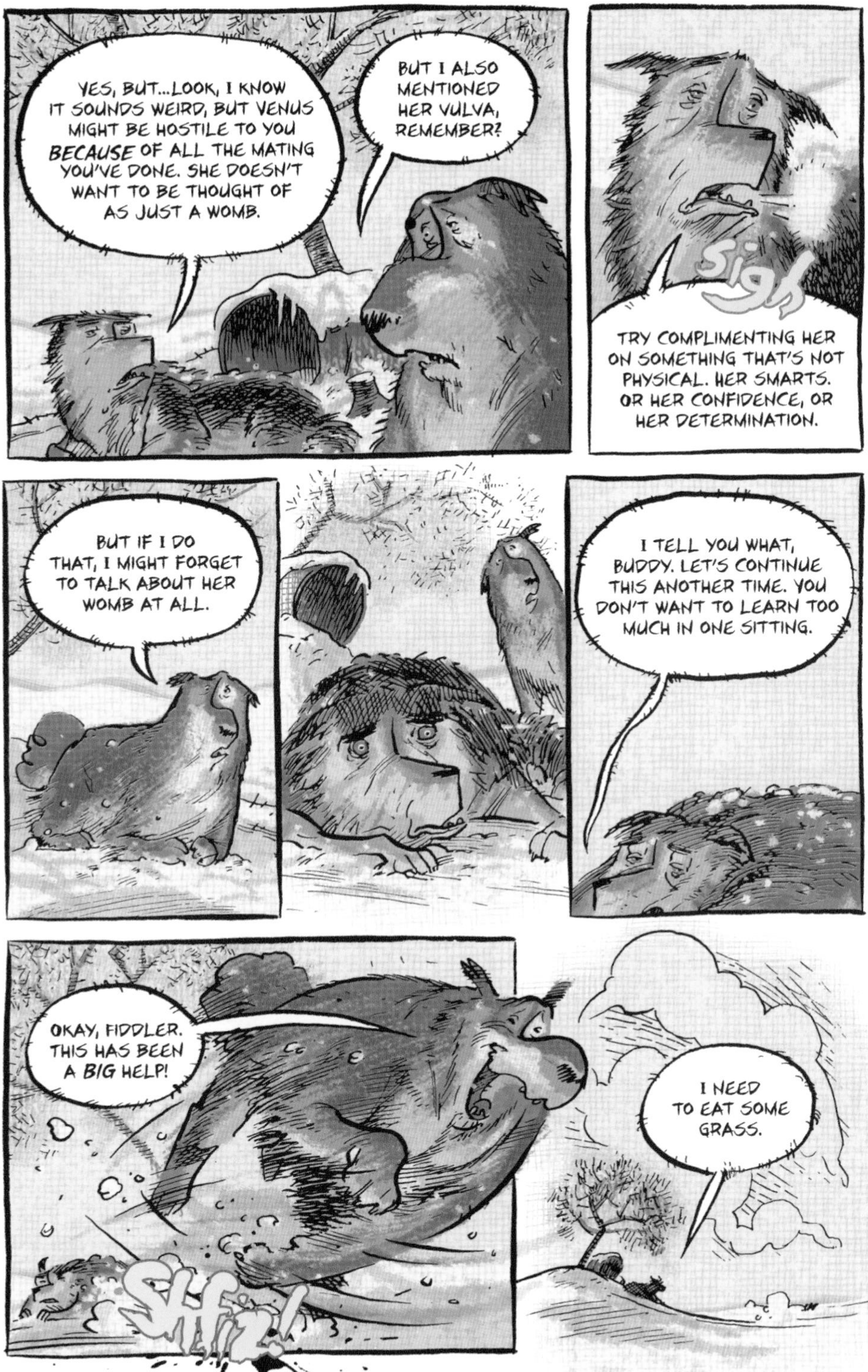
YES, BUT...LOOK, I KNOW IT SOUNDS WEIRD, BUT VENUS MIGHT BE HOSTILE TO YOU *BECAUSE* OF ALL THE MATING YOU'VE DONE. SHE DOESN'T WANT TO BE THOUGHT OF AS JUST A WOMB.
BUT I ALSO MENTIONED HER VULVA, REMEMBER?
SIGH
TRY COMPLIMENTING HER ON SOMETHING THAT'S NOT PHYSICAL. HER SMARTS. OR HER CONFIDENCE, OR HER DETERMINATION.
BUT IF I DO THAT, I MIGHT FORGET TO TALK ABOUT HER WOMB AT ALL.
I TELL YOU WHAT, BUDDY. LET'S CONTINUE THIS ANOTHER TIME. YOU DON'T WANT TO LEARN TOO MUCH IN ONE SITTING.
OKAY, FIDDLER. THIS HAS BEEN A *BIG* HELP!
I NEED TO EAT SOME GRASS.
SHFIZ!

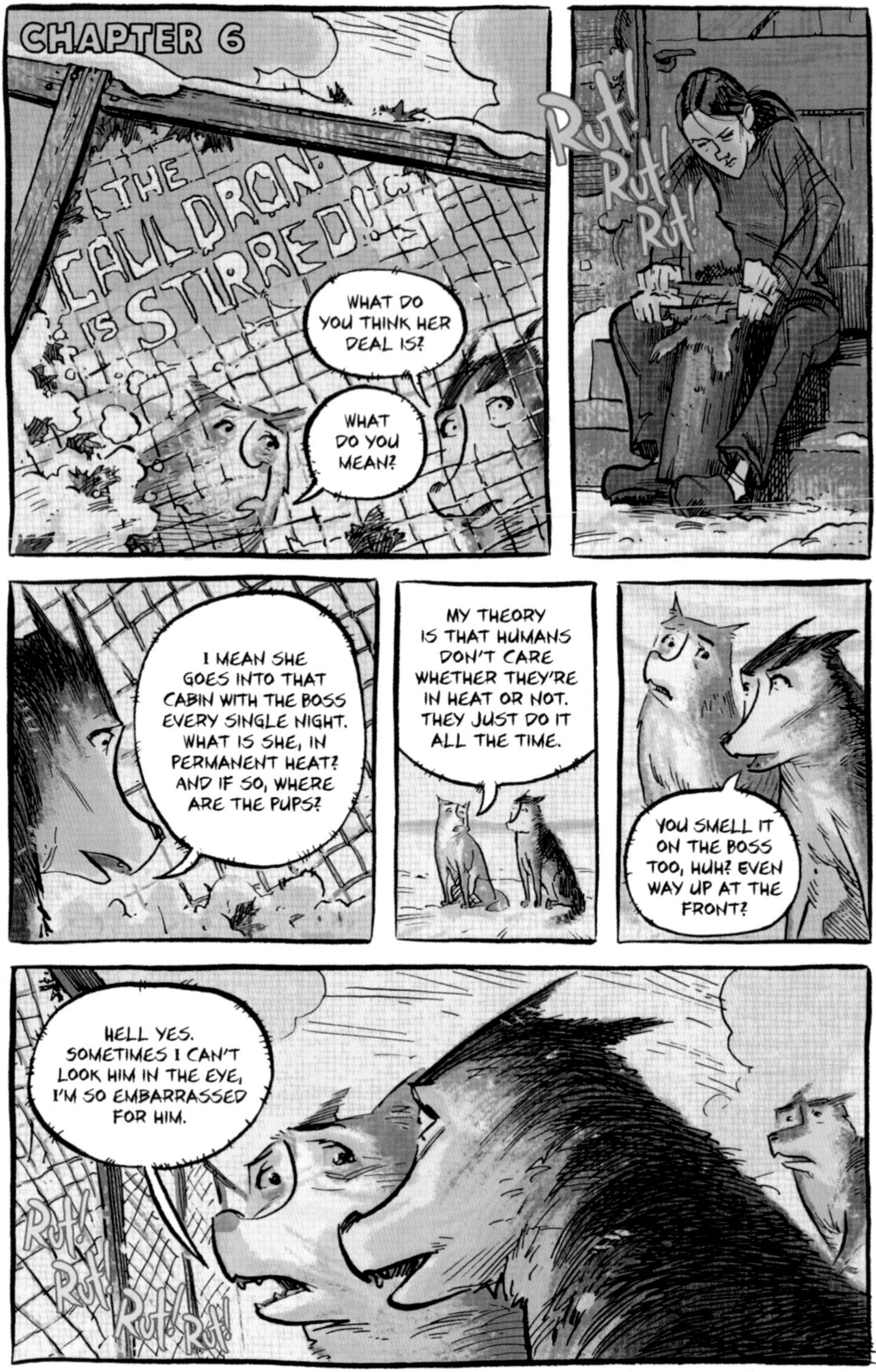
CHAPTER 6
THE CAULDRON IS STIRRED!
WHAT DO YOU THINK HER DEAL IS?
WHAT DO YOU MEAN?
Ruf! Ruf! Ruf!
I MEAN SHE GOES INTO THAT CABIN WITH THE BOSS EVERY SINGLE NIGHT. WHAT IS SHE, IN PERMANENT HEAT? AND IF SO, WHERE ARE THE PUPS?
MY THEORY IS THAT HUMANS DON'T CARE WHETHER THEY'RE IN HEAT OR NOT. THEY JUST DO IT ALL THE TIME.
YOU SMELL IT ON THE BOSS TOO, HUH? EVEN WAY UP AT THE FRONT?
HELL YES. SOMETIMES I CAN'T LOOK HIM IN THE EYE, I'M SO EMBARRASSED FOR HIM.
Ruf! Ruf! Ruf! Ruf!

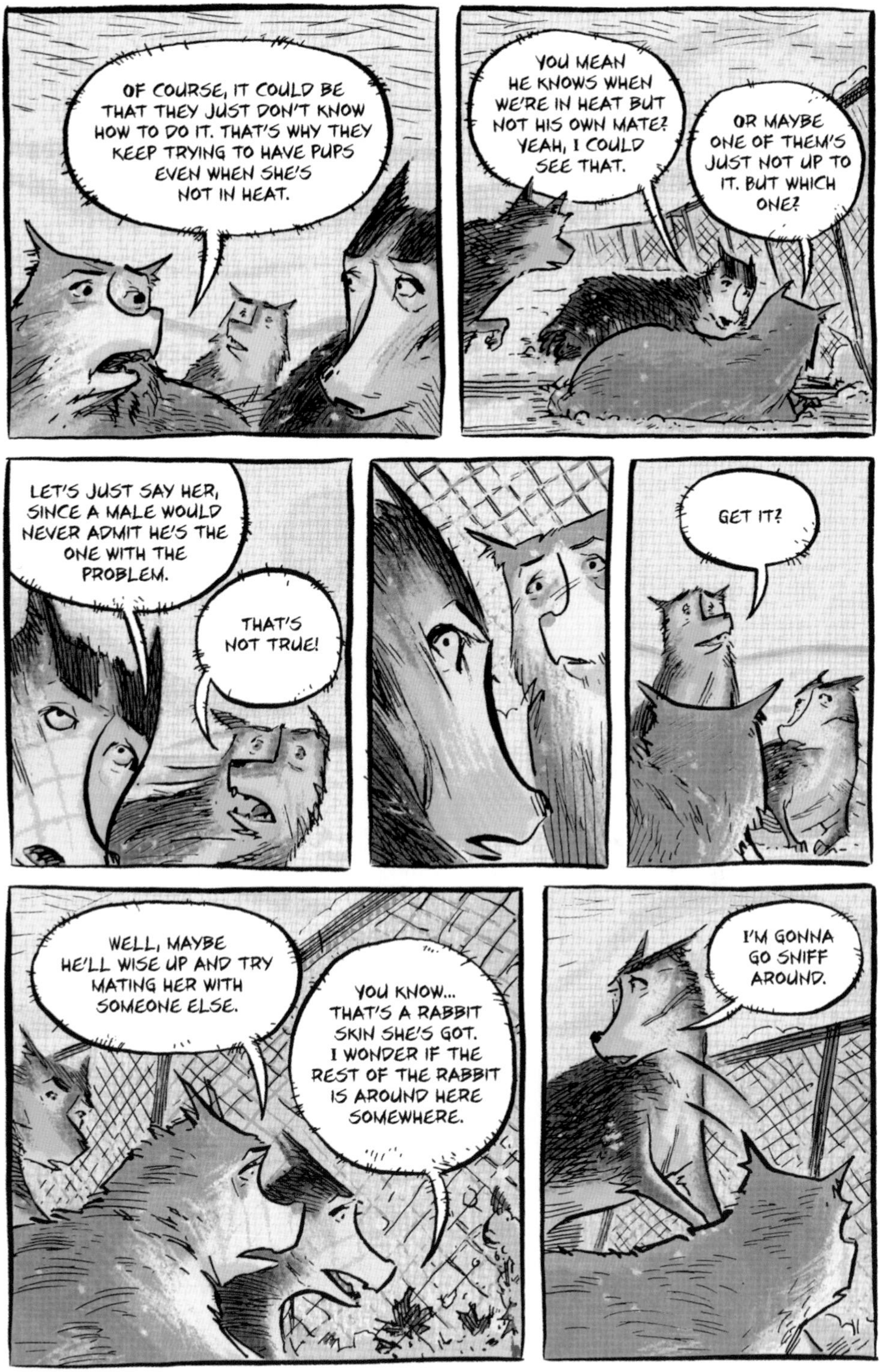
OF COURSE, IT COULD BE THAT THEY JUST DON'T KNOW HOW TO DO IT. THAT'S WHY THEY KEEP TRYING TO HAVE PUPS EVEN WHEN SHE'S NOT IN HEAT.
YOU MEAN HE KNOWS WHEN WE'RE IN HEAT BUT NOT HIS OWN MATE? YEAH, I COULD SEE THAT.
OR MAYBE ONE OF THEM'S JUST NOT UP TO IT. BUT WHICH ONE?
LET'S JUST SAY HER, SINCE A MALE WOULD NEVER ADMIT HE'S THE ONE WITH THE PROBLEM.
THAT'S NOT TRUE!
GET IT?
WELL, MAYBE HE'LL WISE UP AND TRY MATING HER WITH SOMEONE ELSE.
YOU KNOW... THAT'S A RABBIT SKIN SHE'S GOT. I WONDER IF THE REST OF THE RABBIT IS AROUND HERE SOMEWHERE.
I'M GONNA GO SNIFF AROUND.

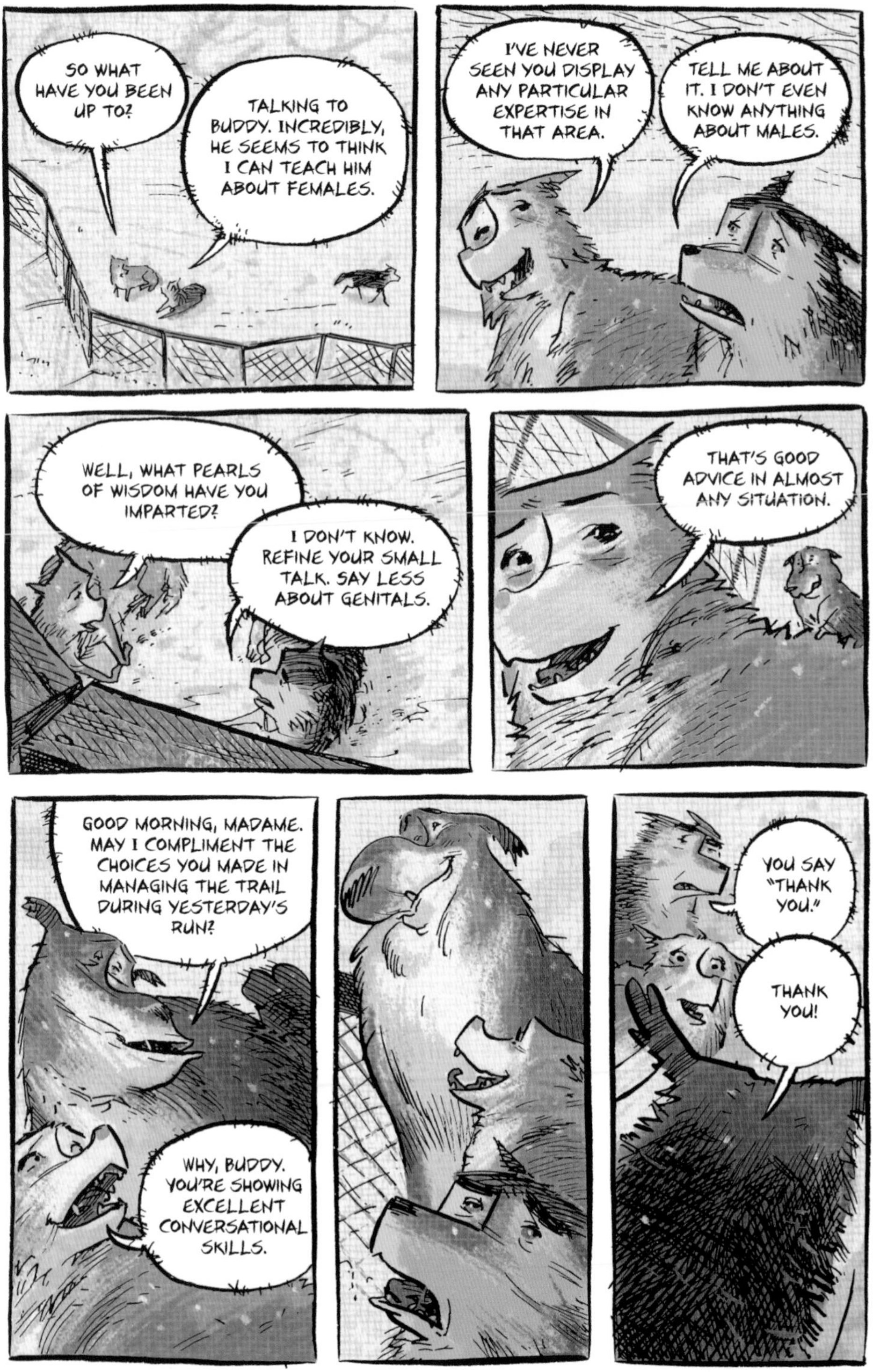
SO WHAT HAVE YOU BEEN UP TO?
TALKING TO BUDDY. INCREDIBLY, HE SEEMS TO THINK I CAN TEACH HIM ABOUT FEMALES.
I'VE NEVER SEEN YOU DISPLAY ANY PARTICULAR EXPERTISE IN THAT AREA.
TELL ME ABOUT IT. I DON'T EVEN KNOW ANYTHING ABOUT MALES.
WELL, WHAT PEARLS OF WISDOM HAVE YOU IMPARTED?
I DON'T KNOW. REFINE YOUR SMALL TALK. SAY LESS ABOUT GENITALS.
THAT'S GOOD ADVICE IN ALMOST ANY SITUATION.
GOOD MORNING, MADAME. MAY I COMPLIMENT THE CHOICES YOU MADE IN MANAGING THE TRAIL DURING YESTERDAY'S RUN?
WHY, BUDDY. YOU'RE SHOWING EXCELLENT CONVERSATIONAL SKILLS.
YOU SAY "THANK YOU."
THANK YOU!

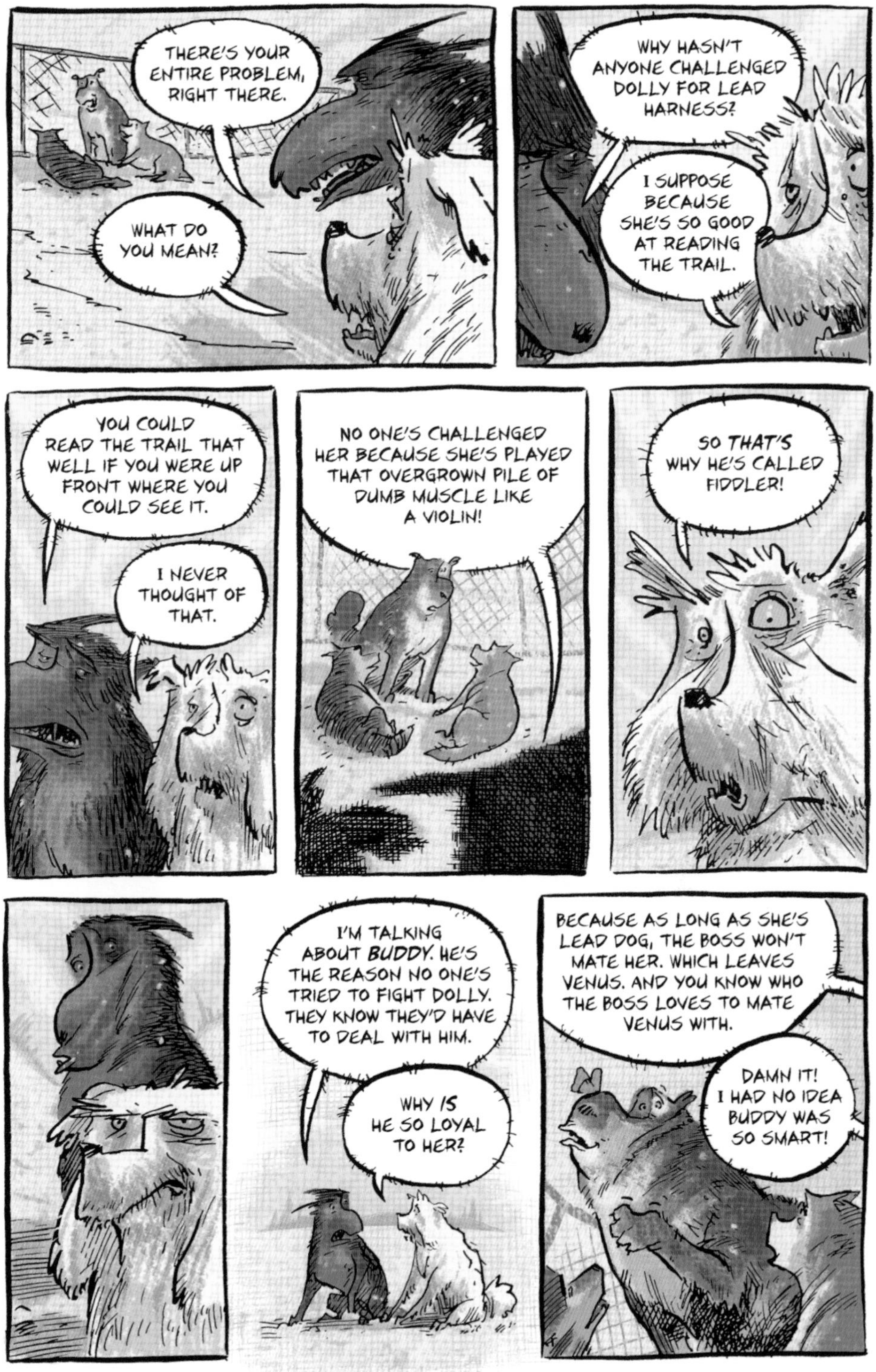
THERE'S YOUR ENTIRE PROBLEM, RIGHT THERE.
WHAT DO YOU MEAN?
WHY HASN'T ANYONE CHALLENGED DOLLY FOR LEAD HARNESS?
I SUPPOSE BECAUSE SHE'S SO GOOD AT READING THE TRAIL.
YOU COULD READ THE TRAIL THAT WELL IF YOU WERE UP FRONT WHERE YOU COULD SEE IT.
I NEVER THOUGHT OF THAT.
NO ONE'S CHALLENGED HER BECAUSE SHE'S PLAYED THAT OVERGROWN PILE OF DUMB MUSCLE LIKE A VIOLIN!
SO *THAT'S* WHY HE'S CALLED FIDDLER!
I'M TALKING ABOUT **BUDDY**. HE'S THE REASON NO ONE'S TRIED TO FIGHT DOLLY. THEY KNOW THEY'D HAVE TO DEAL WITH HIM.
WHY *IS* HE SO LOYAL TO HER?
BECAUSE AS LONG AS SHE'S LEAD DOG, THE BOSS WON'T MATE HER. WHICH LEAVES VENUS. AND YOU KNOW WHO THE BOSS LOVES TO MATE VENUS WITH.
DAMN IT! I HAD NO IDEA BUDDY WAS SO SMART!

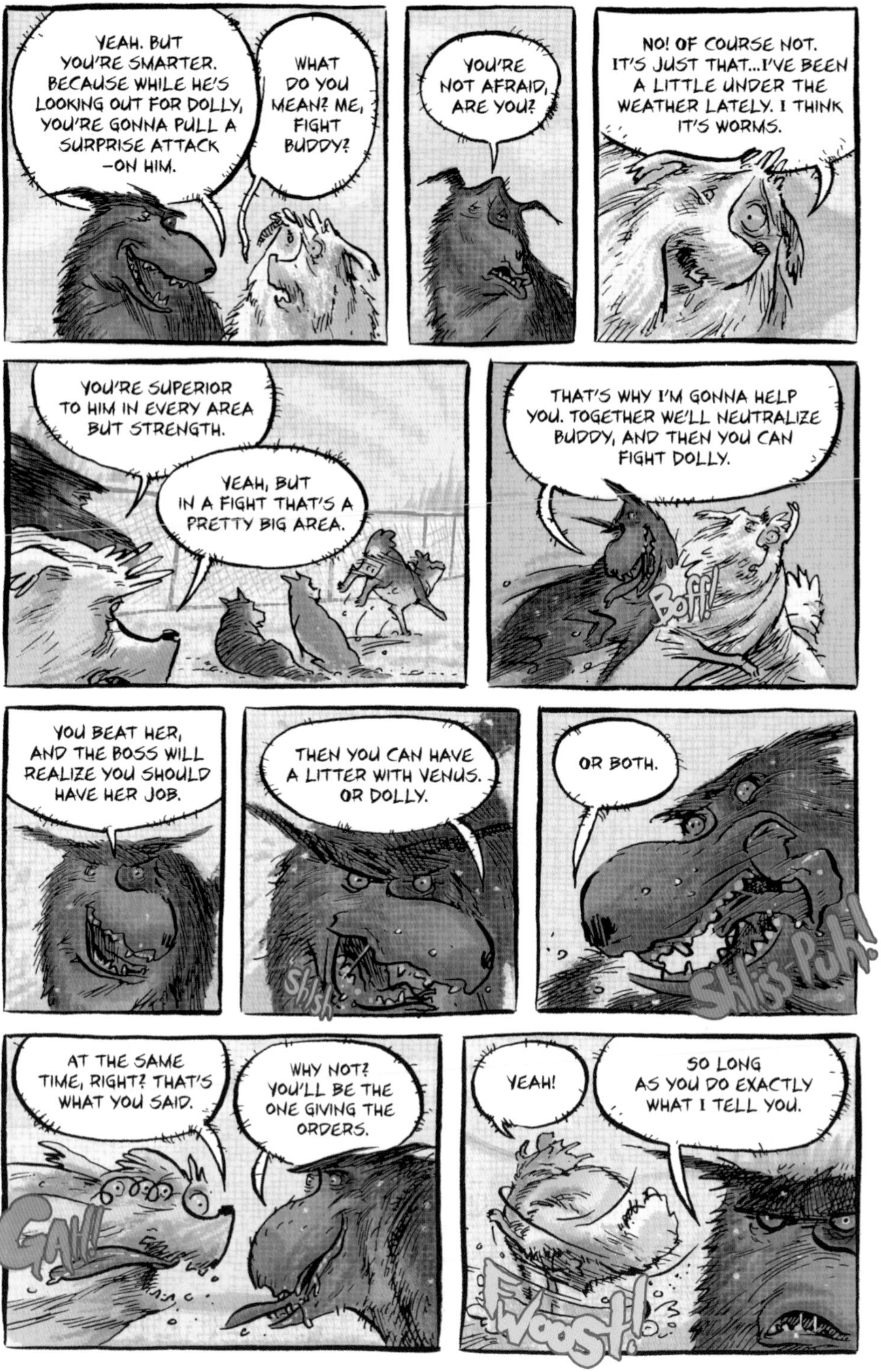
YEAH. BUT YOU'RE SMARTER. BECAUSE WHILE HE'S LOOKING OUT FOR DOLLY, YOU'RE GONNA PULL A SURPRISE ATTACK —ON HIM.
WHAT DO YOU MEAN? ME, FIGHT BUDDY?
YOU'RE NOT AFRAID, ARE YOU?
NO! OF COURSE NOT. IT'S JUST THAT...I'VE BEEN A LITTLE UNDER THE WEATHER LATELY. I THINK IT'S WORMS.
YOU'RE SUPERIOR TO HIM IN EVERY AREA BUT STRENGTH.
YEAH, BUT IN A FIGHT THAT'S A PRETTY BIG AREA.
THAT'S WHY I'M GONNA HELP YOU. TOGETHER WE'LL NEUTRALIZE BUDDY, AND THEN YOU CAN FIGHT DOLLY.
Boff!
YOU BEAT HER, AND THE BOSS WILL REALIZE YOU SHOULD HAVE HER JOB.
THEN YOU CAN HAVE A LITTER WITH VENUS. OR DOLLY.
Shlsh
OR BOTH.
Shliss-Puh!
AT THE SAME TIME, RIGHT? THAT'S WHAT YOU SAID.
Gah!
WHY NOT? YOU'LL BE THE ONE GIVING THE ORDERS.
YEAH!
SO LONG AS YOU DO EXACTLY WHAT I TELL YOU.
Fwoost!

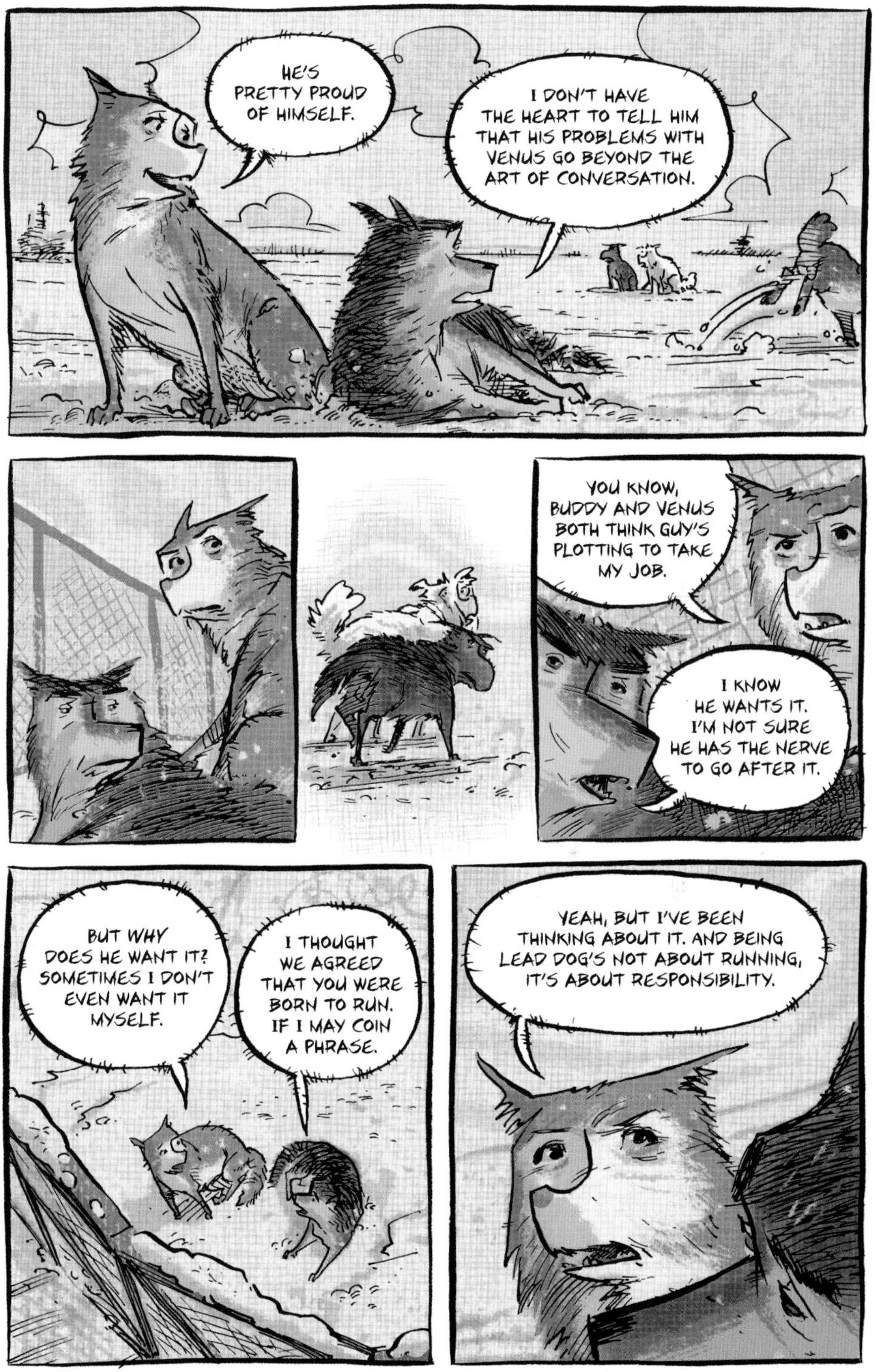
HE'S PRETTY PROUD OF HIMSELF.
I DON'T HAVE THE HEART TO TELL HIM THAT HIS PROBLEMS WITH VENUS GO BEYOND THE ART OF CONVERSATION.
YOU KNOW, BUDDY AND VENUS BOTH THINK GUY'S PLOTTING TO TAKE MY JOB.
I KNOW HE WANTS IT. I'M NOT SURE HE HAS THE NERVE TO GO AFTER IT.
BUT WHY DOES HE WANT IT? SOMETIMES I DON'T EVEN WANT IT MYSELF.
I THOUGHT WE AGREED THAT YOU WERE BORN TO RUN. IF I MAY COIN A PHRASE.
YEAH, BUT I'VE BEEN THINKING ABOUT IT. AND BEING LEAD DOG'S NOT ABOUT RUNNING, IT'S ABOUT RESPONSIBILITY.

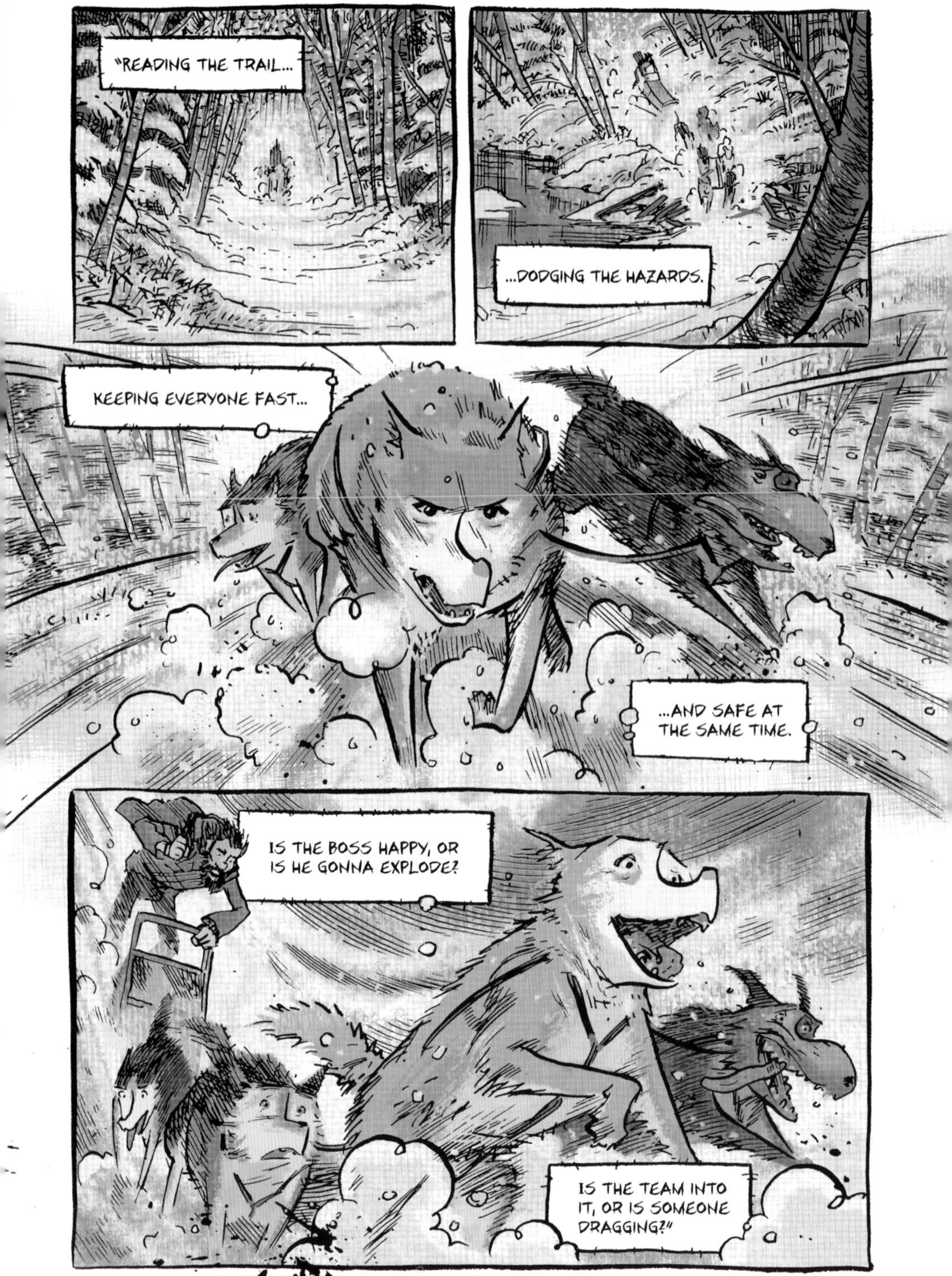

"READING THE TRAIL...
...DODGING THE HAZARDS.
KEEPING EVERYONE FAST...
...AND SAFE AT THE SAME TIME.
IS THE BOSS HAPPY, OR IS HE GONNA EXPLODE?
IS THE TEAM INTO IT, OR IS SOMEONE DRAGGING?"

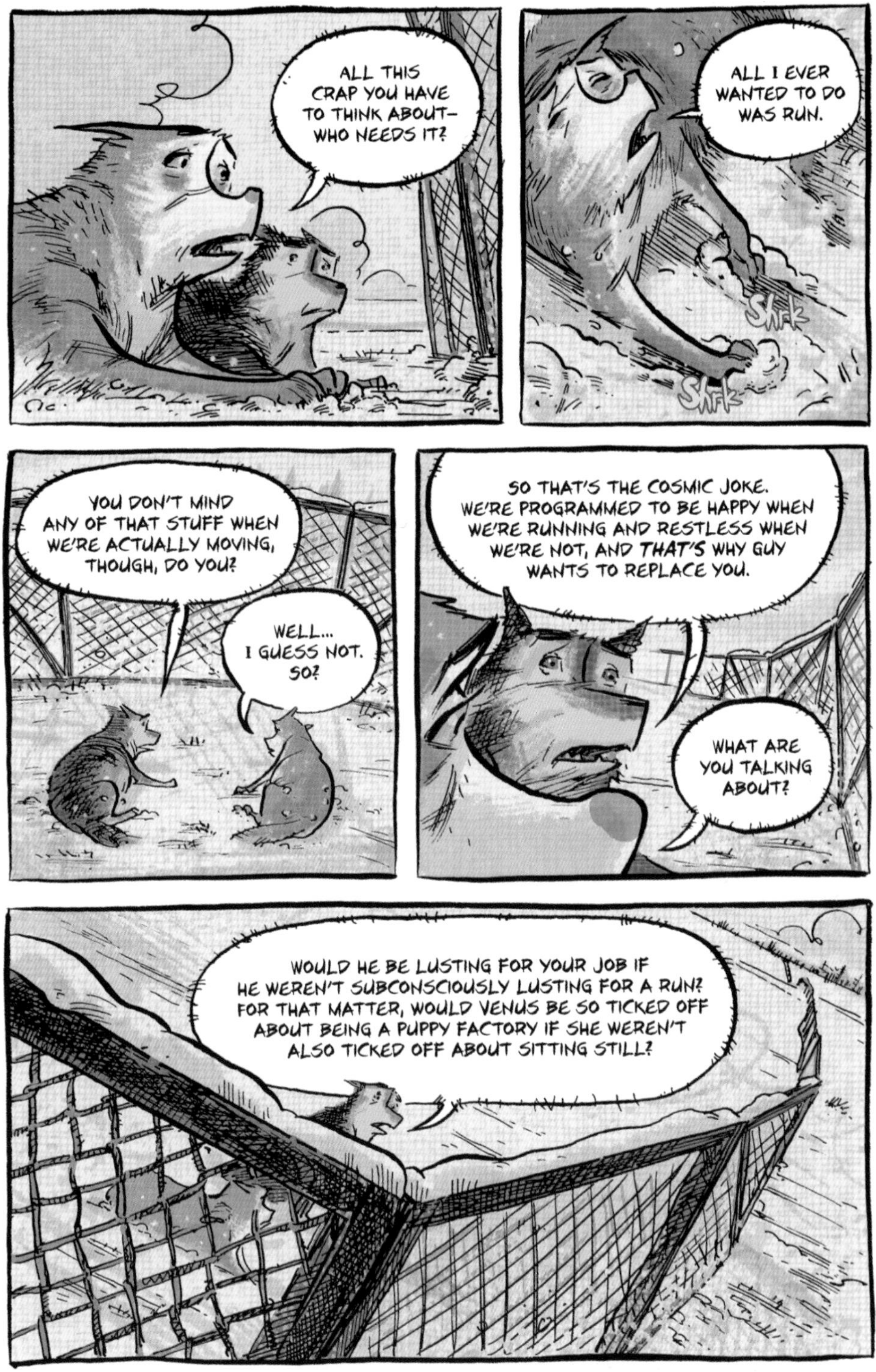
ALL THIS CRAP YOU HAVE TO THINK ABOUT— WHO NEEDS IT?
ALL I EVER WANTED TO DO WAS RUN.
Shrk
Shrk
YOU DON'T MIND ANY OF THAT STUFF WHEN WE'RE ACTUALLY MOVING, THOUGH, DO YOU?
WELL... I GUESS NOT. SO?
SO THAT'S THE COSMIC JOKE. WE'RE PROGRAMMED TO BE HAPPY WHEN WE'RE RUNNING AND RESTLESS WHEN WE'RE NOT, AND THAT'S WHY GUY WANTS TO REPLACE YOU.
WHAT ARE YOU TALKING ABOUT?
WOULD HE BE LUSTING FOR YOUR JOB IF HE WEREN'T SUBCONSCIOUSLY LUSTING FOR A RUN? FOR THAT MATTER, WOULD VENUS BE SO TICKED OFF ABOUT BEING A PUPPY FACTORY IF SHE WEREN'T ALSO TICKED OFF ABOUT SITTING STILL?

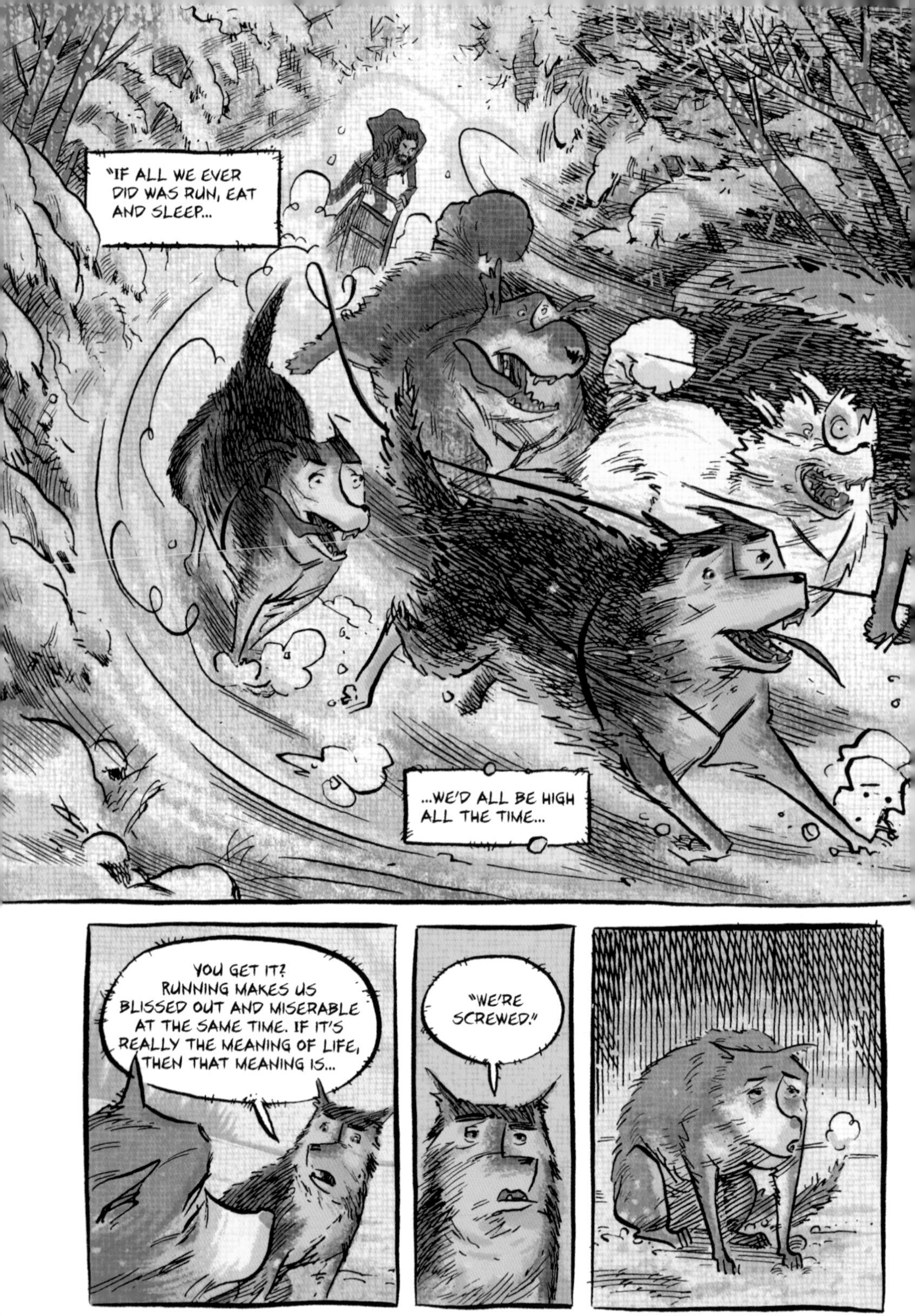
"IF ALL WE EVER DID WAS RUN, EAT AND SLEEP...
...WE'D ALL BE HIGH ALL THE TIME...
YOU GET IT? RUNNING MAKES US BLISSED OUT AND MISERABLE AT THE SAME TIME. IF IT'S REALLY THE MEANING OF LIFE, THEN THAT MEANING IS...
"WE'RE SCREWED."

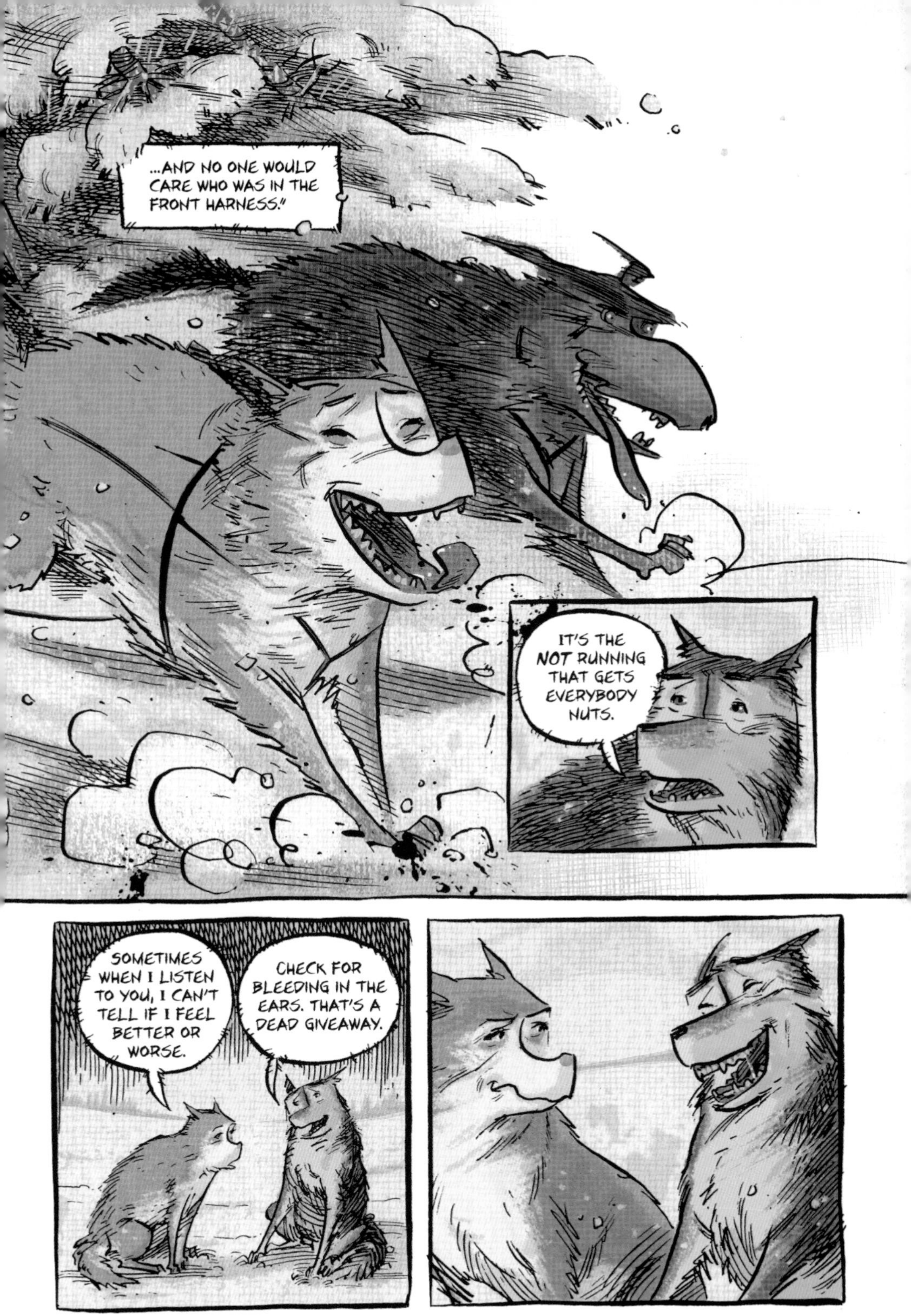
...AND NO ONE WOULD CARE WHO WAS IN THE FRONT HARNESS."
IT'S THE NOT RUNNING THAT GETS EVERYBODY NUTS.
SOMETIMES WHEN I LISTEN TO YOU, I CAN'T TELL IF I FEEL BETTER OR WORSE.
CHECK FOR BLEEDING IN THE EARS. THAT'S A DEAD GIVEAWAY.

# CHAPTER 7

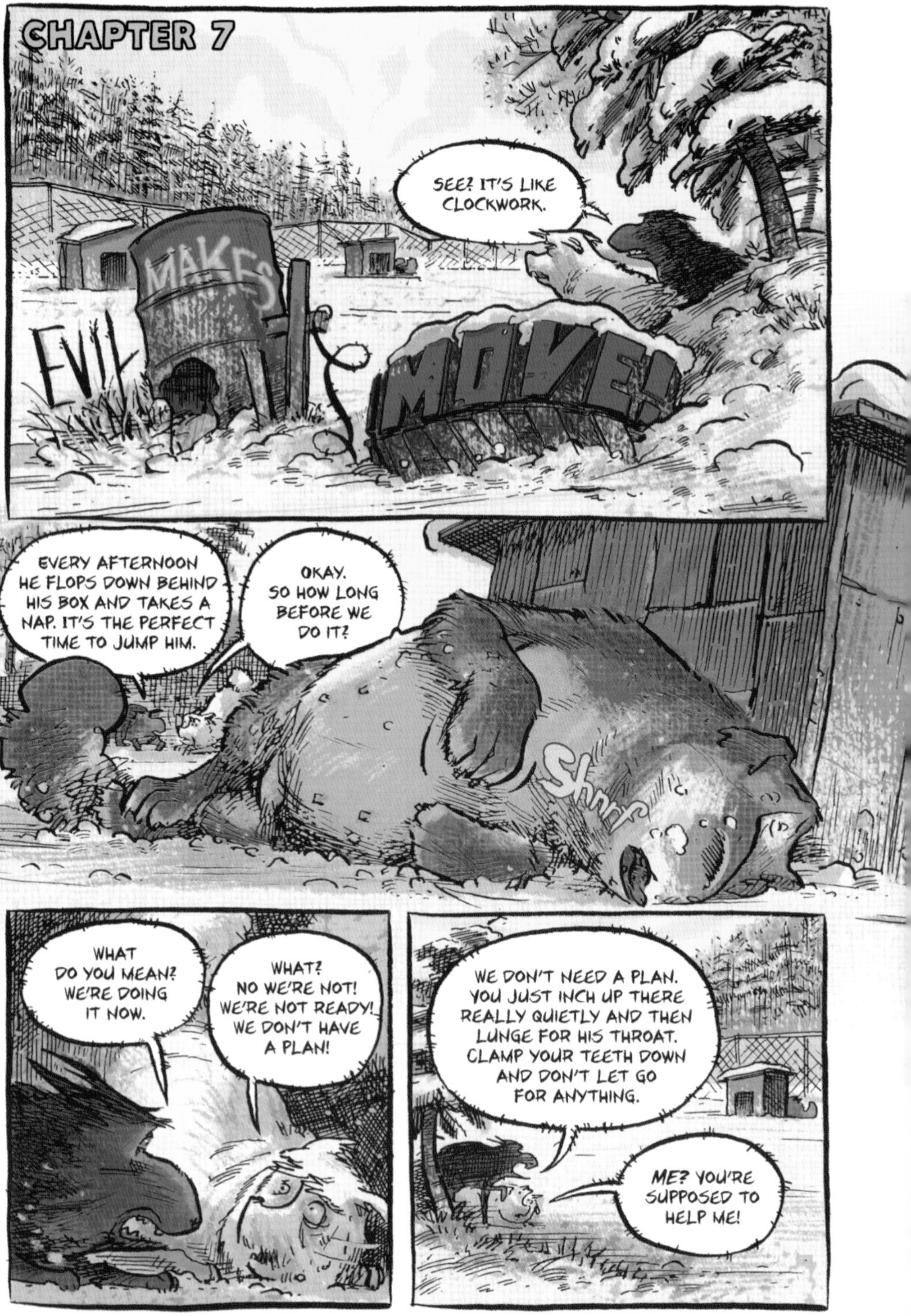

SEE? IT'S LIKE CLOCKWORK.
EVIL
MAKES
MOVE!
EVERY AFTERNOON HE FLOPS DOWN BEHIND HIS BOX AND TAKES A NAP. IT'S THE PERFECT TIME TO JUMP HIM.
OKAY. SO HOW LONG BEFORE WE DO IT?
Shnrf
WHAT DO YOU MEAN? WE'RE DOING IT NOW.
WHAT? NO WE'RE NOT! WE'RE NOT READY! WE DON'T HAVE A PLAN!
WE DON'T NEED A PLAN. YOU JUST INCH UP THERE REALLY QUIETLY AND THEN LUNGE FOR HIS THROAT. CLAMP YOUR TEETH DOWN AND DON'T LET GO FOR ANYTHING.
ME? YOU'RE SUPPOSED TO HELP ME!

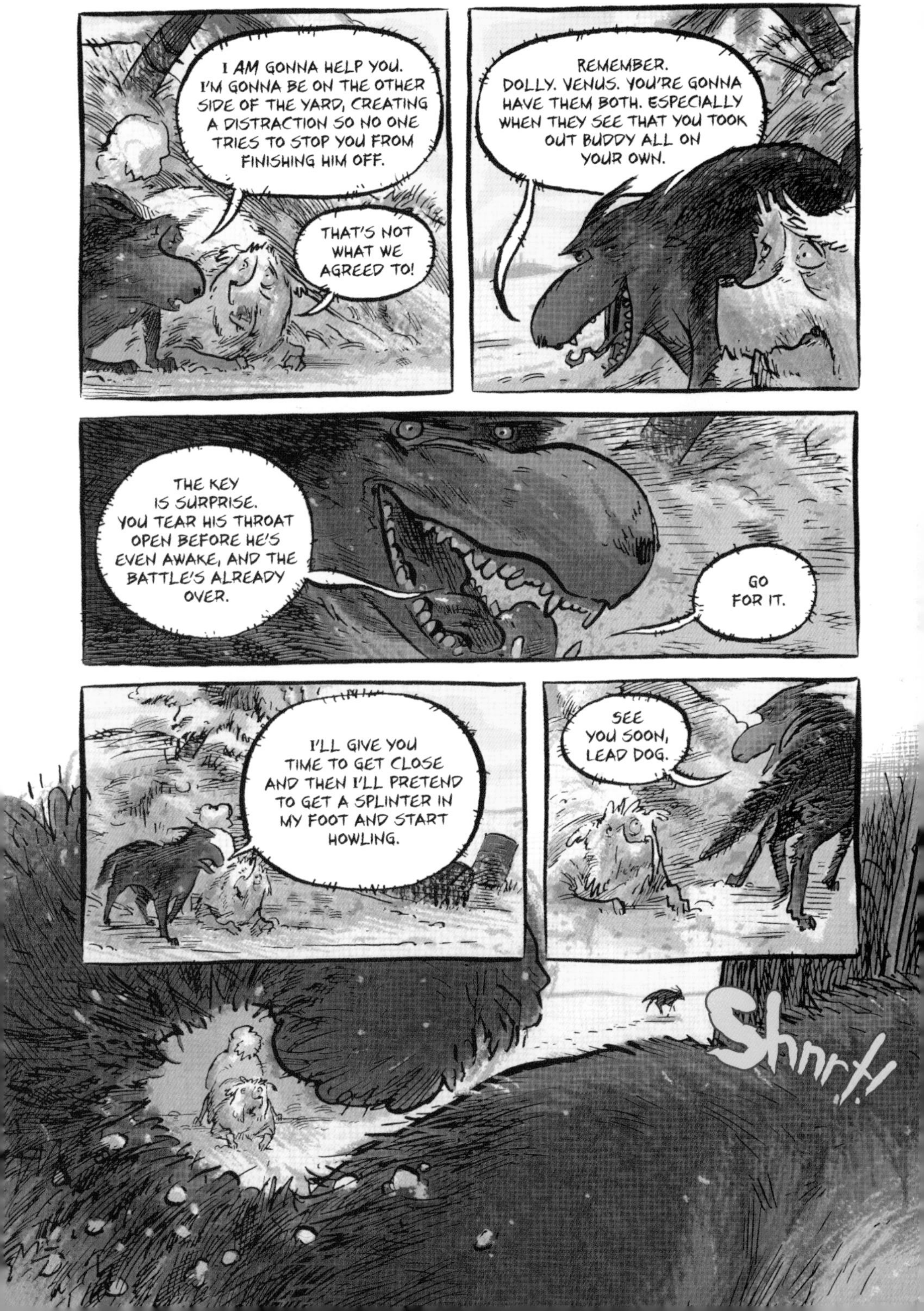
I AM GONNA HELP YOU. I'M GONNA BE ON THE OTHER SIDE OF THE YARD, CREATING A DISTRACTION SO NO ONE TRIES TO STOP YOU FROM FINISHING HIM OFF.
THAT'S NOT WHAT WE AGREED TO!
REMEMBER. DOLLY. VENUS. YOU'RE GONNA HAVE THEM BOTH. ESPECIALLY WHEN THEY SEE THAT YOU TOOK OUT BUDDY ALL ON YOUR OWN.
THE KEY IS SURPRISE. YOU TEAR HIS THROAT OPEN BEFORE HE'S EVEN AWAKE, AND THE BATTLE'S ALREADY OVER.
GO FOR IT.
I'LL GIVE YOU TIME TO GET CLOSE AND THEN I'LL PRETEND TO GET A SPLINTER IN MY FOOT AND START HOWLING.
SEE YOU SOON, LEAD DOG.
Shnrx!

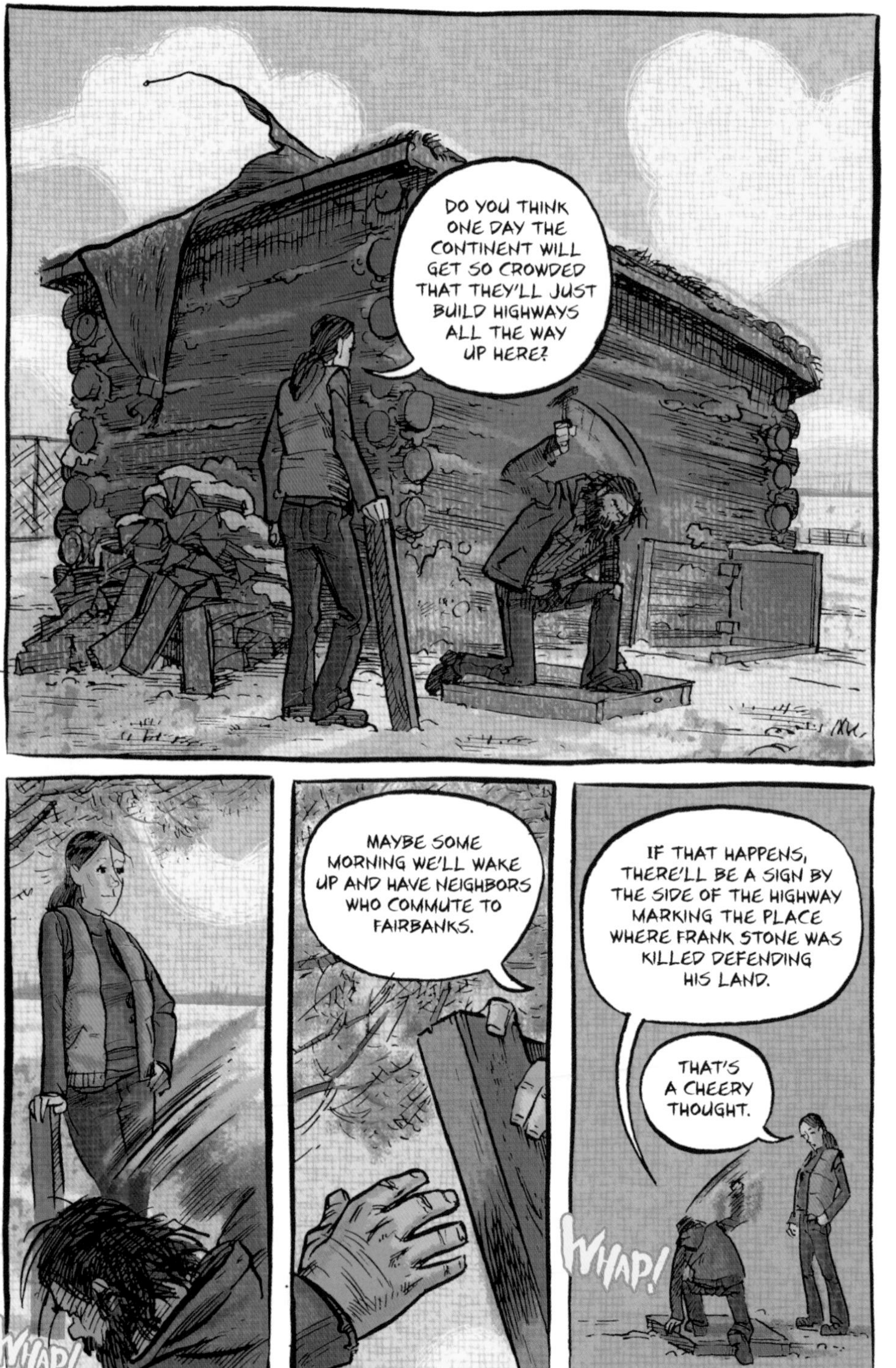
DO YOU THINK ONE DAY THE CONTINENT WILL GET SO CROWDED THAT THEY'LL JUST BUILD HIGHWAYS ALL THE WAY UP HERE?
WHAP!
MAYBE SOME MORNING WE'LL WAKE UP AND HAVE NEIGHBORS WHO COMMUTE TO FAIRBANKS.
IF THAT HAPPENS, THERE'LL BE A SIGN BY THE SIDE OF THE HIGHWAY MARKING THE PLACE WHERE FRANK STONE WAS KILLED DEFENDING HIS LAND.
THAT'S A CHEERY THOUGHT.
WHAP!

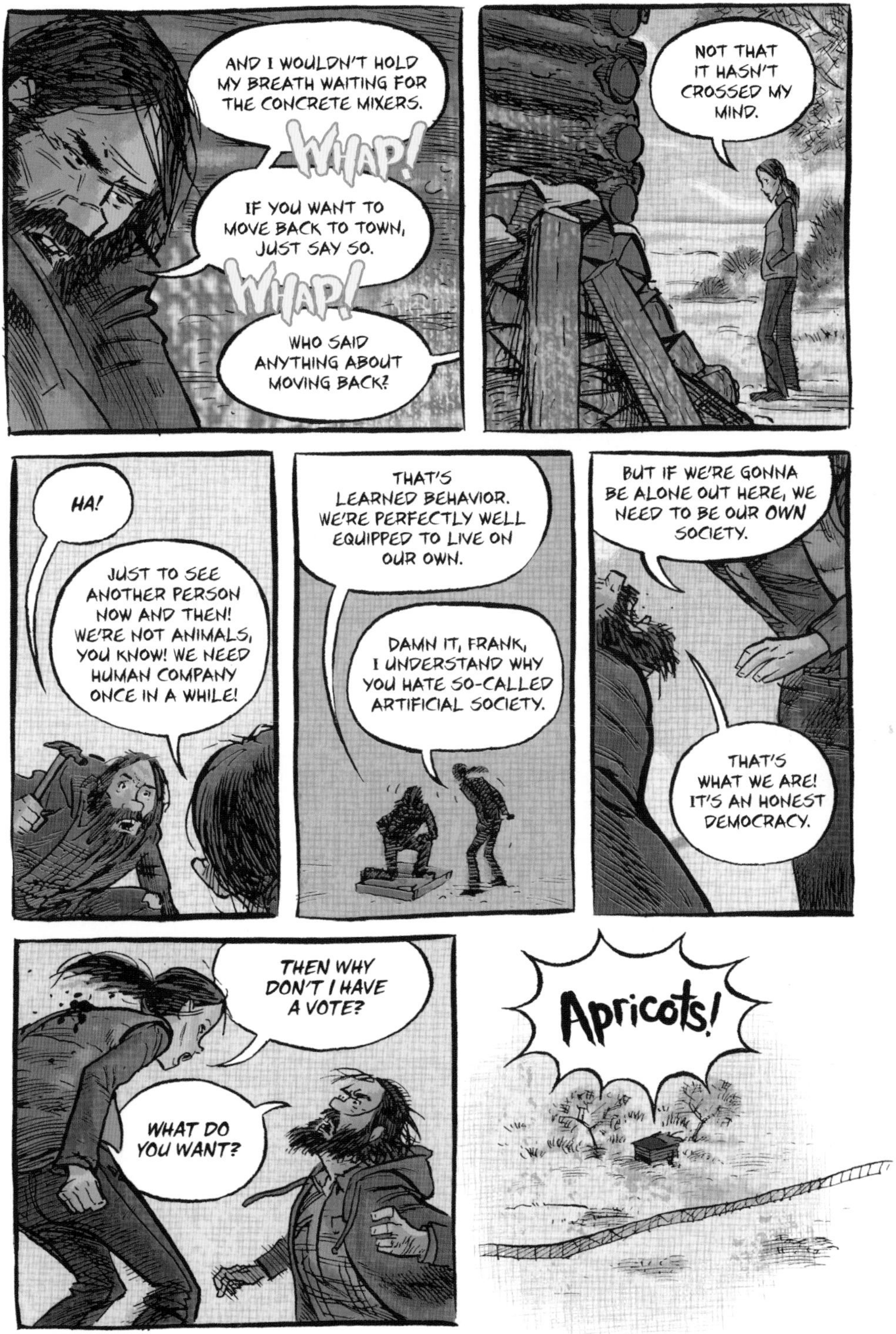
AND I WOULDN'T HOLD MY BREATH WAITING FOR THE CONCRETE MIXERS.
WHAP!
IF YOU WANT TO MOVE BACK TO TOWN, JUST SAY SO.
WHAP!
WHO SAID ANYTHING ABOUT MOVING BACK?
NOT THAT IT HASN'T CROSSED MY MIND.
HA!
JUST TO SEE ANOTHER PERSON NOW AND THEN! WE'RE NOT ANIMALS, YOU KNOW! WE NEED HUMAN COMPANY ONCE IN A WHILE!
THAT'S LEARNED BEHAVIOR. WE'RE PERFECTLY WELL EQUIPPED TO LIVE ON OUR OWN.
DAMN IT, FRANK, I UNDERSTAND WHY YOU HATE SO-CALLED ARTIFICIAL SOCIETY.
BUT IF WE'RE GONNA BE ALONE OUT HERE, WE NEED TO BE OUR OWN SOCIETY.
THAT'S WHAT WE ARE! IT'S AN HONEST DEMOCRACY.
THEN WHY DON'T I HAVE A VOTE?
WHAT DO YOU WANT?
Apricots!

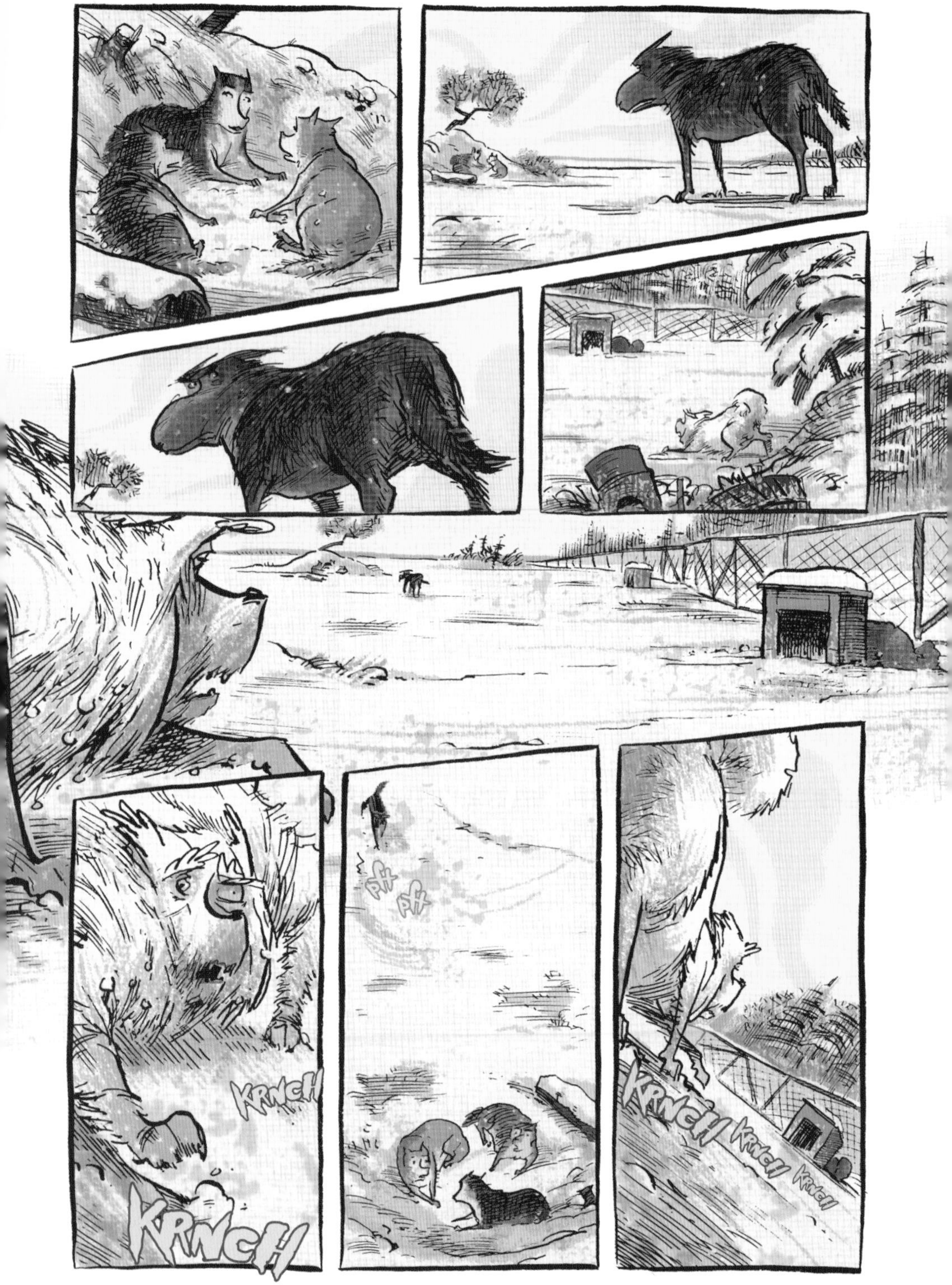
pff
pff
KRNCH
KRNCH
KRNCH
KRNCH
KRNCH
KRNCH

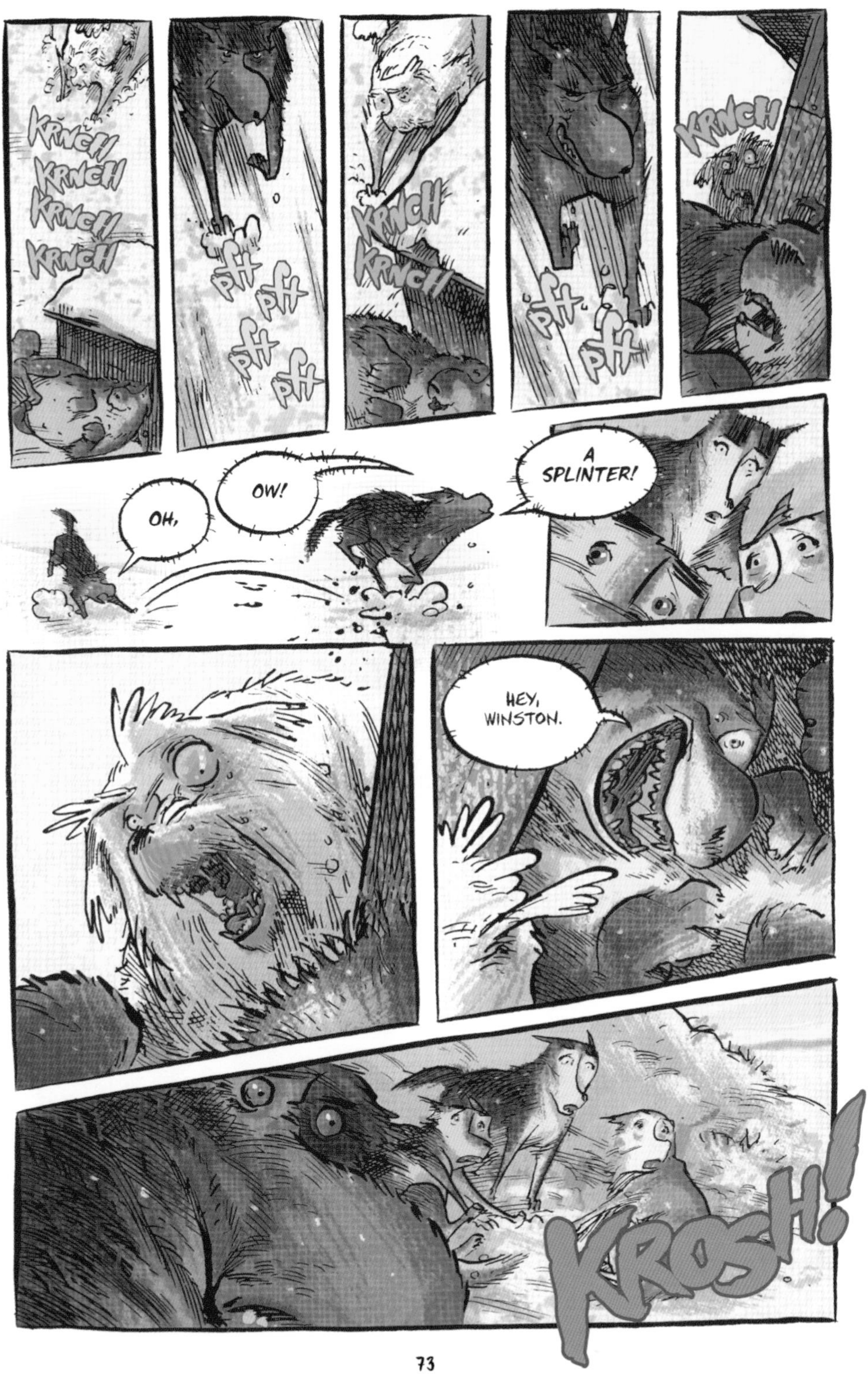
KRNCH
KRNCH
KRNCH
KRNCH
pft
pft
pft
pft
KRNCH
KRNCH
pft
pft
pft
KRNCH
OH,
OW!
A SPLINTER!
HEY, WINSTON.
KROSH!!

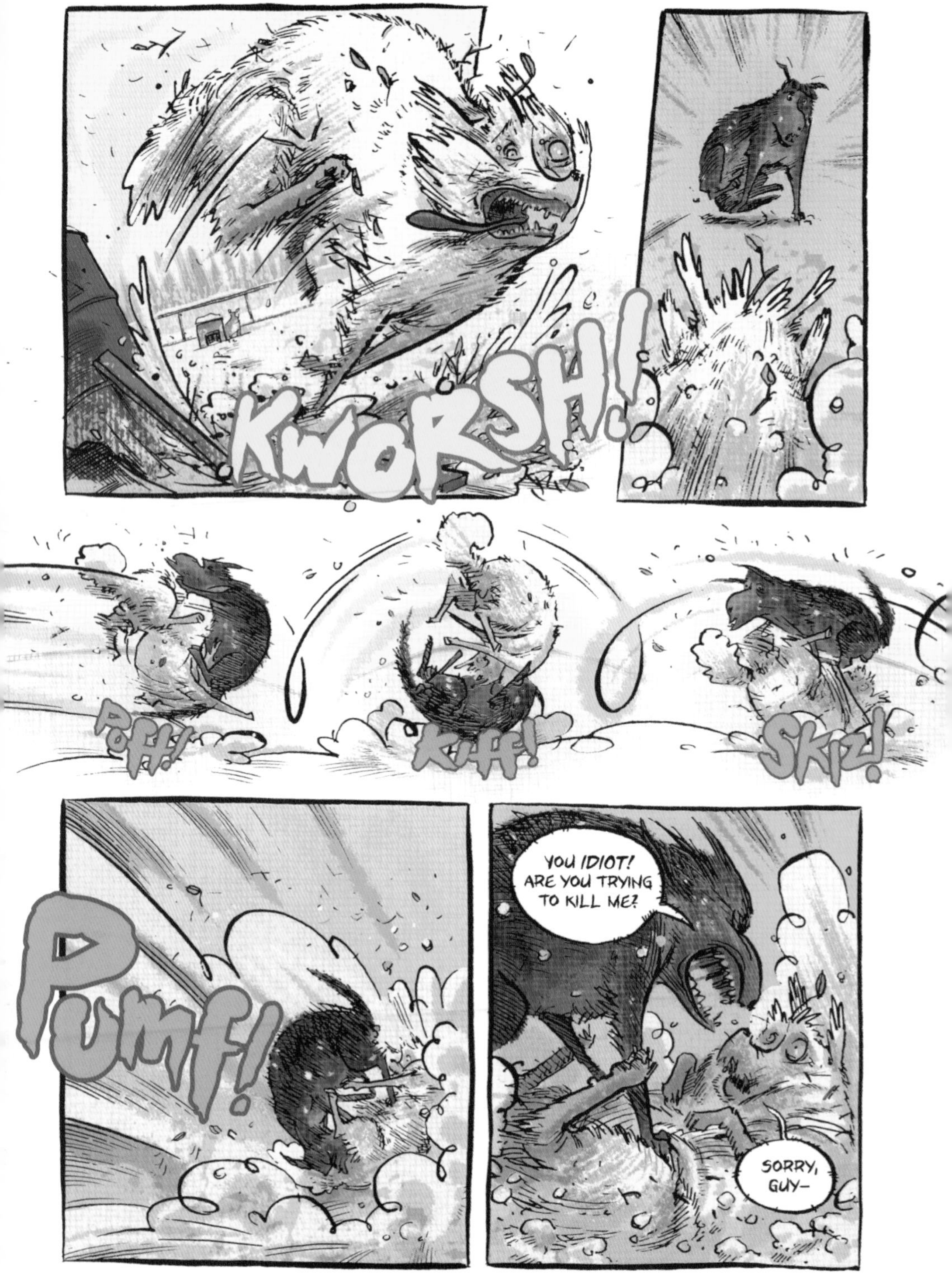
KWORSH!
POFF!
KIFF!
SKIZ!
PUMF!
YOU IDIOT! ARE YOU TRYING TO KILL ME?
SORRY, GUY–

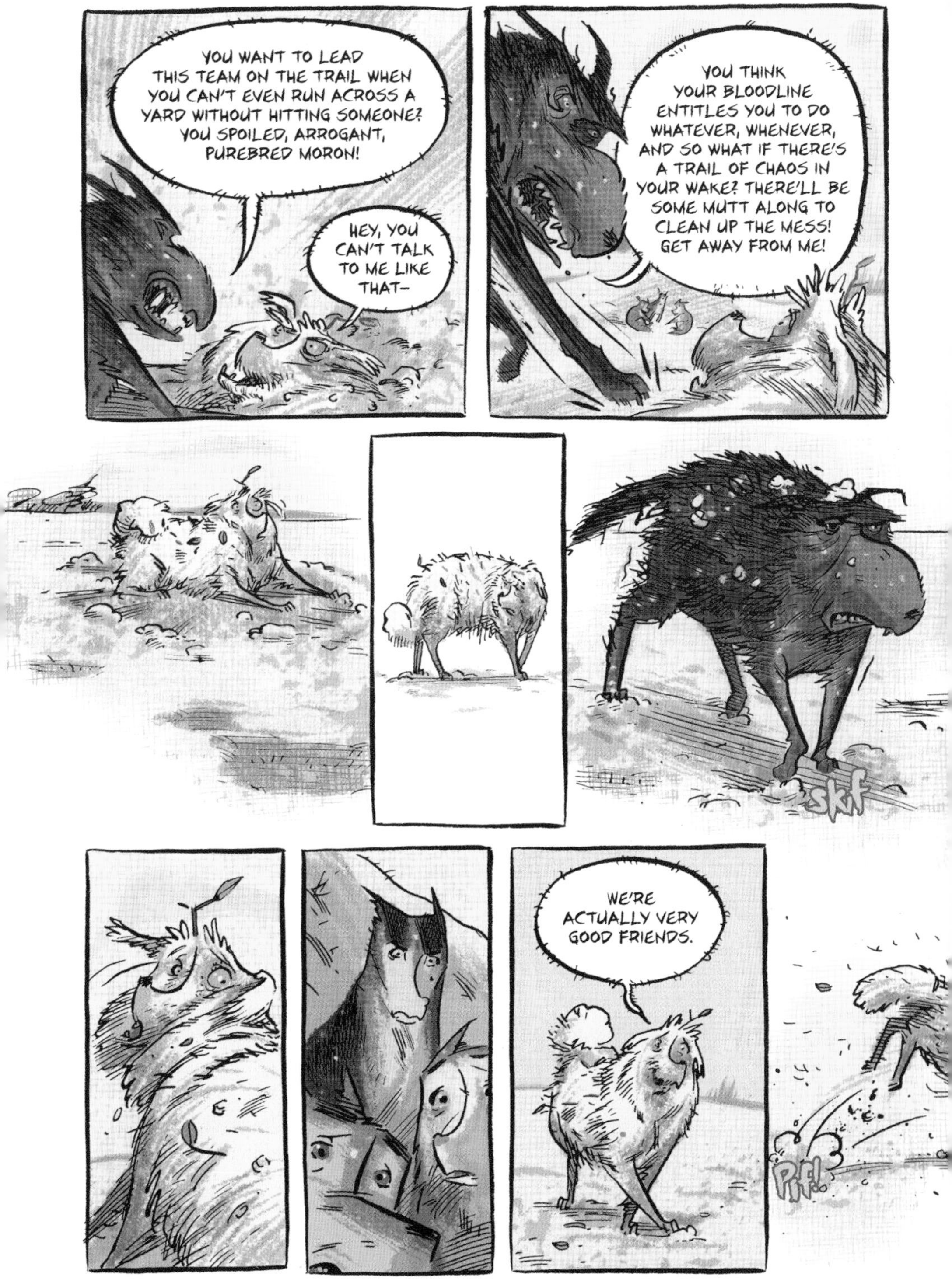
YOU WANT TO LEAD THIS TEAM ON THE TRAIL WHEN YOU CAN'T EVEN RUN ACROSS A YARD WITHOUT HITTING SOMEONE? YOU SPOILED, ARROGANT, PUREBRED MORON!
HEY, YOU CAN'T TALK TO ME LIKE THAT–
YOU THINK YOUR BLOODLINE ENTITLES YOU TO DO WHATEVER, WHENEVER, AND SO WHAT IF THERE'S A TRAIL OF CHAOS IN YOUR WAKE? THERE'LL BE SOME MUTT ALONG TO CLEAN UP THE MESS! GET AWAY FROM ME!
skf
WE'RE ACTUALLY VERY GOOD FRIENDS.
Pif!

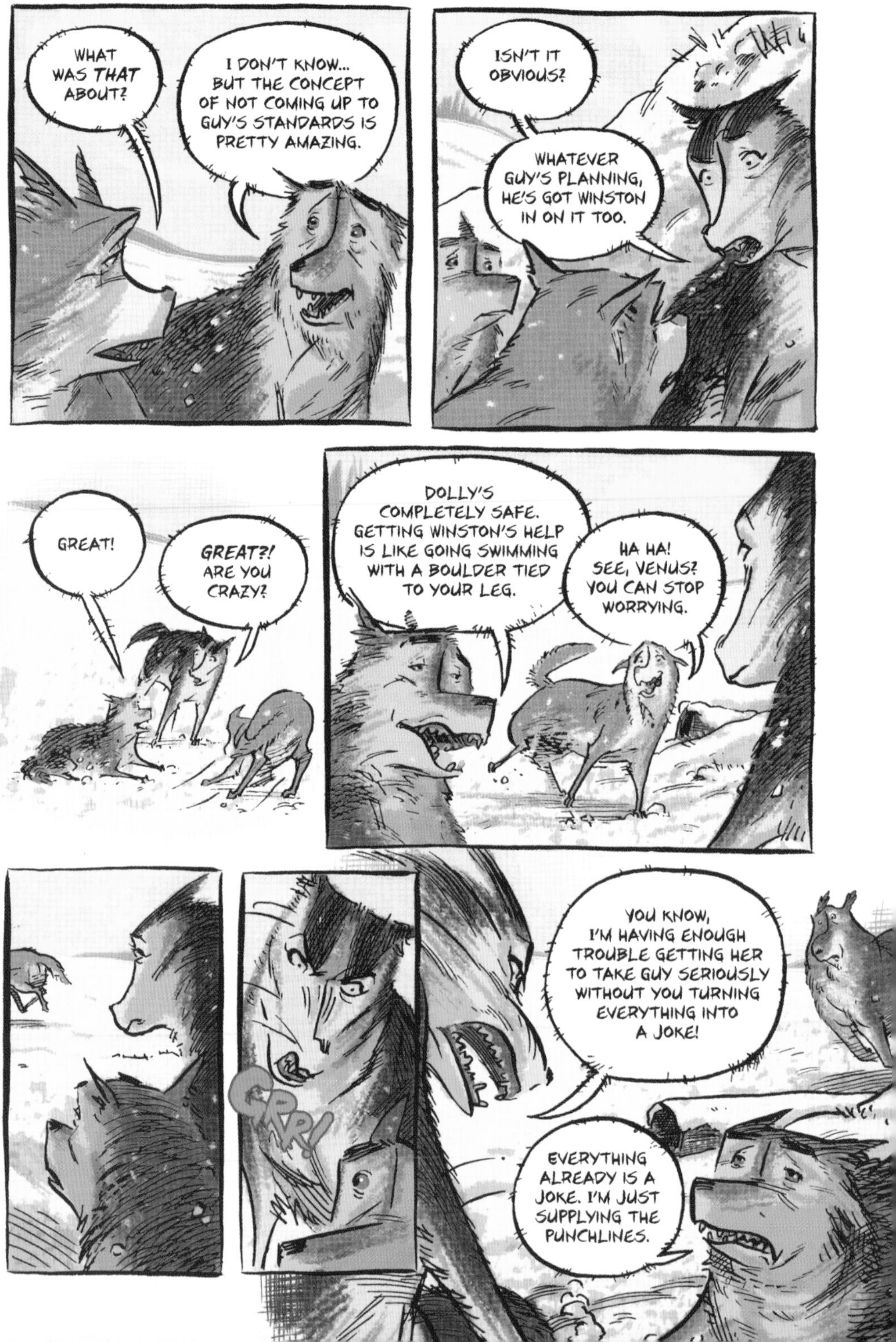
WHAT WAS THAT ABOUT?
I DON'T KNOW... BUT THE CONCEPT OF NOT COMING UP TO GUY'S STANDARDS IS PRETTY AMAZING.
ISN'T IT OBVIOUS?
WHATEVER GUY'S PLANNING, HE'S GOT WINSTON IN ON IT TOO.
GREAT!
GREAT?! ARE YOU CRAZY?
DOLLY'S COMPLETELY SAFE. GETTING WINSTON'S HELP IS LIKE GOING SWIMMING WITH A BOULDER TIED TO YOUR LEG.
HA HA! SEE, VENUS? YOU CAN STOP WORRYING.
GRR!
YOU KNOW, I'M HAVING ENOUGH TROUBLE GETTING HER TO TAKE GUY SERIOUSLY WITHOUT YOU TURNING EVERYTHING INTO A JOKE!
EVERYTHING ALREADY IS A JOKE. I'M JUST SUPPLYING THE PUNCHLINES.

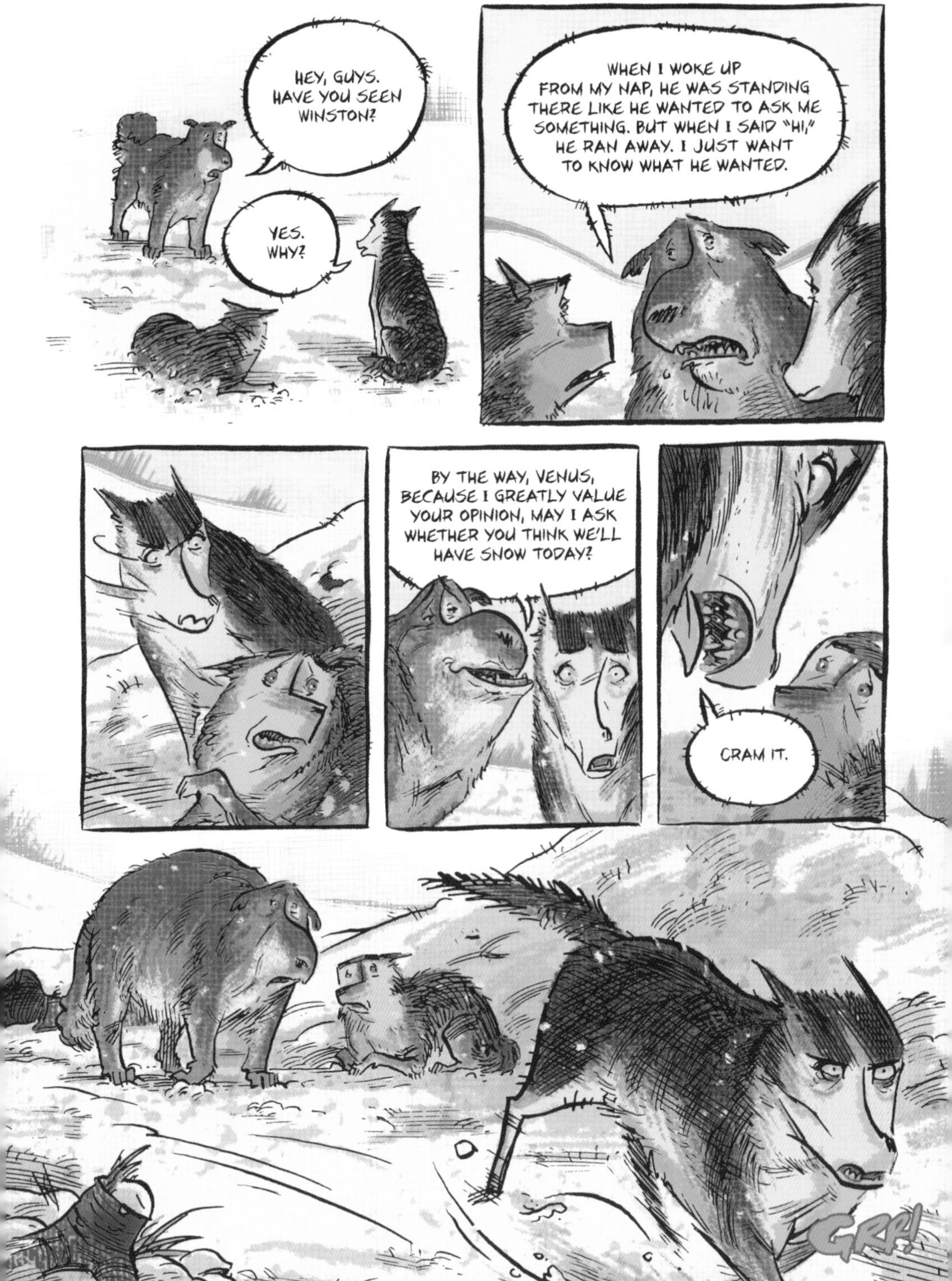
HEY, GUYS. HAVE YOU SEEN WINSTON?
YES. WHY?
WHEN I WOKE UP FROM MY NAP, HE WAS STANDING THERE LIKE HE WANTED TO ASK ME SOMETHING. BUT WHEN I SAID "HI," HE RAN AWAY. I JUST WANT TO KNOW WHAT HE WANTED.
BY THE WAY, VENUS, BECAUSE I GREATLY VALUE YOUR OPINION, MAY I ASK WHETHER YOU THINK WE'LL HAVE SNOW TODAY?
CRAM IT.
GRR!

# CHAPTER 8

DISASTER IN WHITE!

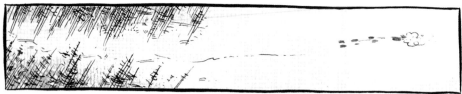

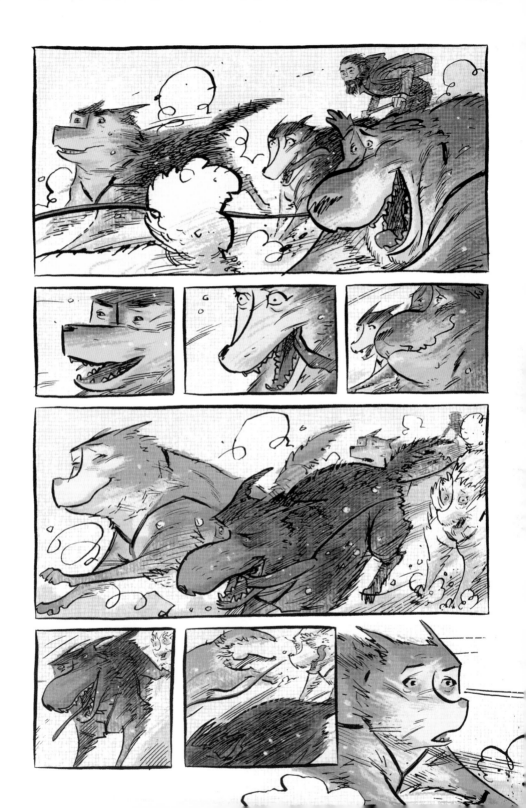

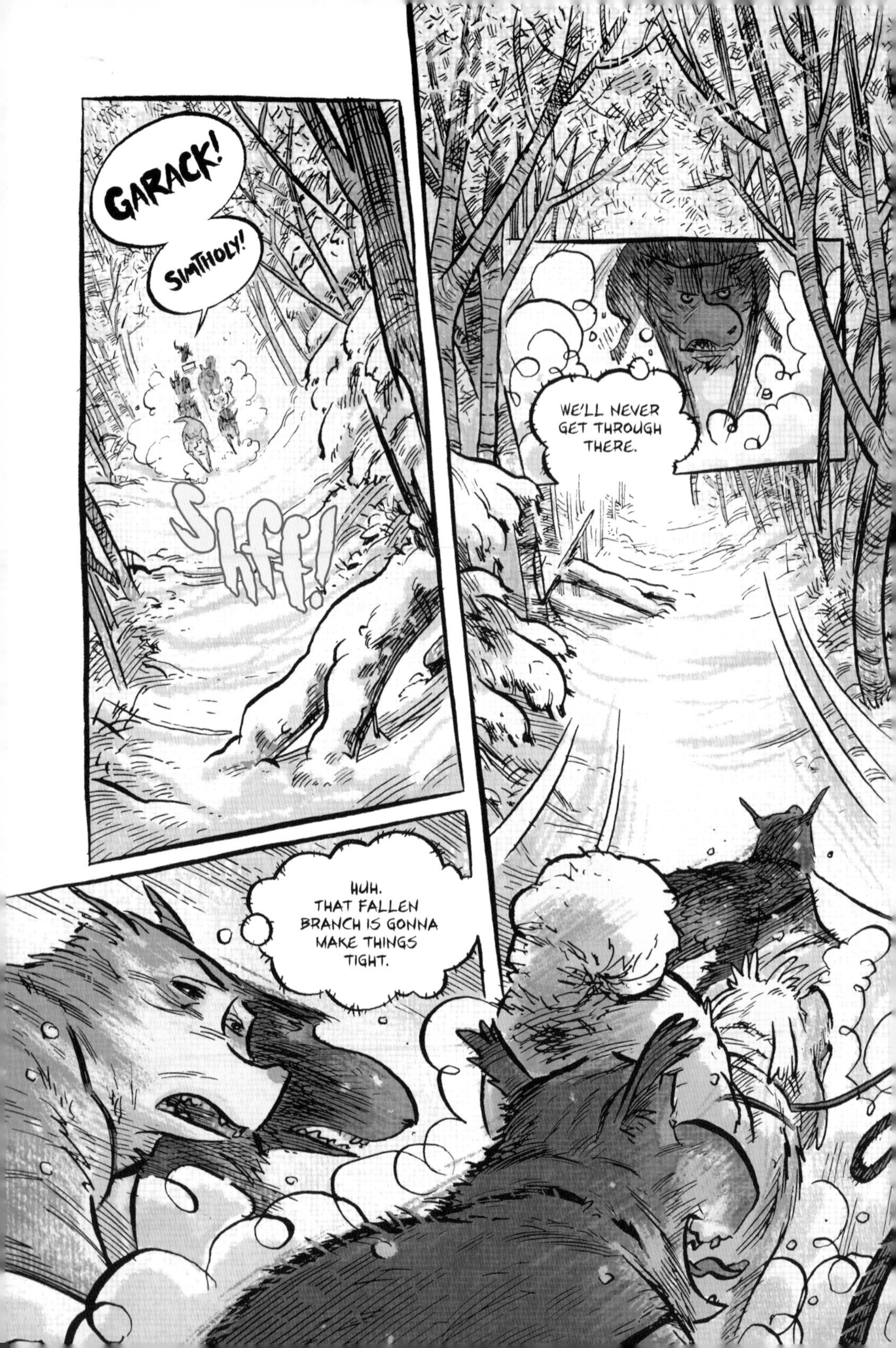
GARACK!
SIMTHOLY!
SHFF!
WE'LL NEVER GET THROUGH THERE.
HUH. THAT FALLEN BRANCH IS GONNA MAKE THINGS TIGHT.

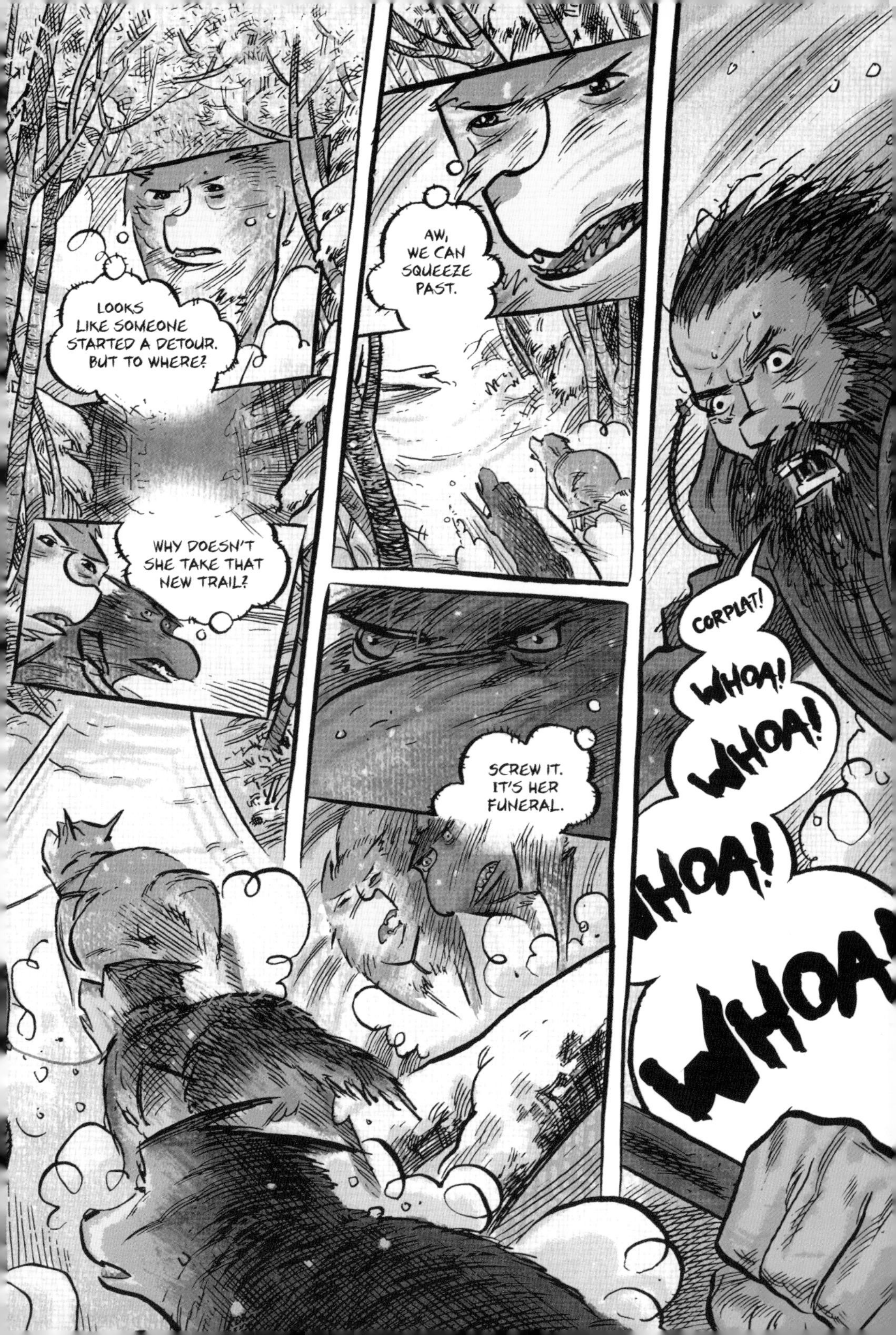
LOOKS LIKE SOMEONE STARTED A DETOUR. BUT TO WHERE?
WHY DOESN'T SHE TAKE THAT NEW TRAIL?
AW, WE CAN SQUEEZE PAST.
SCREW IT. IT'S HER FUNERAL.
CORPLAT!
WHOA!
WHOA!
WHOA!
WHOA!

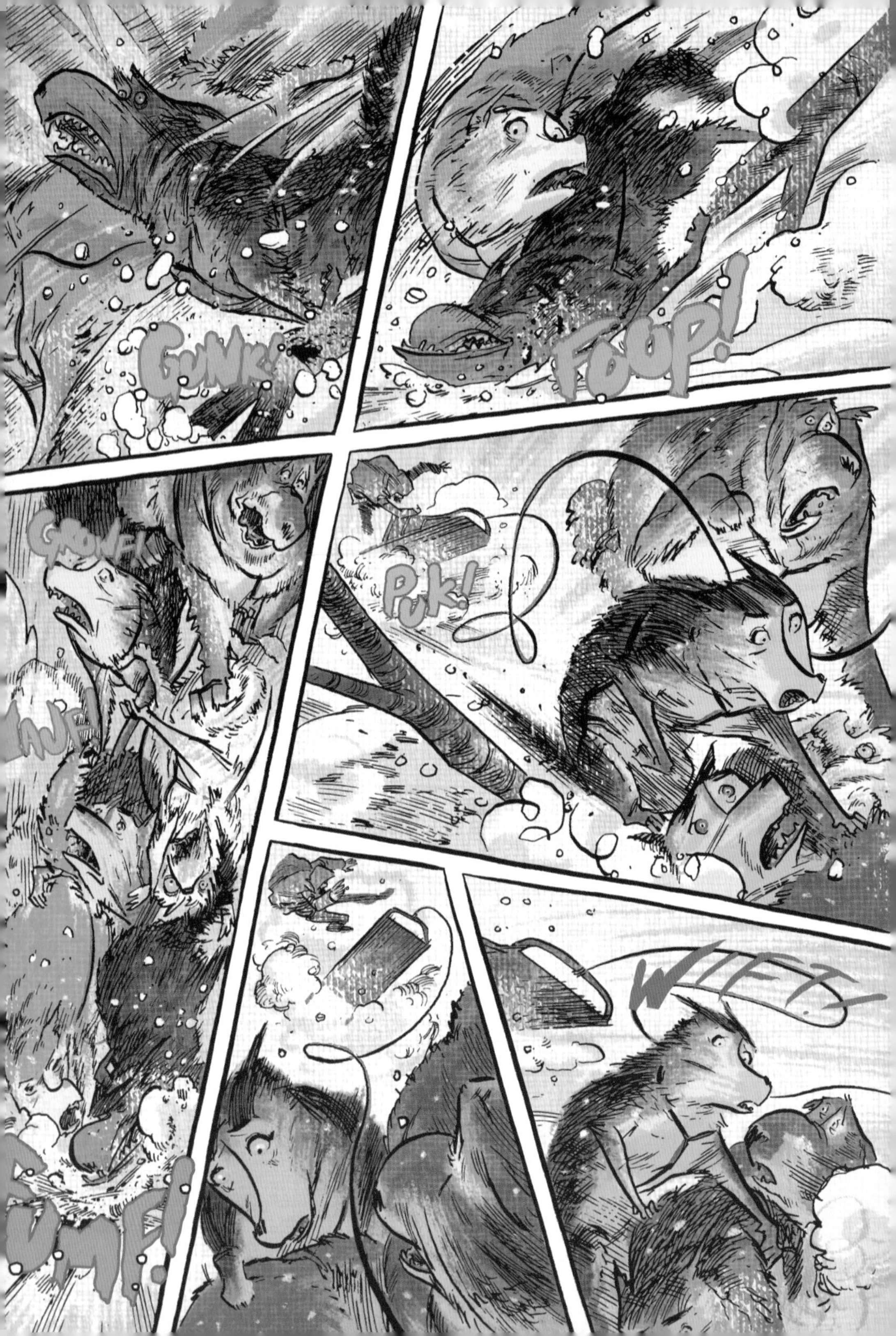
GUNK!
FOOP!
GRONF!
PUK!

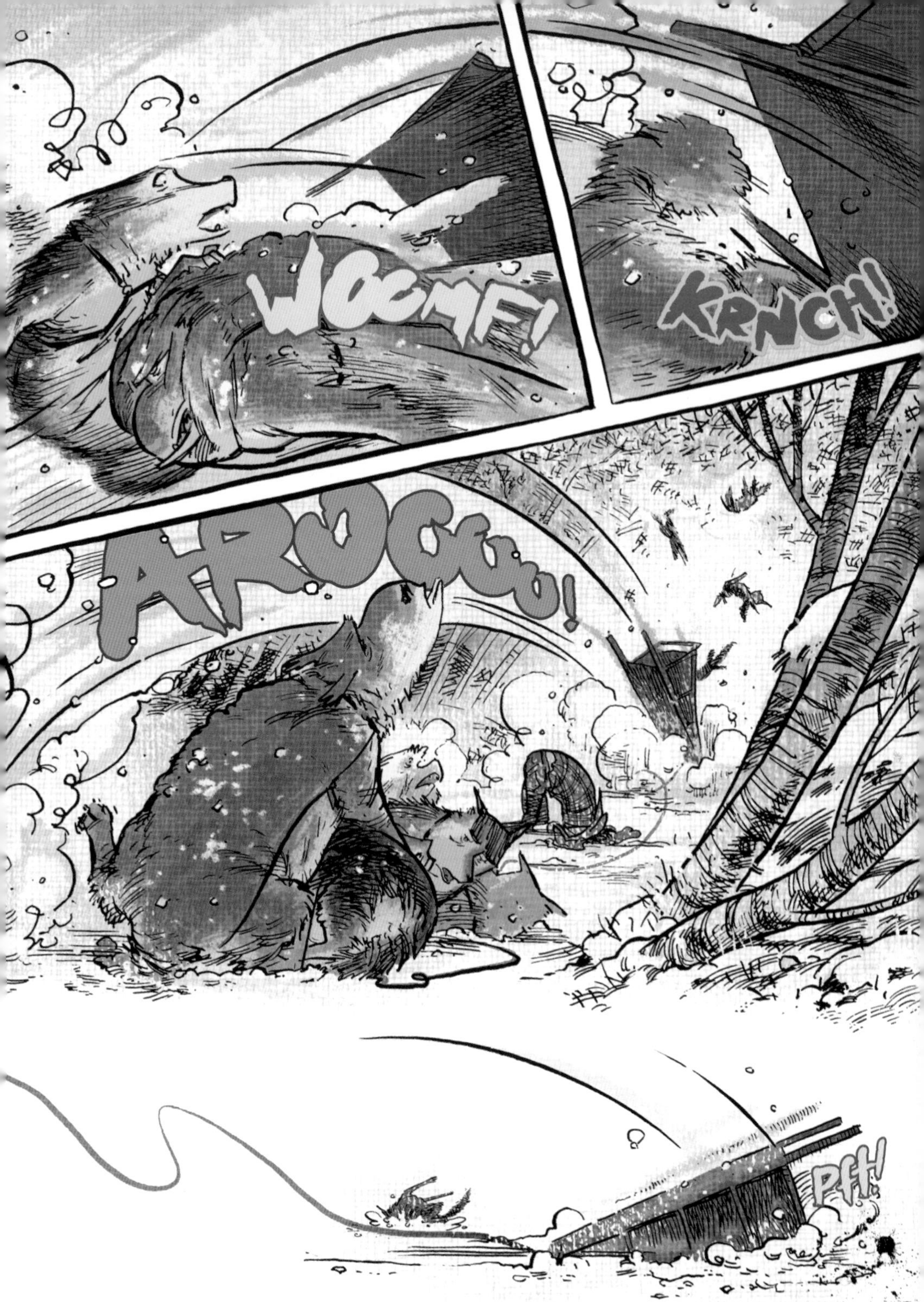
WOOMF!
KRNCH!
AROOOOOO!
PFF!

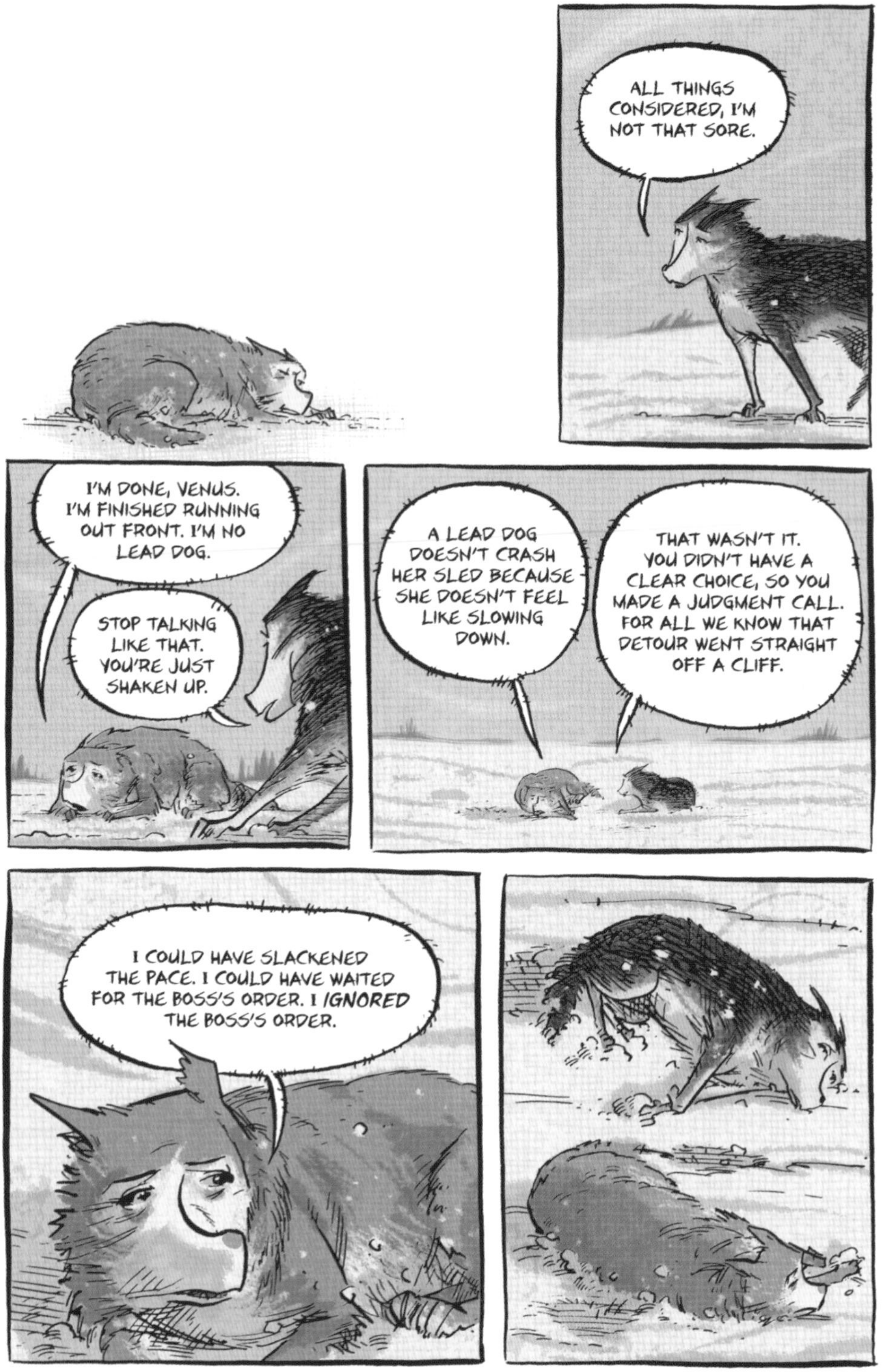
ALL THINGS CONSIDERED, I'M NOT THAT SORE.
I'M DONE, VENUS. I'M FINISHED RUNNING OUT FRONT. I'M NO LEAD DOG.
STOP TALKING LIKE THAT. YOU'RE JUST SHAKEN UP.
A LEAD DOG DOESN'T CRASH HER SLED BECAUSE SHE DOESN'T FEEL LIKE SLOWING DOWN.
THAT WASN'T IT. YOU DIDN'T HAVE A CLEAR CHOICE, SO YOU MADE A JUDGMENT CALL. FOR ALL WE KNOW THAT DETOUR WENT STRAIGHT OFF A CLIFF.
I COULD HAVE SLACKENED THE PACE. I COULD HAVE WAITED FOR THE BOSS'S ORDER. I *IGNORED* THE BOSS'S ORDER.

WHAT IF WE'D BEEN ANOTHER TEN MILES INTO THE WOODS? MY ARROGANCE COULD HAVE KILLED US ALL.

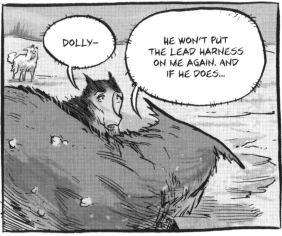

DOLLY—

HE WON'T PUT THE LEAD HARNESS ON ME AGAIN. AND IF HE DOES...

...I WON'T TAKE IT.

SPFF!

WHAT DO YOU WANT?

NOTHING!

Spkt!

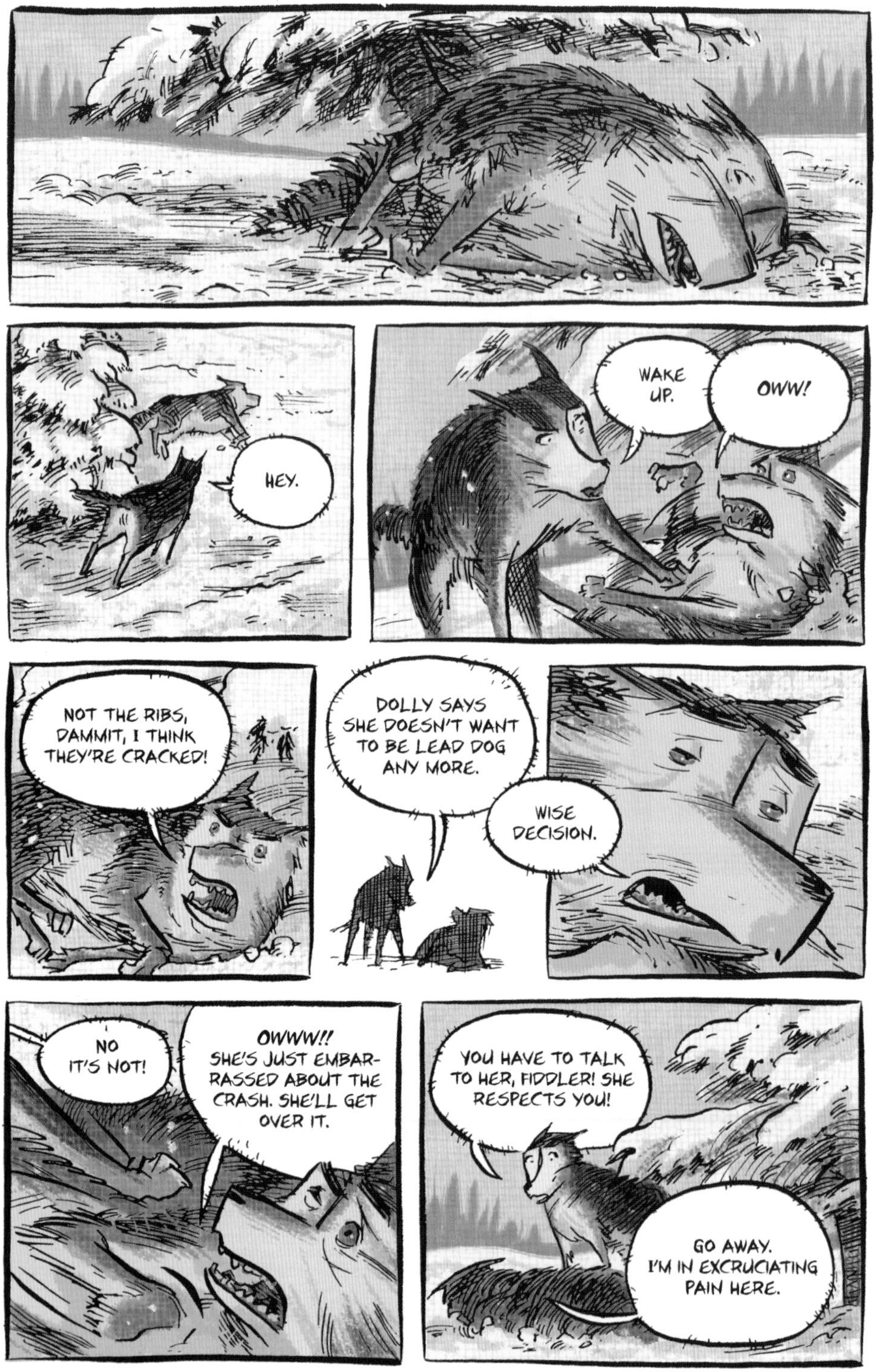
HEY.
WAKE UP.
OWW!
NOT THE RIBS, DAMMIT, I THINK THEY'RE CRACKED!
DOLLY SAYS SHE DOESN'T WANT TO BE LEAD DOG ANY MORE.
WISE DECISION.
NO IT'S NOT!
OWWW!! SHE'S JUST EMBARRASSED ABOUT THE CRASH. SHE'LL GET OVER IT.
YOU HAVE TO TALK TO HER, FIDDLER! SHE RESPECTS YOU!
GO AWAY. I'M IN EXCRUCIATING PAIN HERE.

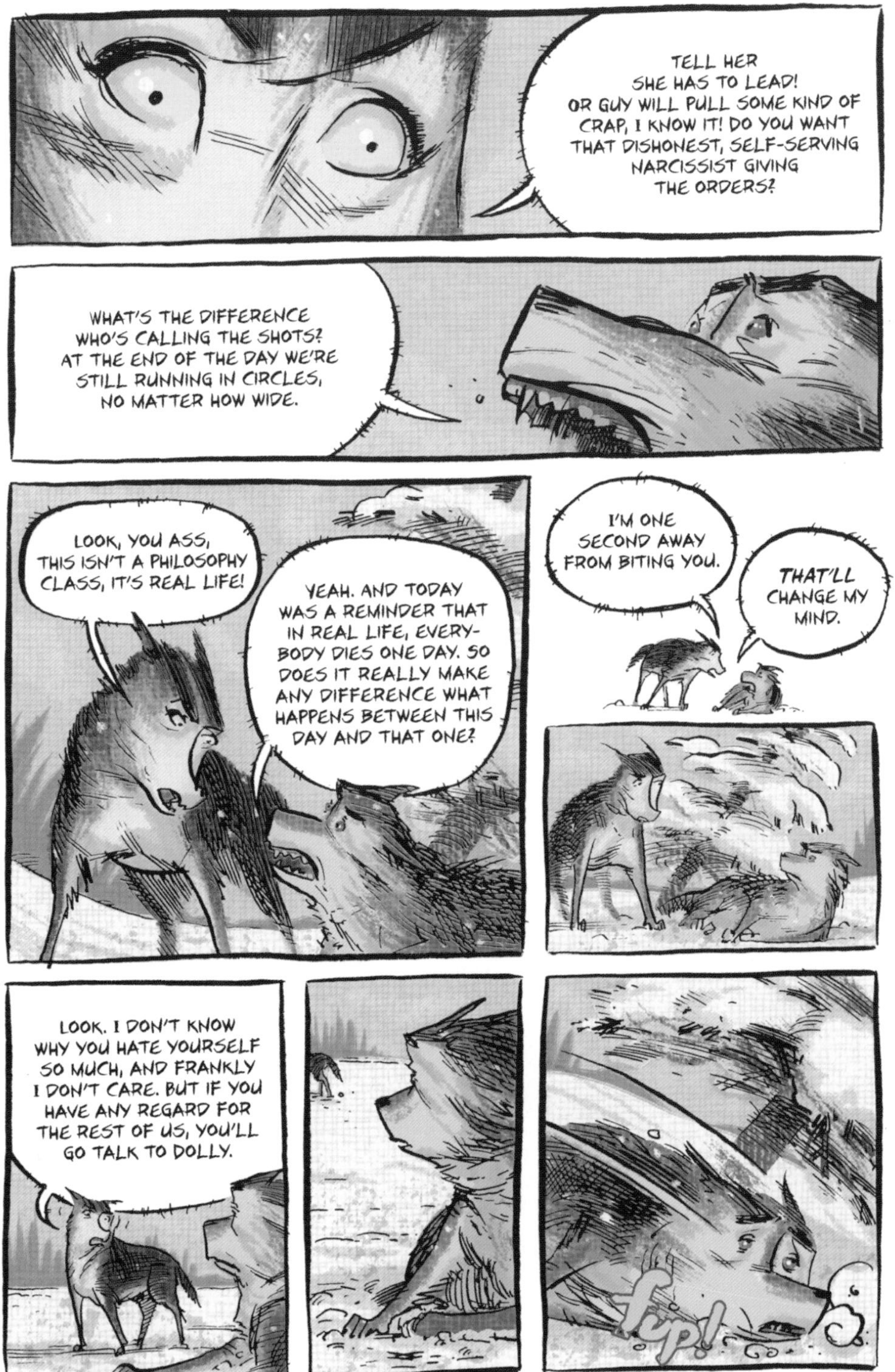
TELL HER SHE HAS TO LEAD! OR GUY WILL PULL SOME KIND OF CRAP, I KNOW IT! DO YOU WANT THAT DISHONEST, SELF-SERVING NARCISSIST GIVING THE ORDERS?
WHAT'S THE DIFFERENCE WHO'S CALLING THE SHOTS? AT THE END OF THE DAY WE'RE STILL RUNNING IN CIRCLES, NO MATTER HOW WIDE.
LOOK, YOU ASS, THIS ISN'T A PHILOSOPHY CLASS, IT'S REAL LIFE!
YEAH. AND TODAY WAS A REMINDER THAT IN REAL LIFE, EVERY-BODY DIES ONE DAY. SO DOES IT REALLY MAKE ANY DIFFERENCE WHAT HAPPENS BETWEEN THIS DAY AND THAT ONE?
I'M ONE SECOND AWAY FROM BITING YOU.
*THAT'LL* CHANGE MY MIND.
LOOK. I DON'T KNOW WHY YOU HATE YOURSELF SO MUCH, AND FRANKLY I DON'T CARE. BUT IF YOU HAVE ANY REGARD FOR THE REST OF US, YOU'LL GO TALK TO DOLLY.
FUP!

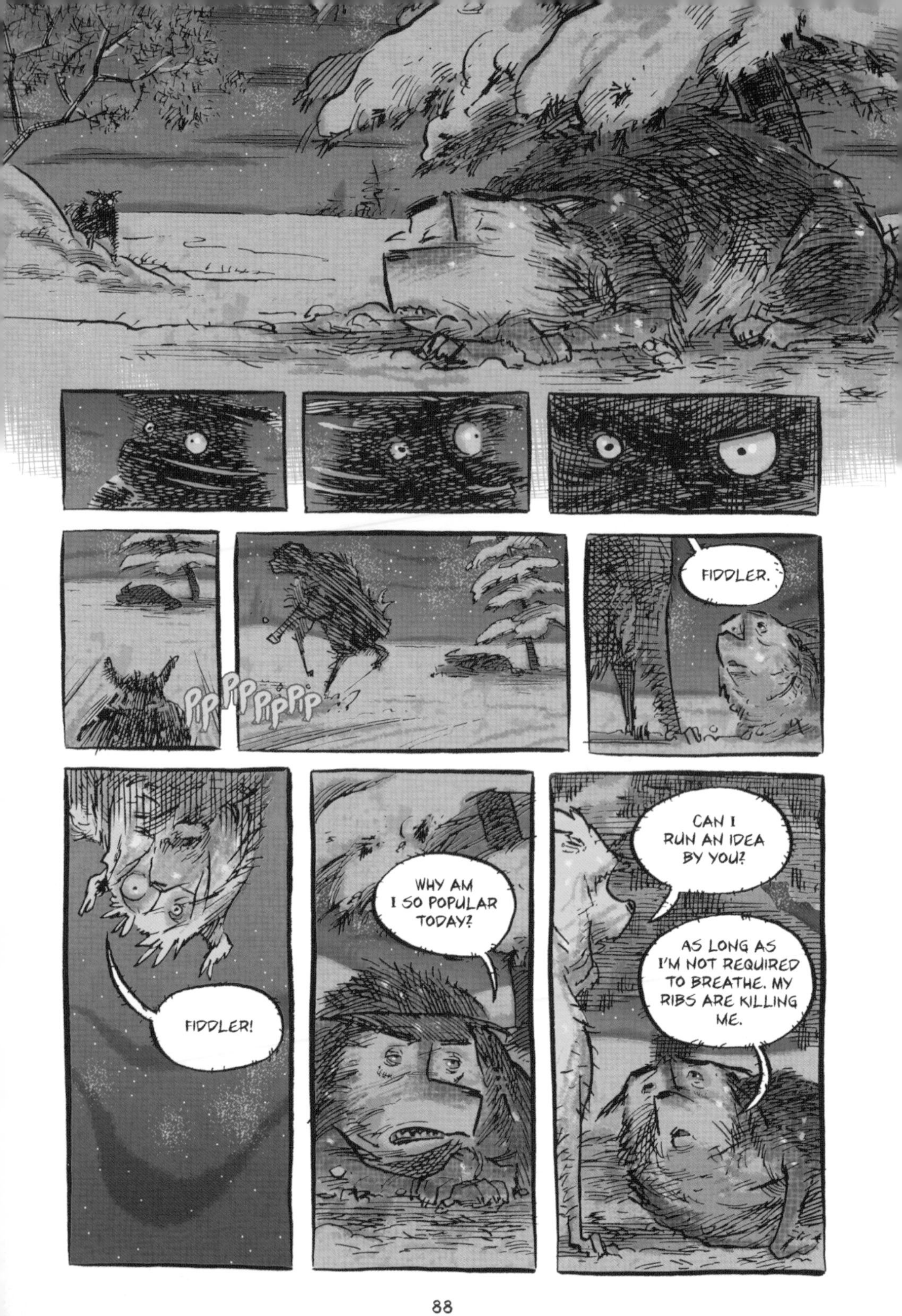
PIPPIPPIPPIP
FIDDLER.
FIDDLER!
WHY AM I SO POPULAR TODAY?
CAN I RUN AN IDEA BY YOU?
AS LONG AS I'M NOT REQUIRED TO BREATHE. MY RIBS ARE KILLING ME.

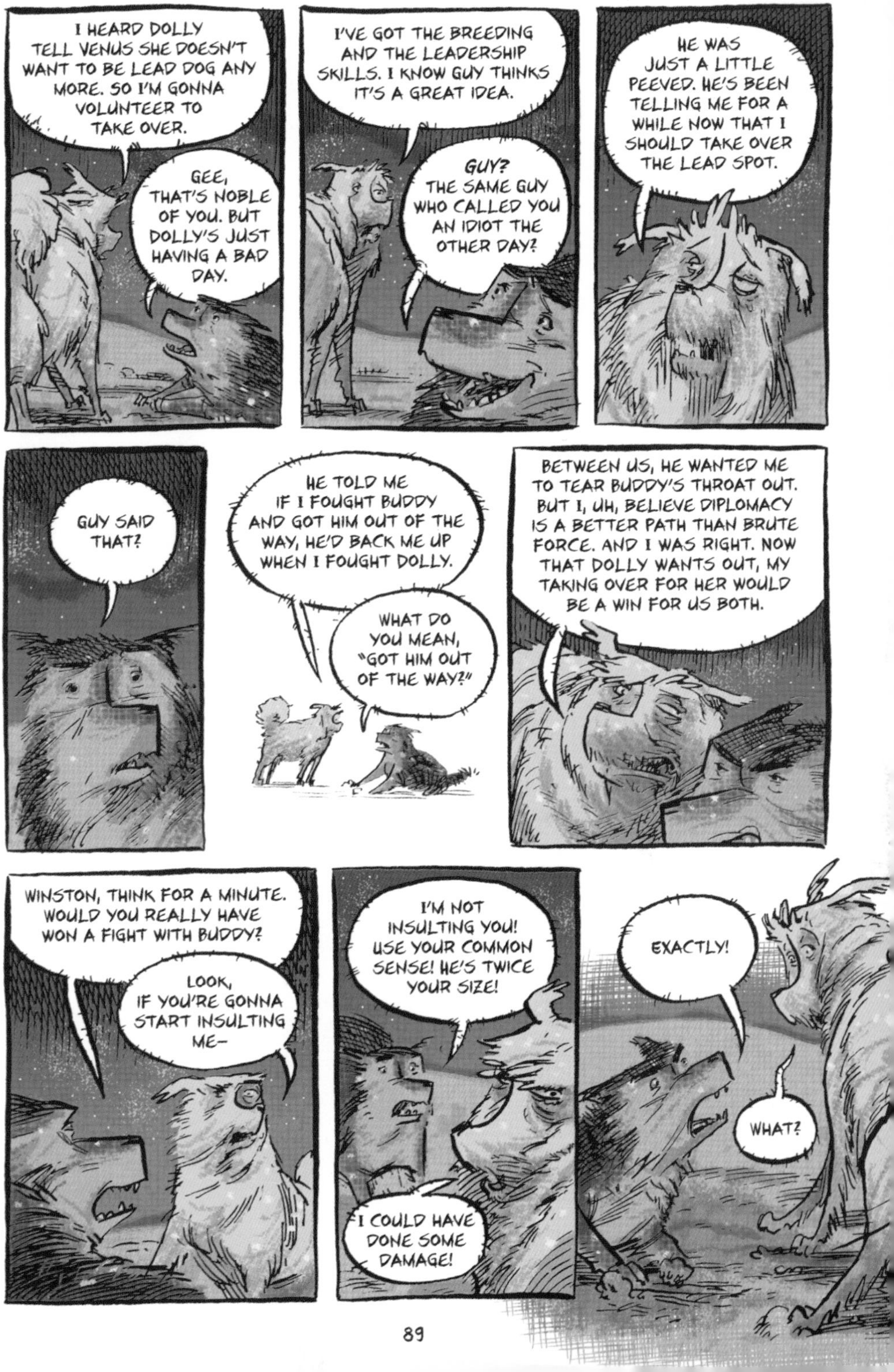
I HEARD DOLLY TELL VENUS SHE DOESN'T WANT TO BE LEAD DOG ANY MORE. SO I'M GONNA VOLUNTEER TO TAKE OVER.
GEE, THAT'S NOBLE OF YOU. BUT DOLLY'S JUST HAVING A BAD DAY.
I'VE GOT THE BREEDING AND THE LEADERSHIP SKILLS. I KNOW GUY THINKS IT'S A GREAT IDEA.
GUY? THE SAME GUY WHO CALLED YOU AN IDIOT THE OTHER DAY?
HE WAS JUST A LITTLE PEEVED. HE'S BEEN TELLING ME FOR A WHILE NOW THAT I SHOULD TAKE OVER THE LEAD SPOT.
GUY SAID THAT?
HE TOLD ME IF I FOUGHT BUDDY AND GOT HIM OUT OF THE WAY, HE'D BACK ME UP WHEN I FOUGHT DOLLY.
WHAT DO YOU MEAN, "GOT HIM OUT OF THE WAY?"
BETWEEN US, HE WANTED ME TO TEAR BUDDY'S THROAT OUT. BUT I, UH, BELIEVE DIPLOMACY IS A BETTER PATH THAN BRUTE FORCE. AND I WAS RIGHT. NOW THAT DOLLY WANTS OUT, MY TAKING OVER FOR HER WOULD BE A WIN FOR US BOTH.
WINSTON, THINK FOR A MINUTE. WOULD YOU REALLY HAVE WON A FIGHT WITH BUDDY?
LOOK, IF YOU'RE GONNA START INSULTING ME–
I'M NOT INSULTING YOU! USE YOUR COMMON SENSE! HE'S TWICE YOUR SIZE!
I COULD HAVE DONE SOME DAMAGE!
EXACTLY!
WHAT?

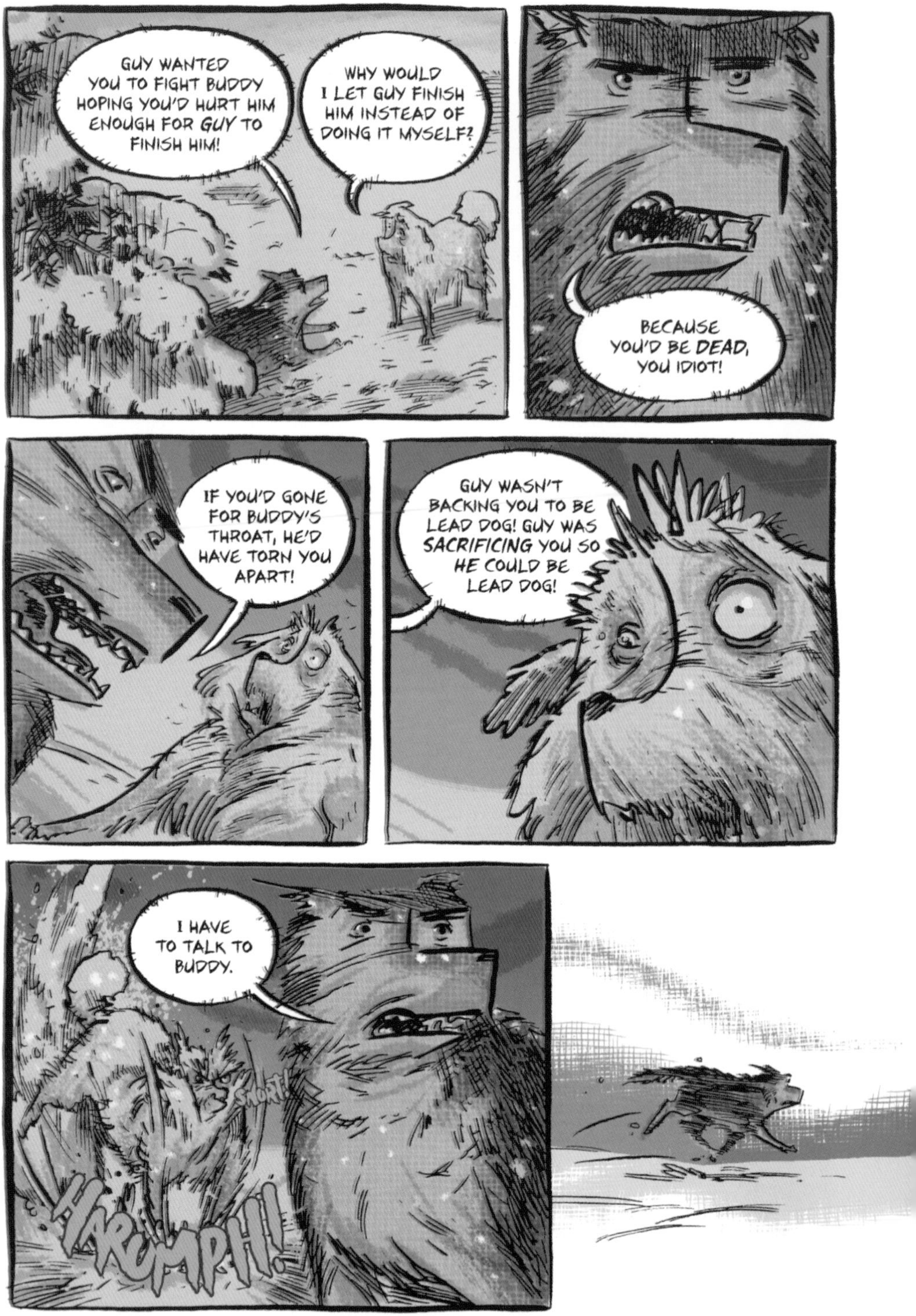
GUY WANTED YOU TO FIGHT BUDDY HOPING YOU'D HURT HIM ENOUGH FOR GUY TO FINISH HIM!
WHY WOULD I LET GUY FINISH HIM INSTEAD OF DOING IT MYSELF?
BECAUSE YOU'D BE DEAD, YOU IDIOT!
IF YOU'D GONE FOR BUDDY'S THROAT, HE'D HAVE TORN YOU APART!
GUY WASN'T BACKING YOU TO BE LEAD DOG! GUY WAS SACRIFICING YOU SO HE COULD BE LEAD DOG!
I HAVE TO TALK TO BUDDY.
SNORT!
HARUMPH!

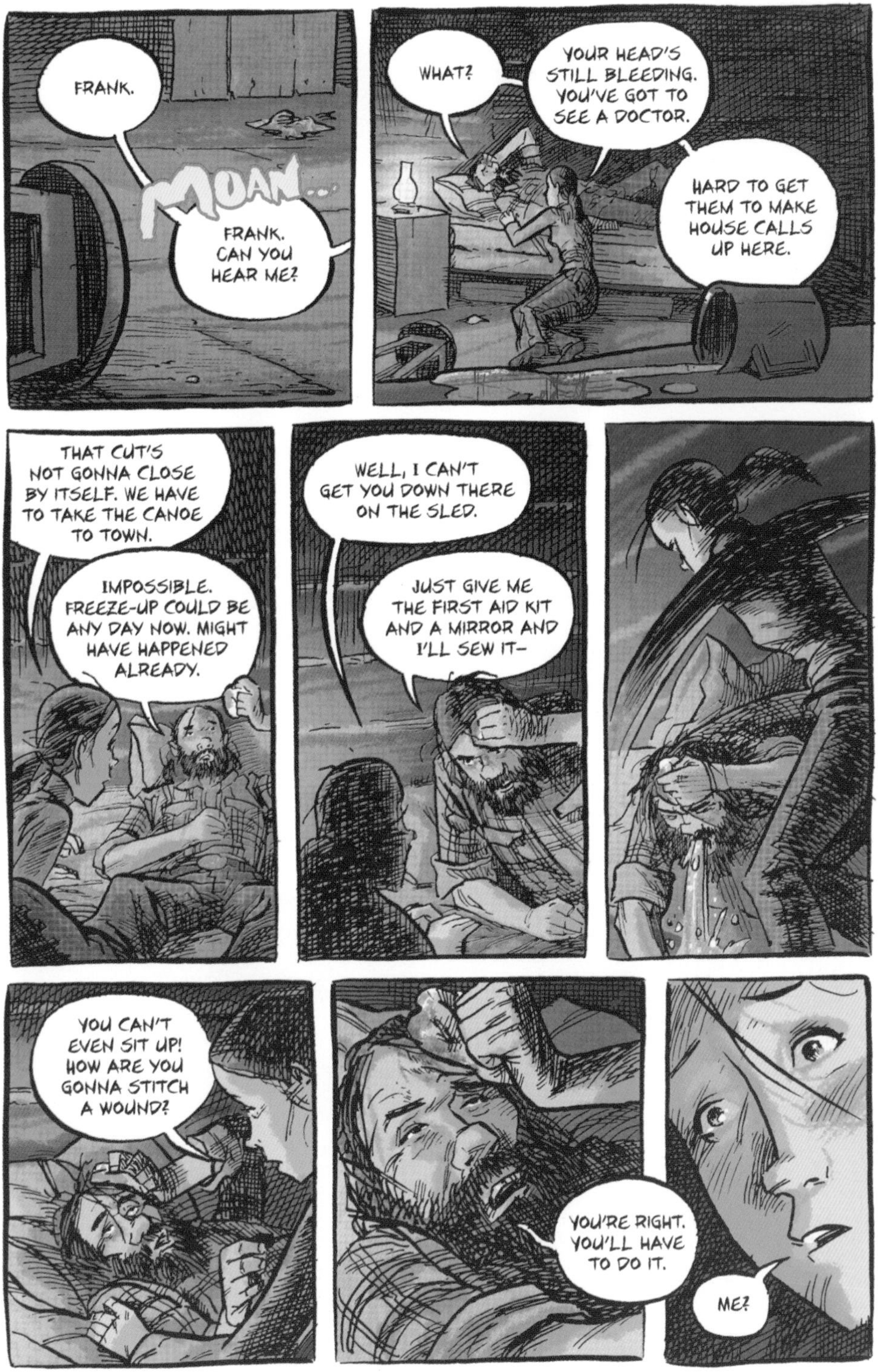
FRANK.
MOAN...
FRANK. CAN YOU HEAR ME?
WHAT?
YOUR HEAD'S STILL BLEEDING. YOU'VE GOT TO SEE A DOCTOR.
HARD TO GET THEM TO MAKE HOUSE CALLS UP HERE.
THAT CUT'S NOT GONNA CLOSE BY ITSELF. WE HAVE TO TAKE THE CANOE TO TOWN.
IMPOSSIBLE. FREEZE-UP COULD BE ANY DAY NOW. MIGHT HAVE HAPPENED ALREADY.
WELL, I CAN'T GET YOU DOWN THERE ON THE SLED.
JUST GIVE ME THE FIRST AID KIT AND A MIRROR AND I'LL SEW IT–
YOU CAN'T EVEN SIT UP! HOW ARE YOU GONNA STITCH A WOUND?
YOU'RE RIGHT. YOU'LL HAVE TO DO IT.
ME?

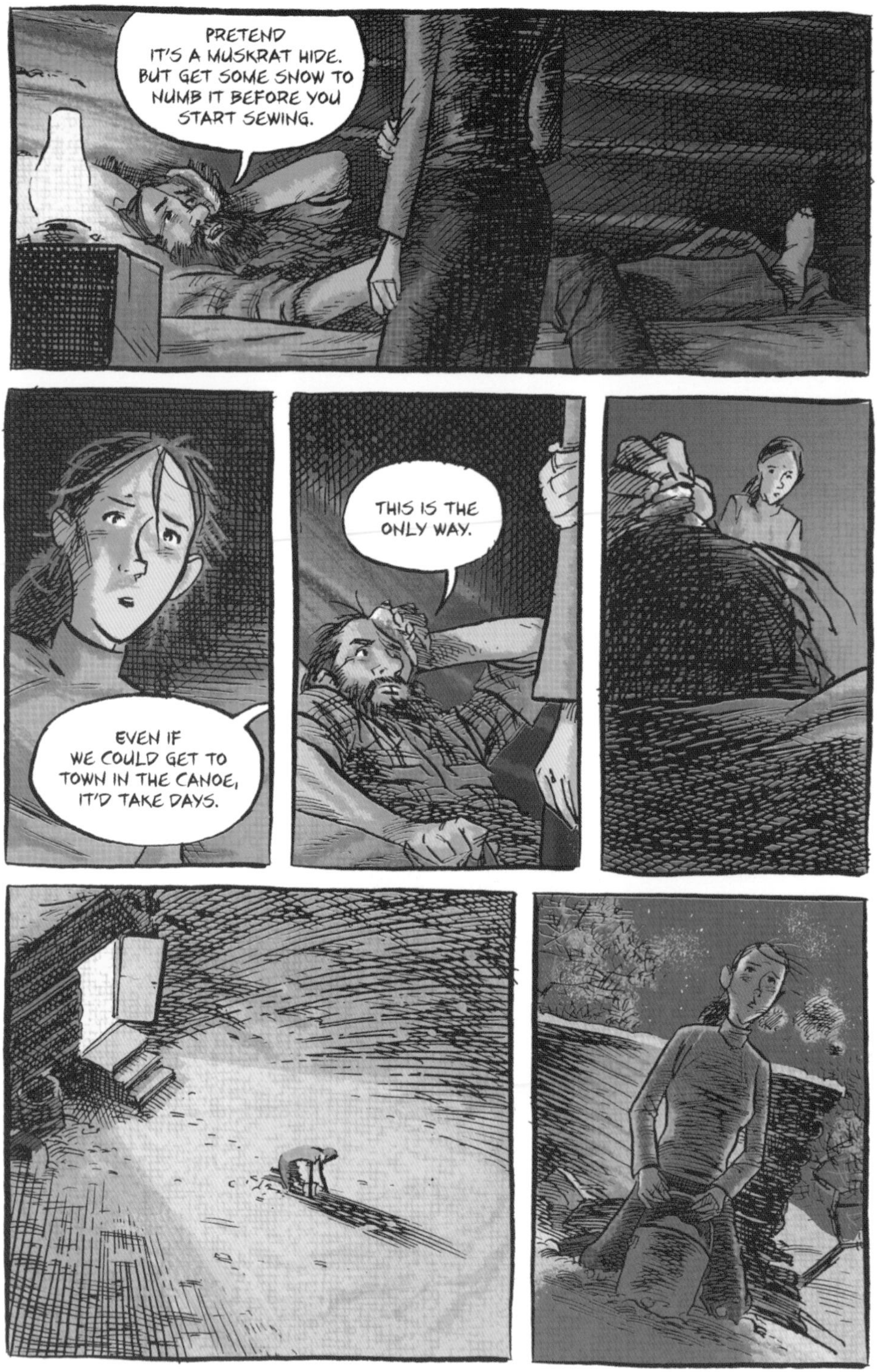
PRETEND IT'S A MUSKRAT HIDE. BUT GET SOME SNOW TO NUMB IT BEFORE YOU START SEWING.
EVEN IF WE COULD GET TO TOWN IN THE CANOE, IT'D TAKE DAYS.
THIS IS THE ONLY WAY.

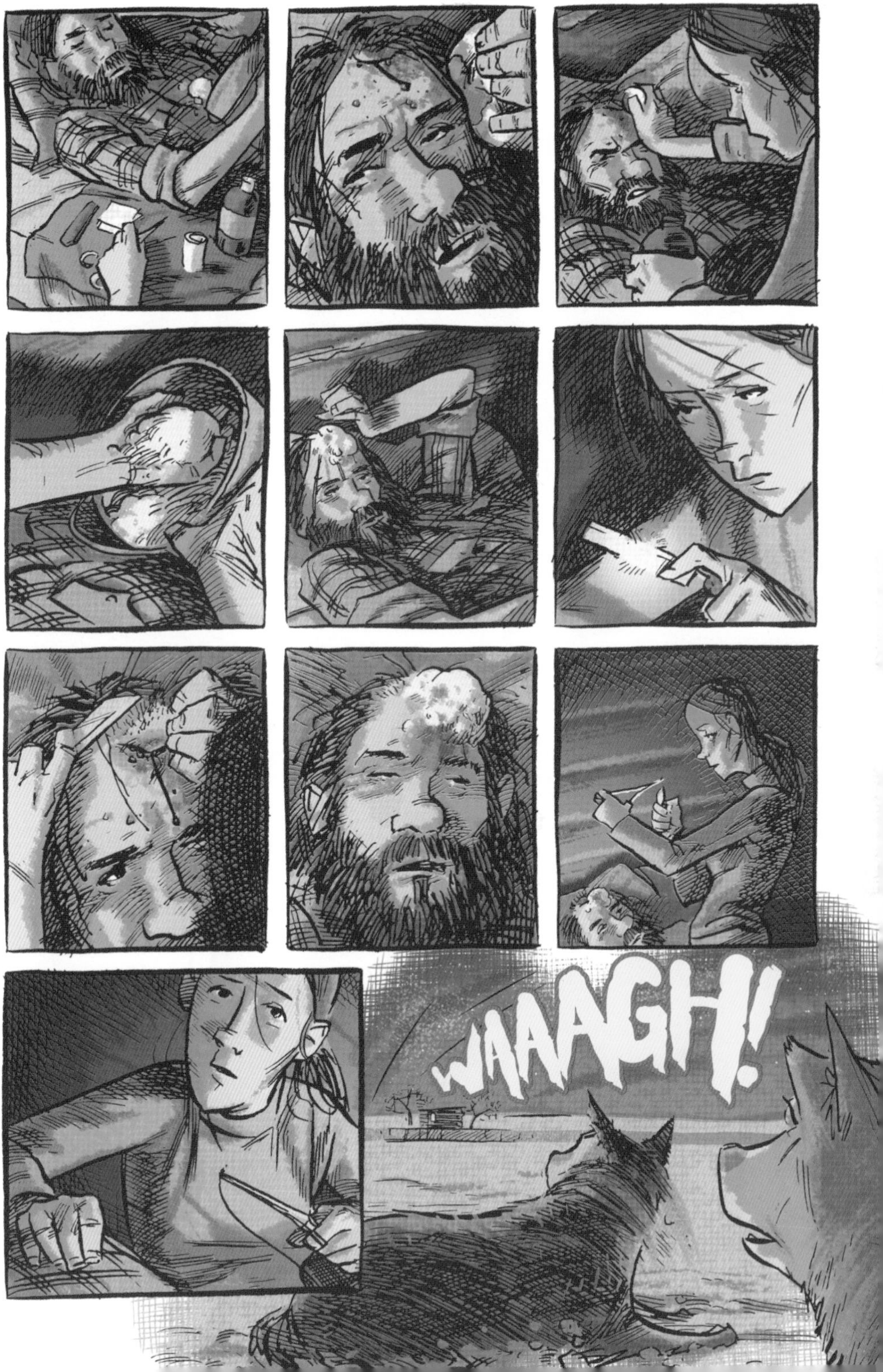
WAAAGH!

# CHAPTER 9

BUDDY, LISTEN.

THIS SITUATION WITH GUY IS A LOT MORE SERIOUS THAN—

—WHAT'S WRONG WITH YOUR LEG?

HUH? NOTHING, IT'S JUST A LITTLE BRUISE.

IT LOOKS WORSE THAN A BRUISE. WHAT HAPPENED?

THE SLED WAS COMING DOWN ON VENUS SO I PUSHED HER OUT OF THE WAY, AND...

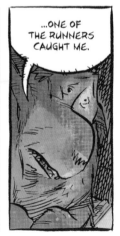

...ONE OF THE RUNNERS CAUGHT ME.

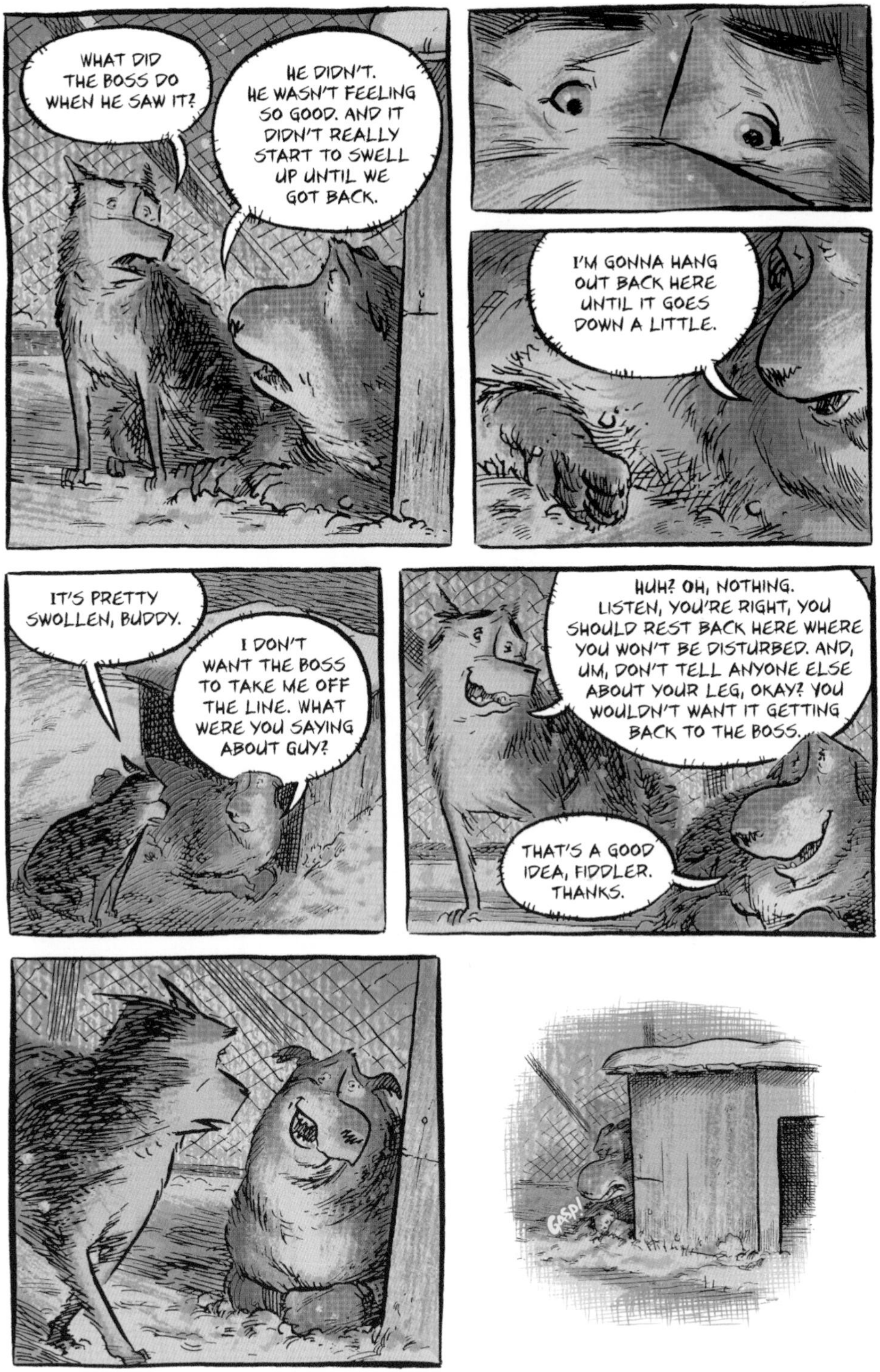
WHAT DID THE BOSS DO WHEN HE SAW IT?
HE DIDN'T. HE WASN'T FEELING SO GOOD. AND IT DIDN'T REALLY START TO SWELL UP UNTIL WE GOT BACK.
I'M GONNA HANG OUT BACK HERE UNTIL IT GOES DOWN A LITTLE.
IT'S PRETTY SWOLLEN, BUDDY.
I DON'T WANT THE BOSS TO TAKE ME OFF THE LINE. WHAT WERE YOU SAYING ABOUT GUY?
HUH? OH, NOTHING. LISTEN, YOU'RE RIGHT, YOU SHOULD REST BACK HERE WHERE YOU WON'T BE DISTURBED. AND, UM, DON'T TELL ANYONE ELSE ABOUT YOUR LEG, OKAY? YOU WOULDN'T WANT IT GETTING BACK TO THE BOSS.
THAT'S A GOOD IDEA, FIDDLER. THANKS.
GASP!

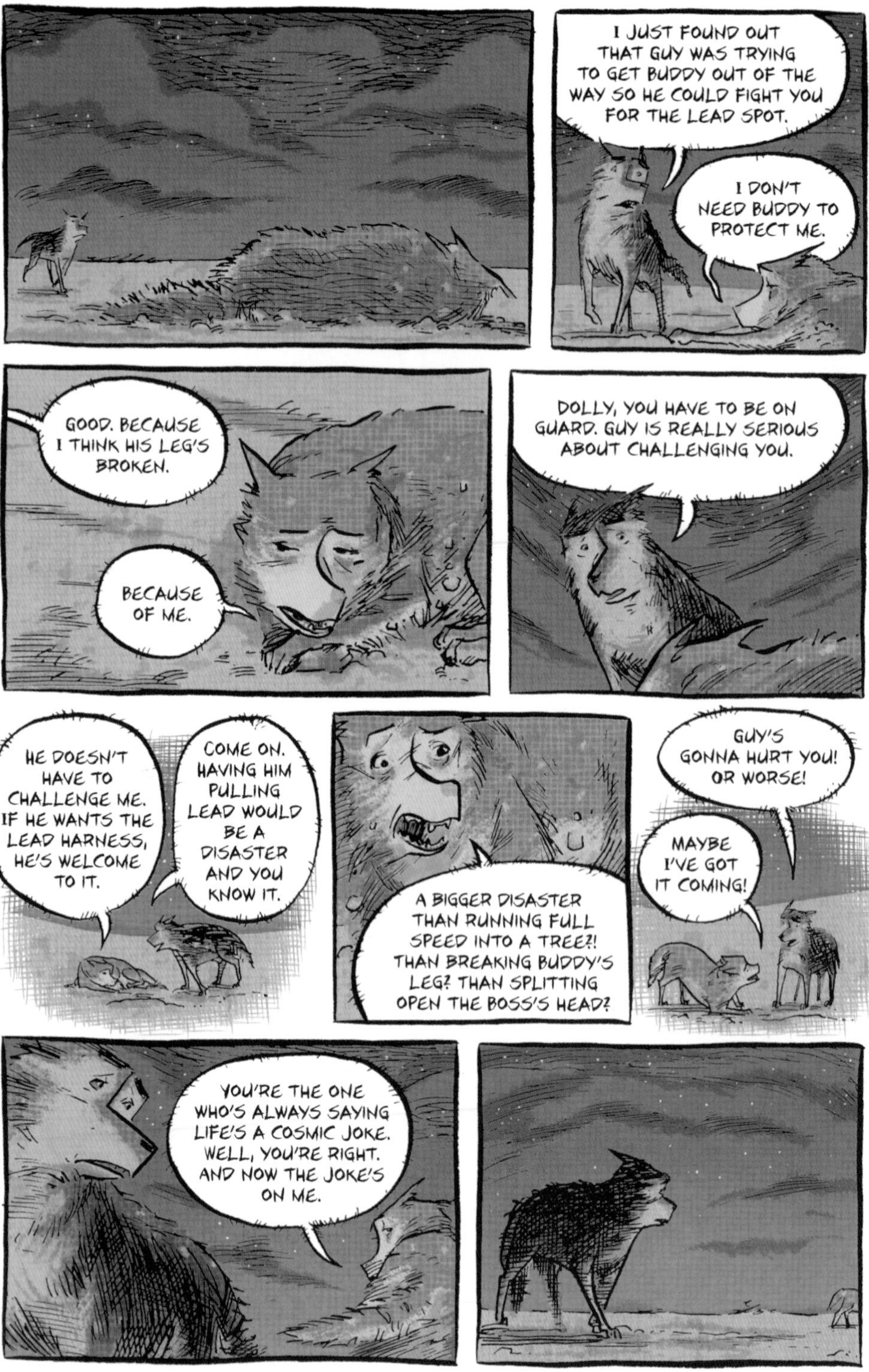
I JUST FOUND OUT THAT GUY WAS TRYING TO GET BUDDY OUT OF THE WAY SO HE COULD FIGHT YOU FOR THE LEAD SPOT.
I DON'T NEED BUDDY TO PROTECT ME.
GOOD. BECAUSE I THINK HIS LEG'S BROKEN.
BECAUSE OF ME.
DOLLY, YOU HAVE TO BE ON GUARD. GUY IS REALLY SERIOUS ABOUT CHALLENGING YOU.
HE DOESN'T HAVE TO CHALLENGE ME. IF HE WANTS THE LEAD HARNESS, HE'S WELCOME TO IT.
COME ON. HAVING HIM PULLING LEAD WOULD BE A DISASTER AND YOU KNOW IT.
A BIGGER DISASTER THAN RUNNING FULL SPEED INTO A TREE?! THAN BREAKING BUDDY'S LEG? THAN SPLITTING OPEN THE BOSS'S HEAD?
GUY'S GONNA HURT YOU! OR WORSE!
MAYBE I'VE GOT IT COMING!
YOU'RE THE ONE WHO'S ALWAYS SAYING LIFE'S A COSMIC JOKE. WELL, YOU'RE RIGHT. AND NOW THE JOKE'S ON ME.

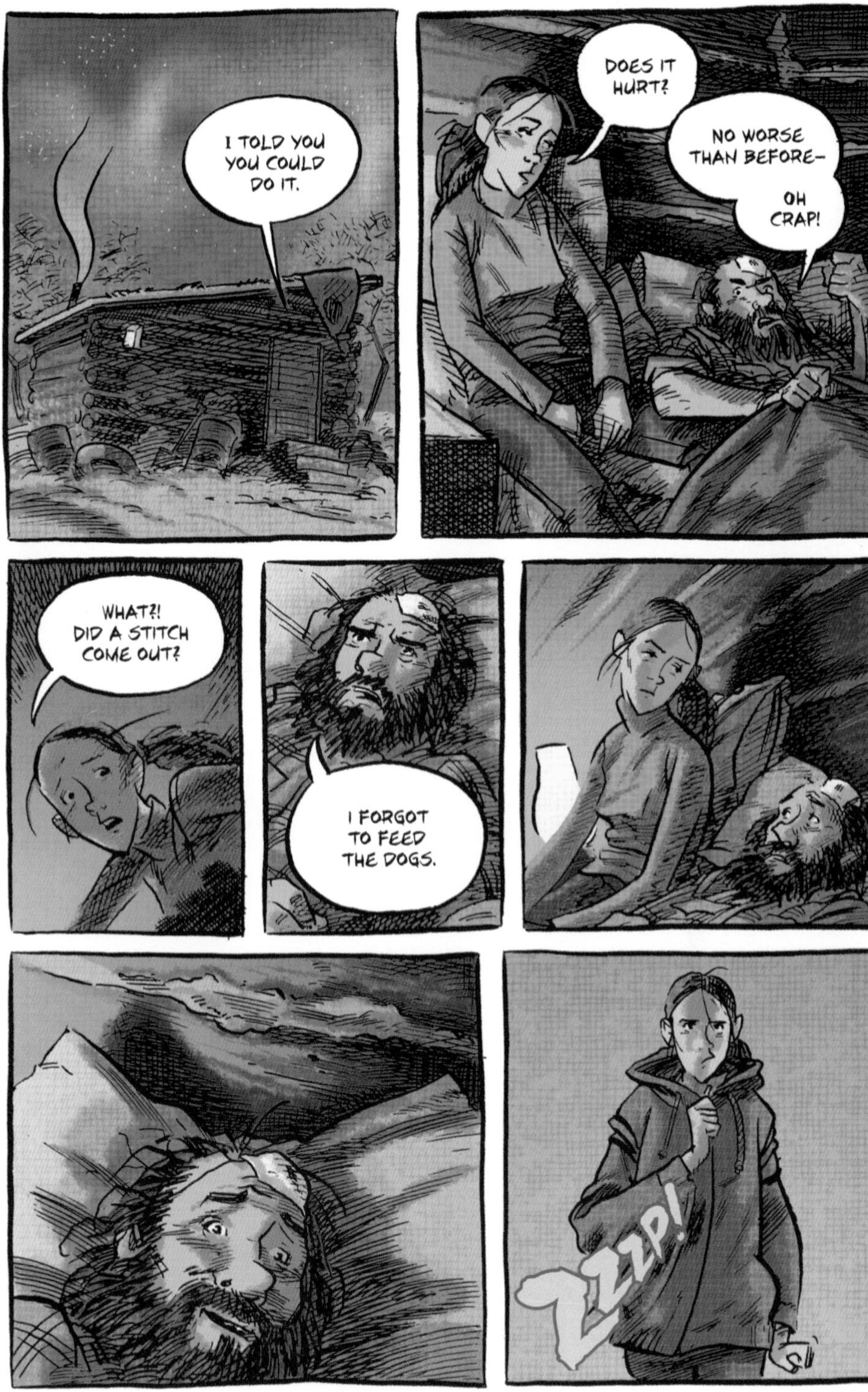
I TOLD YOU YOU COULD DO IT.
DOES IT HURT?
NO WORSE THAN BEFORE-
OH CRAP!
WHAT?! DID A STITCH COME OUT?
I FORGOT TO FEED THE DOGS.
ZZZP!

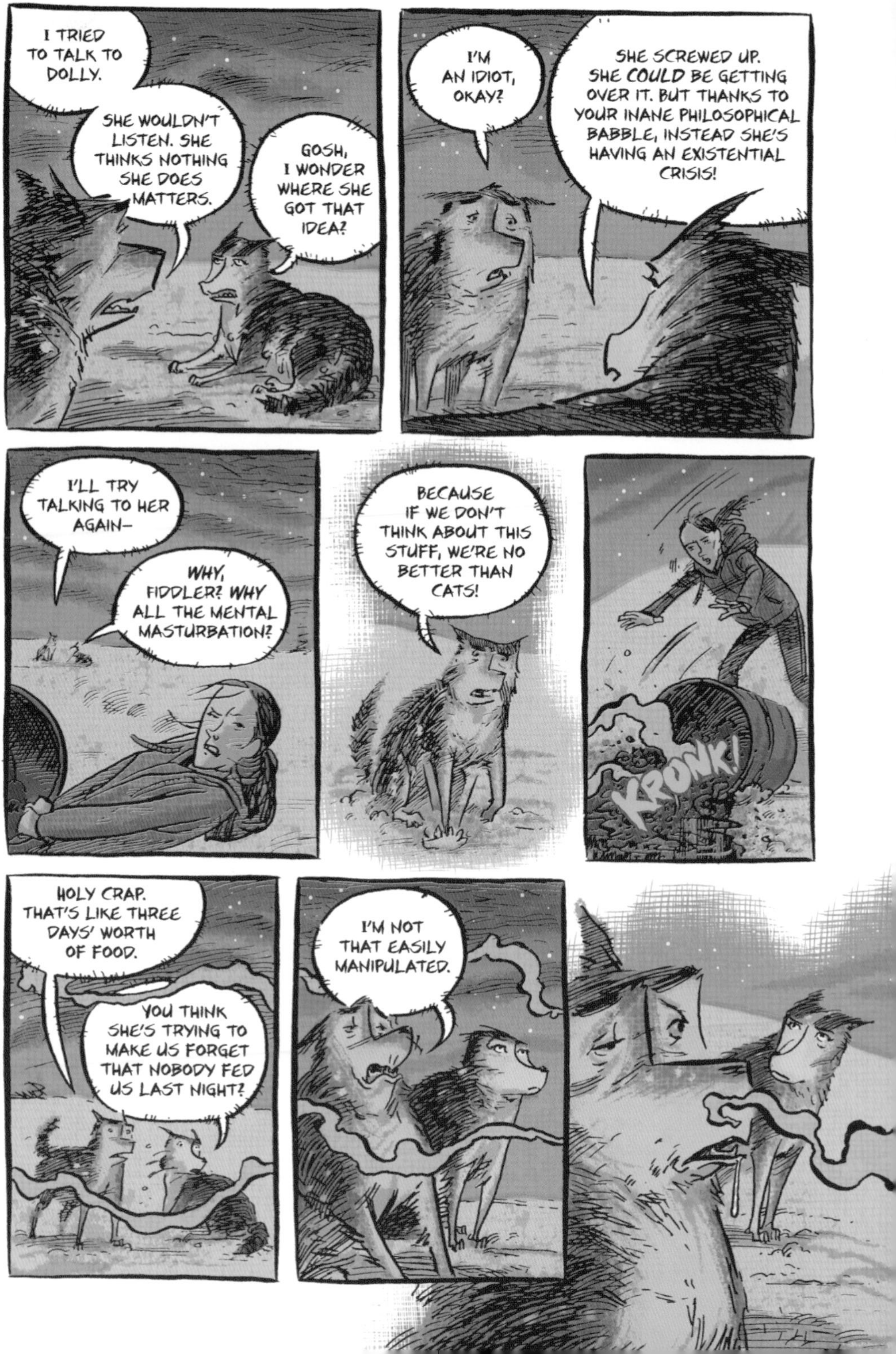
I TRIED TO TALK TO DOLLY.
SHE WOULDN'T LISTEN. SHE THINKS NOTHING SHE DOES MATTERS.
GOSH, I WONDER WHERE SHE GOT THAT IDEA?
I'M AN IDIOT, OKAY?
SHE SCREWED UP. SHE COULD BE GETTING OVER IT. BUT THANKS TO YOUR INANE PHILOSOPHICAL BABBLE, INSTEAD SHE'S HAVING AN EXISTENTIAL CRISIS!
I'LL TRY TALKING TO HER AGAIN–
WHY, FIDDLER? WHY ALL THE MENTAL MASTURBATION?
BECAUSE IF WE DON'T THINK ABOUT THIS STUFF, WE'RE NO BETTER THAN CATS!
KRONK!
HOLY CRAP. THAT'S LIKE THREE DAYS' WORTH OF FOOD.
YOU THINK SHE'S TRYING TO MAKE US FORGET THAT NOBODY FED US LAST NIGHT?
I'M NOT THAT EASILY MANIPULATED.

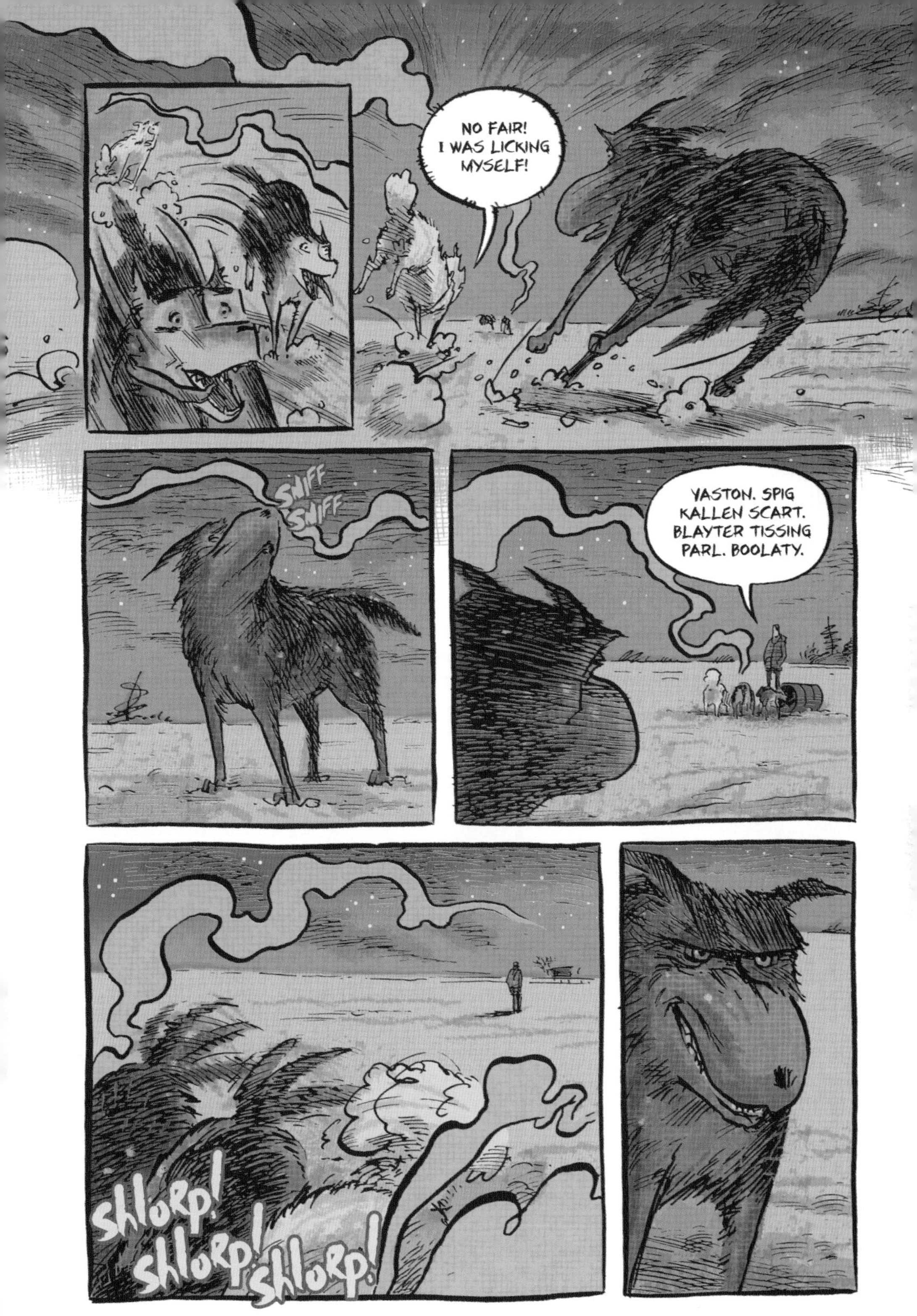
NO FAIR! I WAS LICKING MYSELF!
SNIFF SNIFF
YASTON. SPIG KALLEN SCART. BLAYTER TISSING PARL. BOOLATY.
SHLORP! SHLORP! SHLORP!

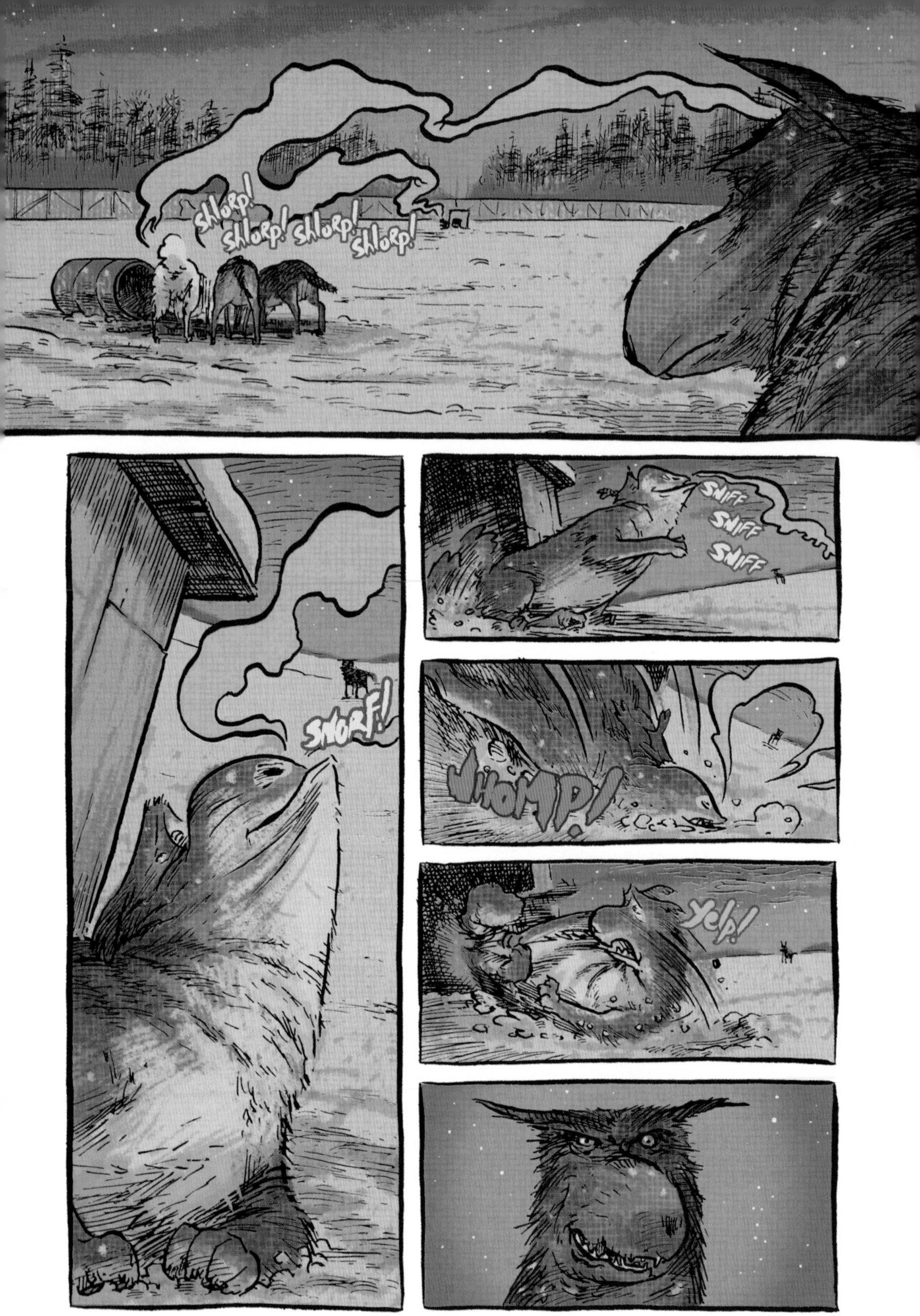
Shlorp!
Shlorp!
Shlorp!
Shlorp!
SNORF!
SNIFF
SNIFF
SNIFF
WHOMP!
Yelp!

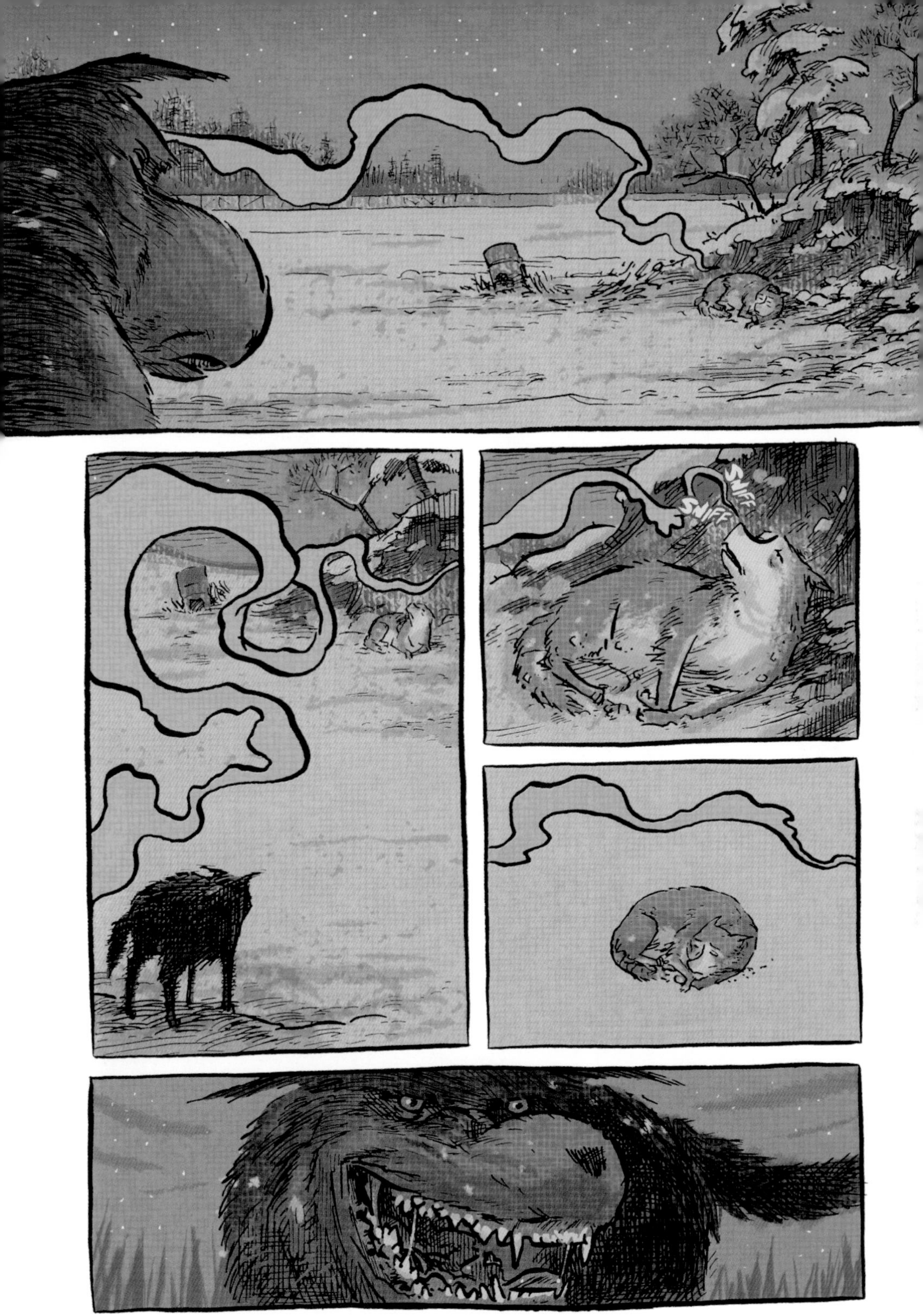
SNIFF
SNIFF

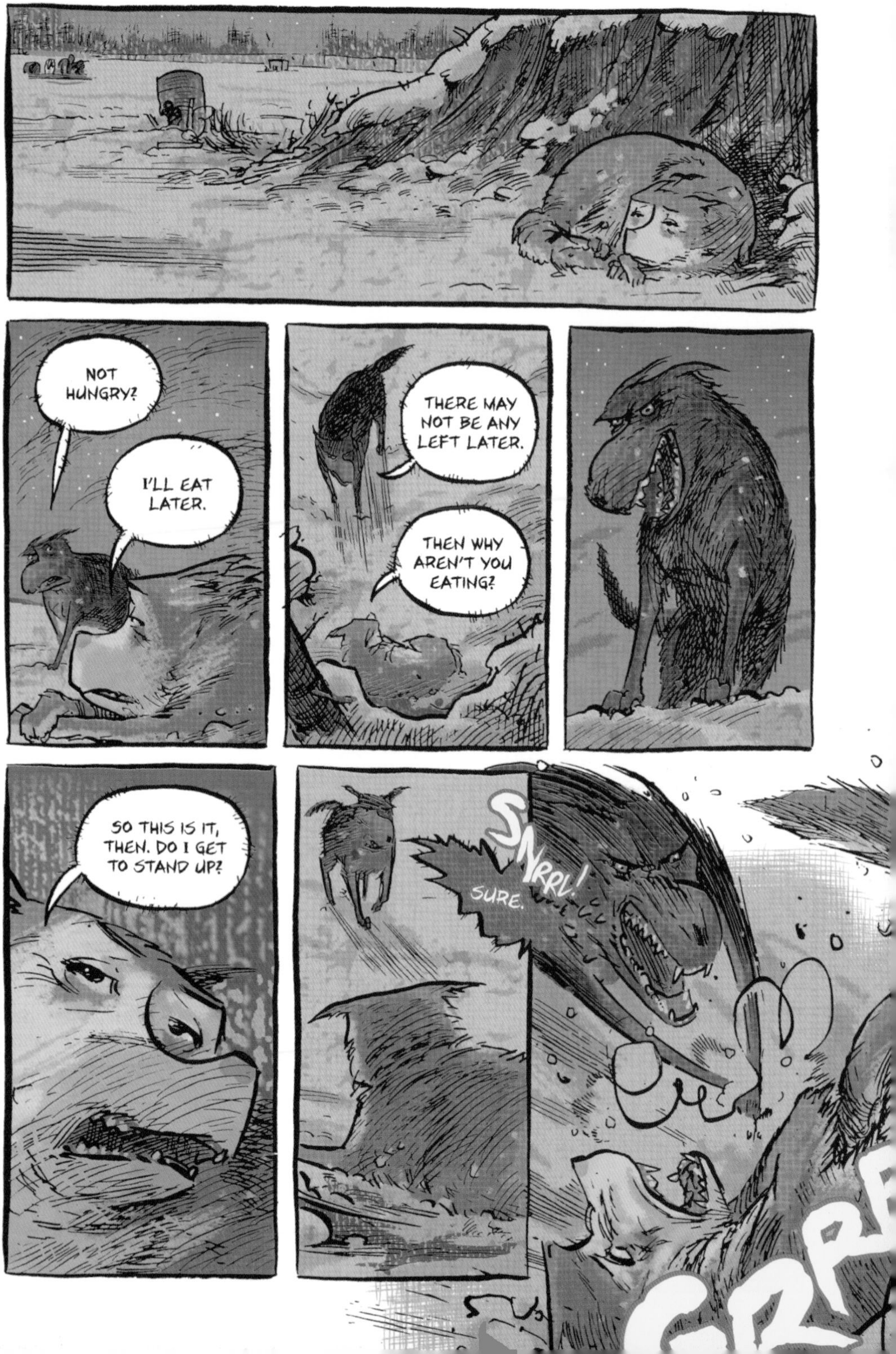
NOT HUNGRY?
I'LL EAT LATER.
THERE MAY NOT BE ANY LEFT LATER.
THEN WHY AREN'T YOU EATING?
SO THIS IS IT, THEN. DO I GET TO STAND UP?
SNRRL!
SURE.

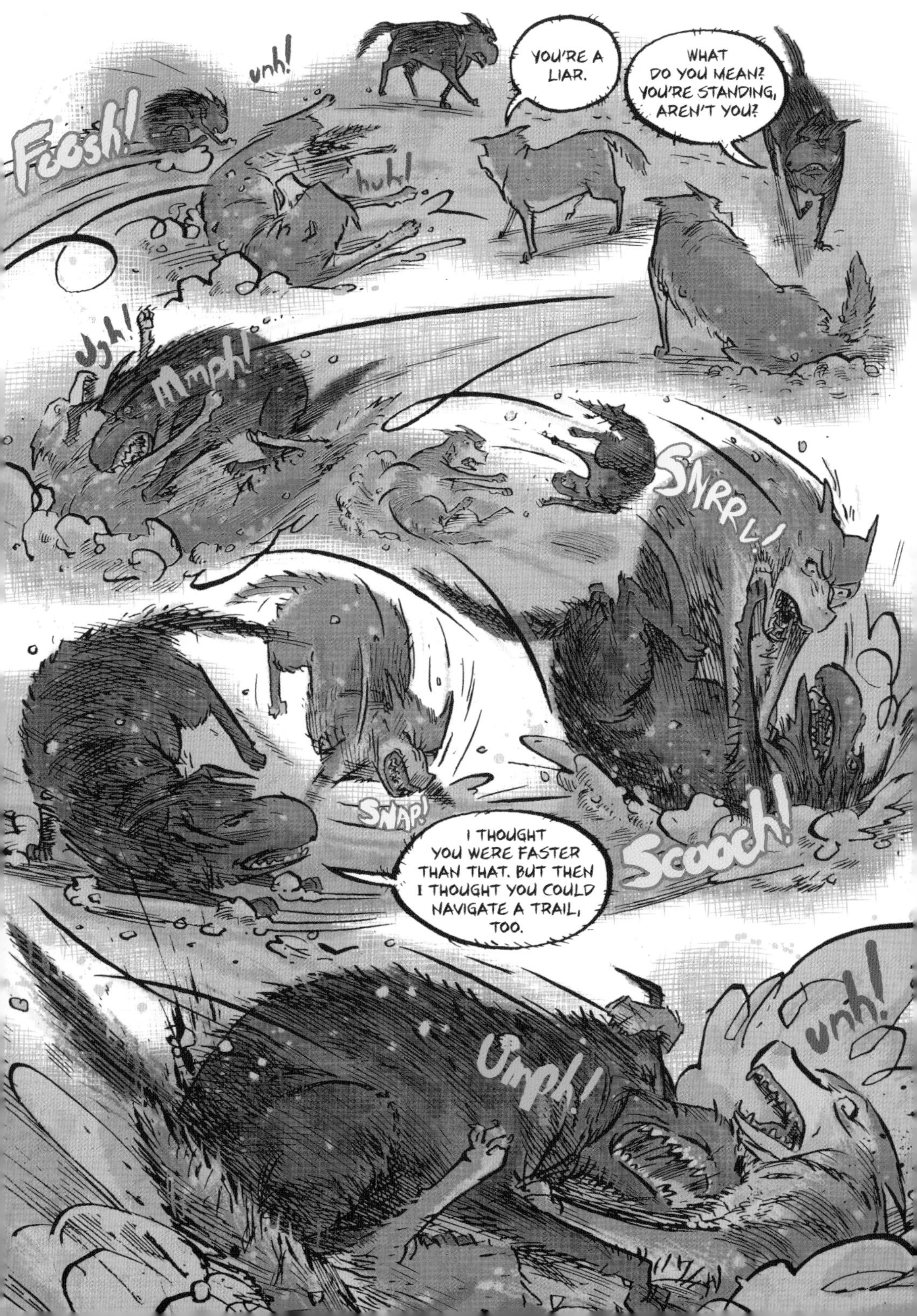
Foosh!
unh!
huh!
YOU'RE A LIAR.
WHAT DO YOU MEAN? YOU'RE STANDING, AREN'T YOU?
Ugh!
Mmph!
SNRRL!
SNAP!
Scooch!
I THOUGHT YOU WERE FASTER THAN THAT. BUT THEN I THOUGHT YOU COULD NAVIGATE A TRAIL, TOO.
Umph!
unh!

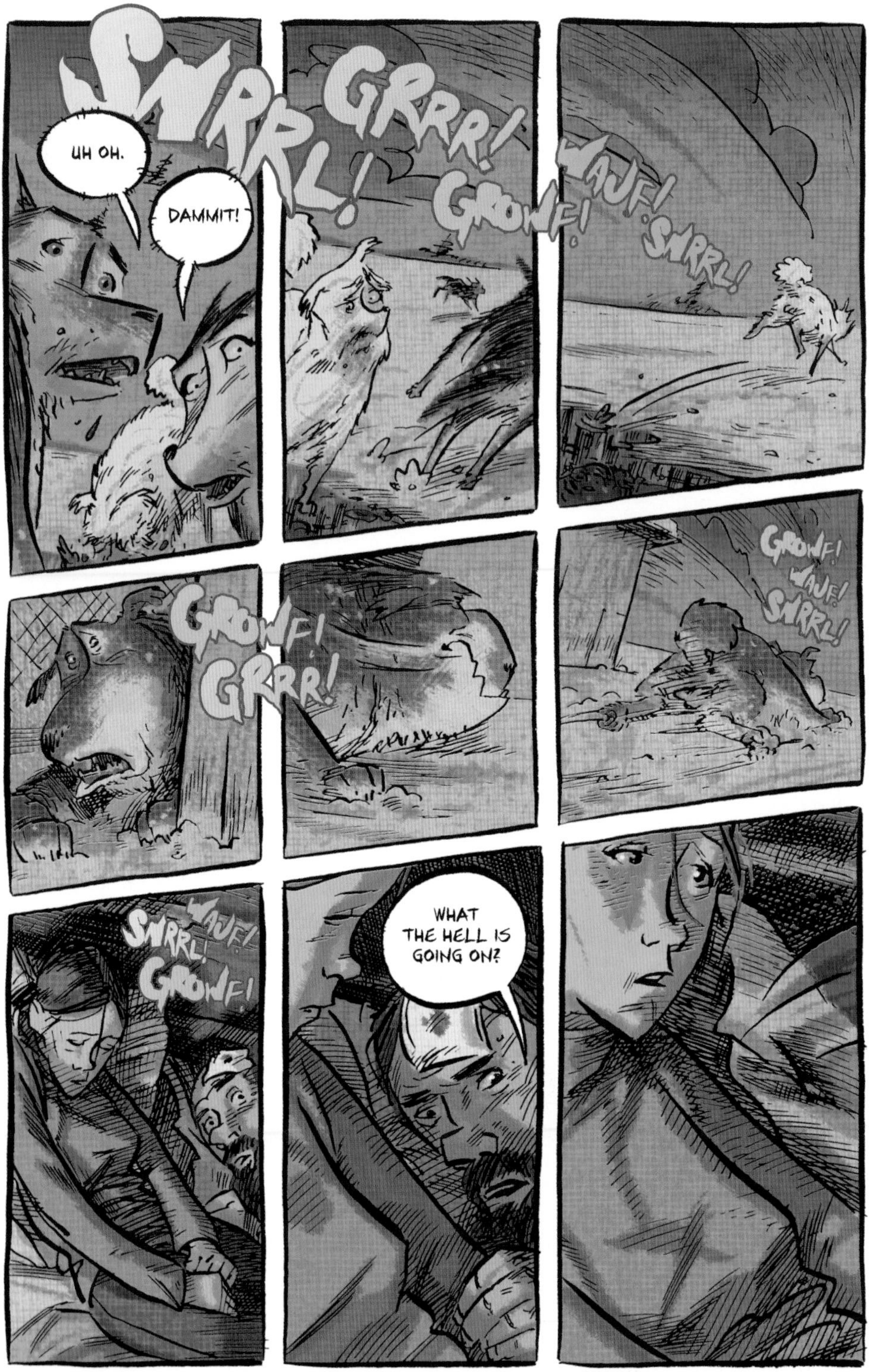
SNRRL!
UH OH.
DAMMIT!
GRRRR!
WAUF!
GROWF!
SNRRL!
GROWF!
GRRR!
GROWF!
WAUF!
SNRRL!
WAUF!
SNRRL!
GROWF!
WHAT THE HELL IS GOING ON?

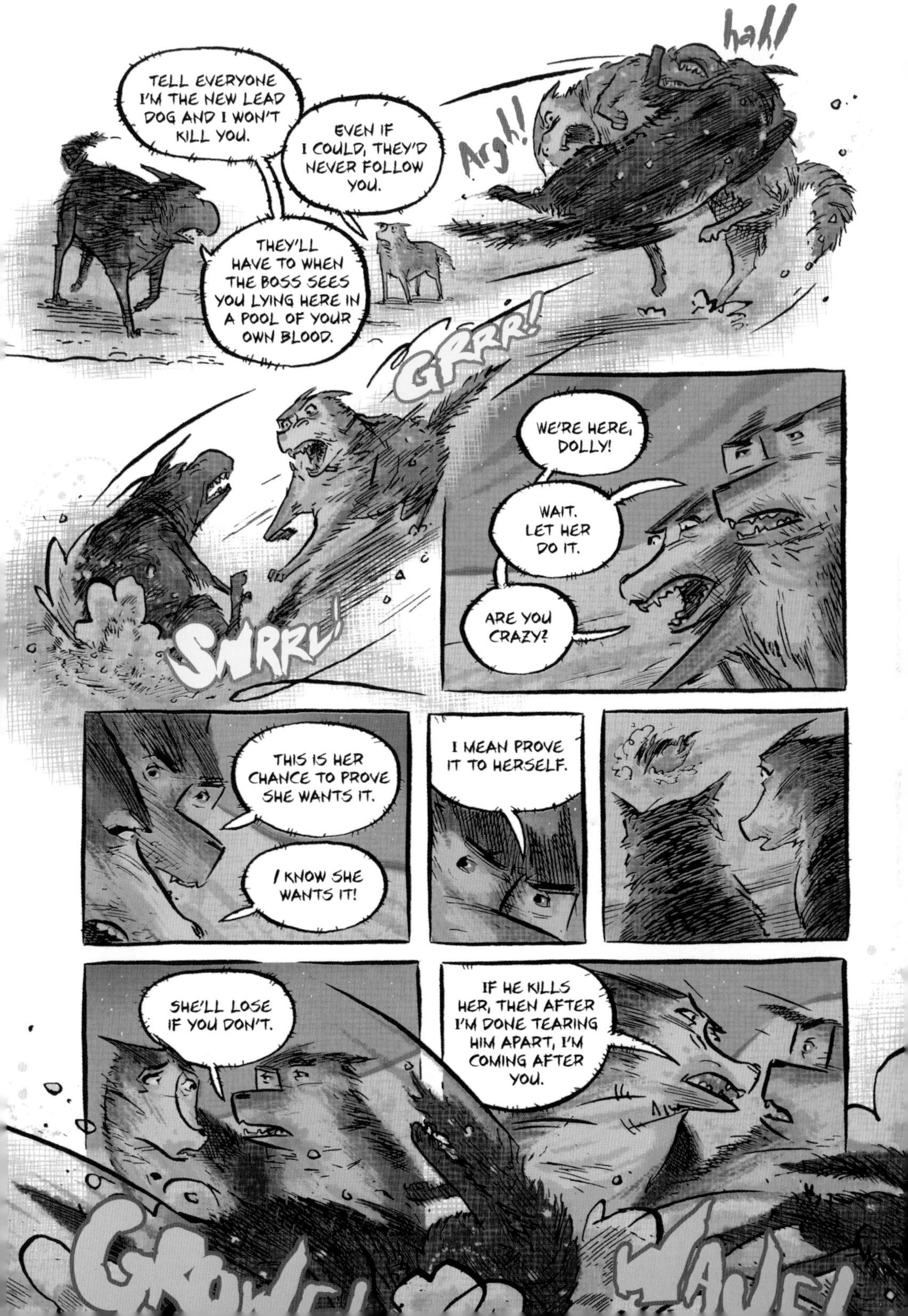

TELL EVERYONE I'M THE NEW LEAD DOG AND I WON'T KILL YOU.
EVEN IF I COULD, THEY'D NEVER FOLLOW YOU.
THEY'LL HAVE TO WHEN THE BOSS SEES YOU LYING HERE IN A POOL OF YOUR OWN BLOOD.
hah!
Argh!
GRRR!
SNRRL!
WE'RE HERE, DOLLY!
WAIT. LET HER DO IT.
ARE YOU CRAZY?
THIS IS HER CHANCE TO PROVE SHE WANTS IT.
I KNOW SHE WANTS IT!
I MEAN PROVE IT TO HERSELF.
SHE'LL LOSE IF YOU DON'T.
IF HE KILLS HER, THEN AFTER I'M DONE TEARING HIM APART, I'M COMING AFTER YOU.

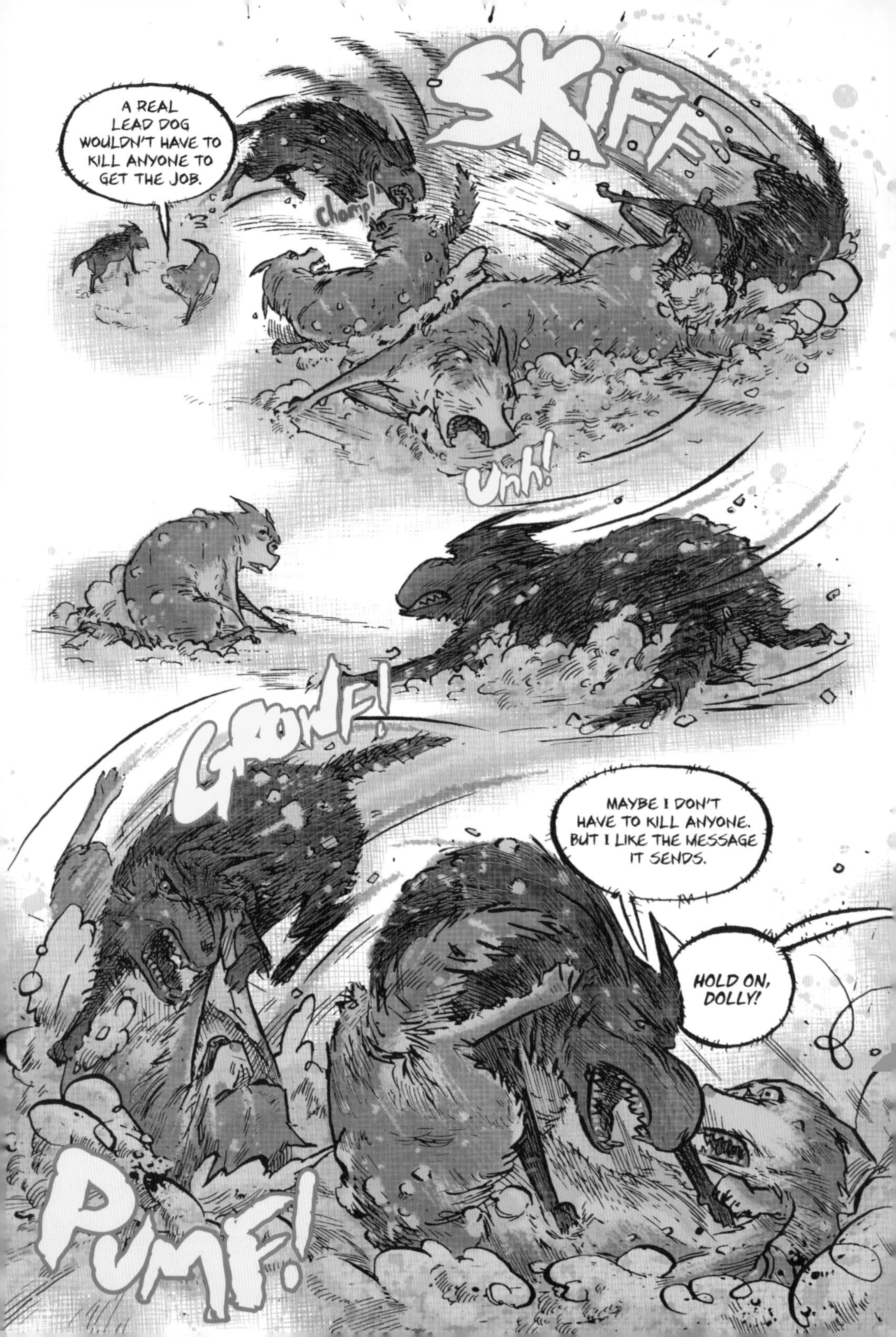
A REAL LEAD DOG WOULDN'T HAVE TO KILL ANYONE TO GET THE JOB.
Chomp!
SKIFF
Unh!
GROWF!
MAYBE I DON'T HAVE TO KILL ANYONE. BUT I LIKE THE MESSAGE IT SENDS.
HOLD ON, DOLLY!
PUMF!

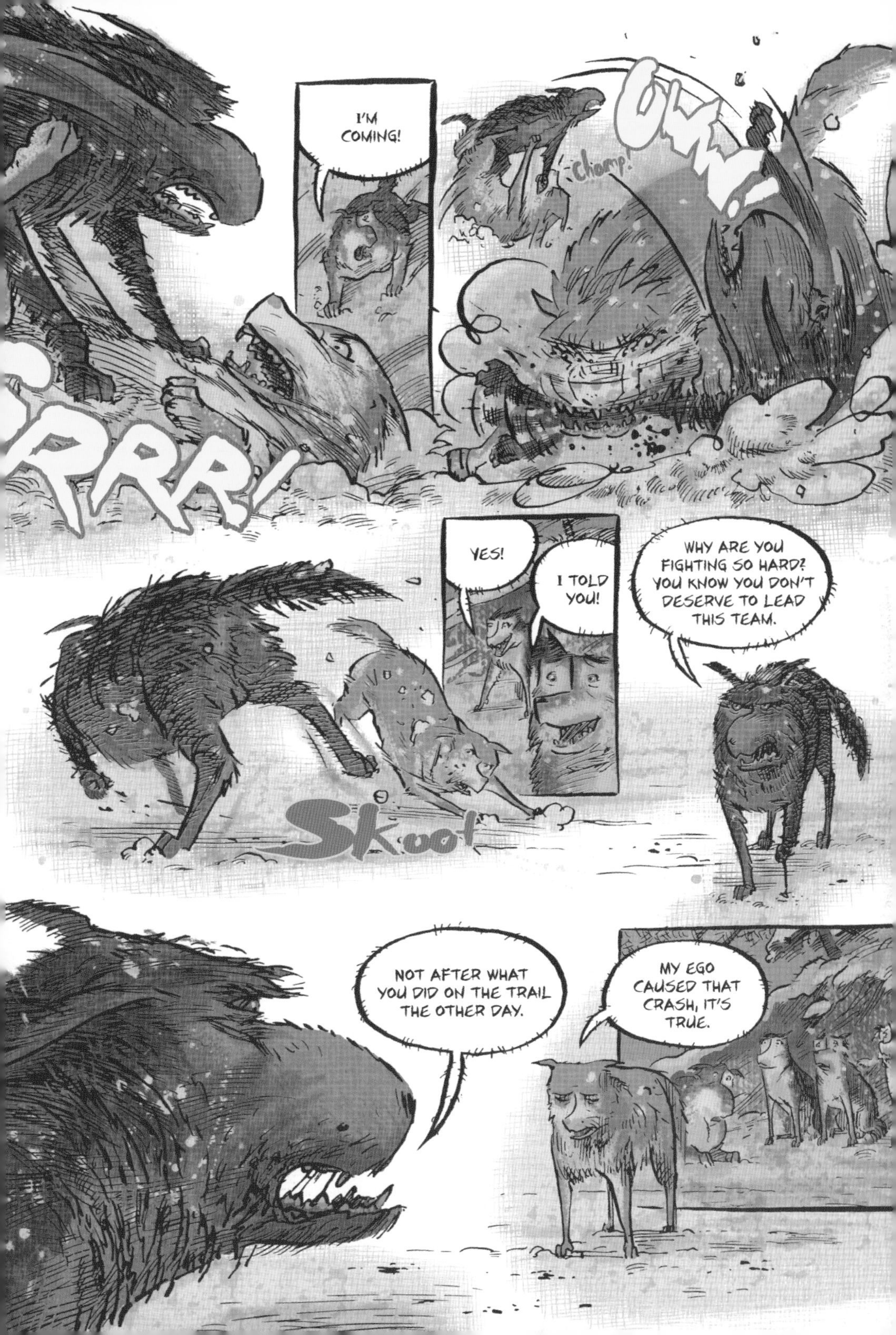

RRRR!
I'M COMING!
Champ!
OW!
YES!
I TOLD YOU!
WHY ARE YOU FIGHTING SO HARD? YOU KNOW YOU DON'T DESERVE TO LEAD THIS TEAM.
Skoot
NOT AFTER WHAT YOU DID ON THE TRAIL THE OTHER DAY.
MY EGO CAUSED THAT CRASH, IT'S TRUE.

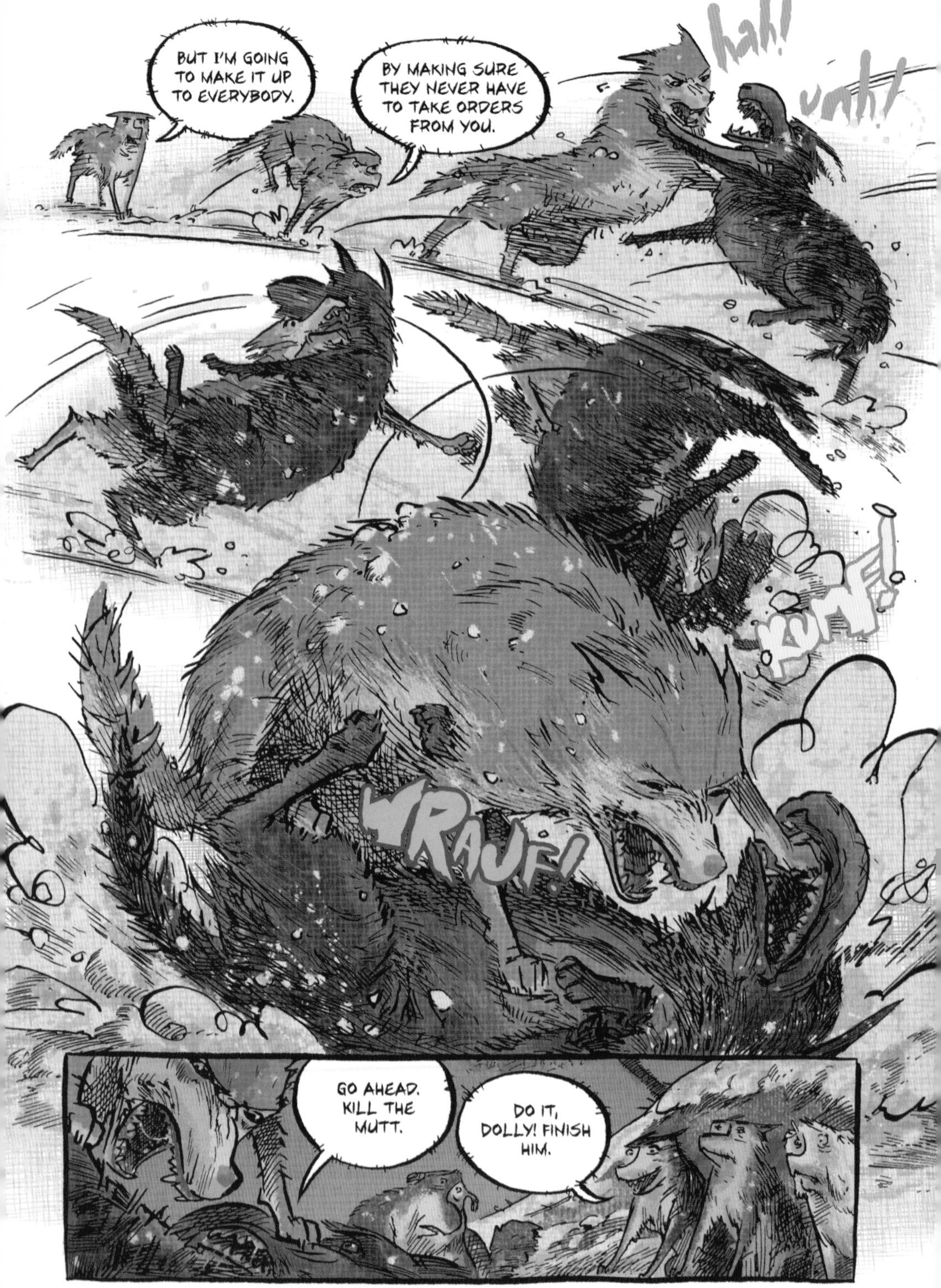
BUT I'M GOING TO MAKE IT UP TO EVERYBODY.
BY MAKING SURE THEY NEVER HAVE TO TAKE ORDERS FROM YOU.
hah!
unh!
KUMF!
WRAUF!
GO AHEAD. KILL THE MUTT.
DO IT, DOLLY! FINISH HIM.

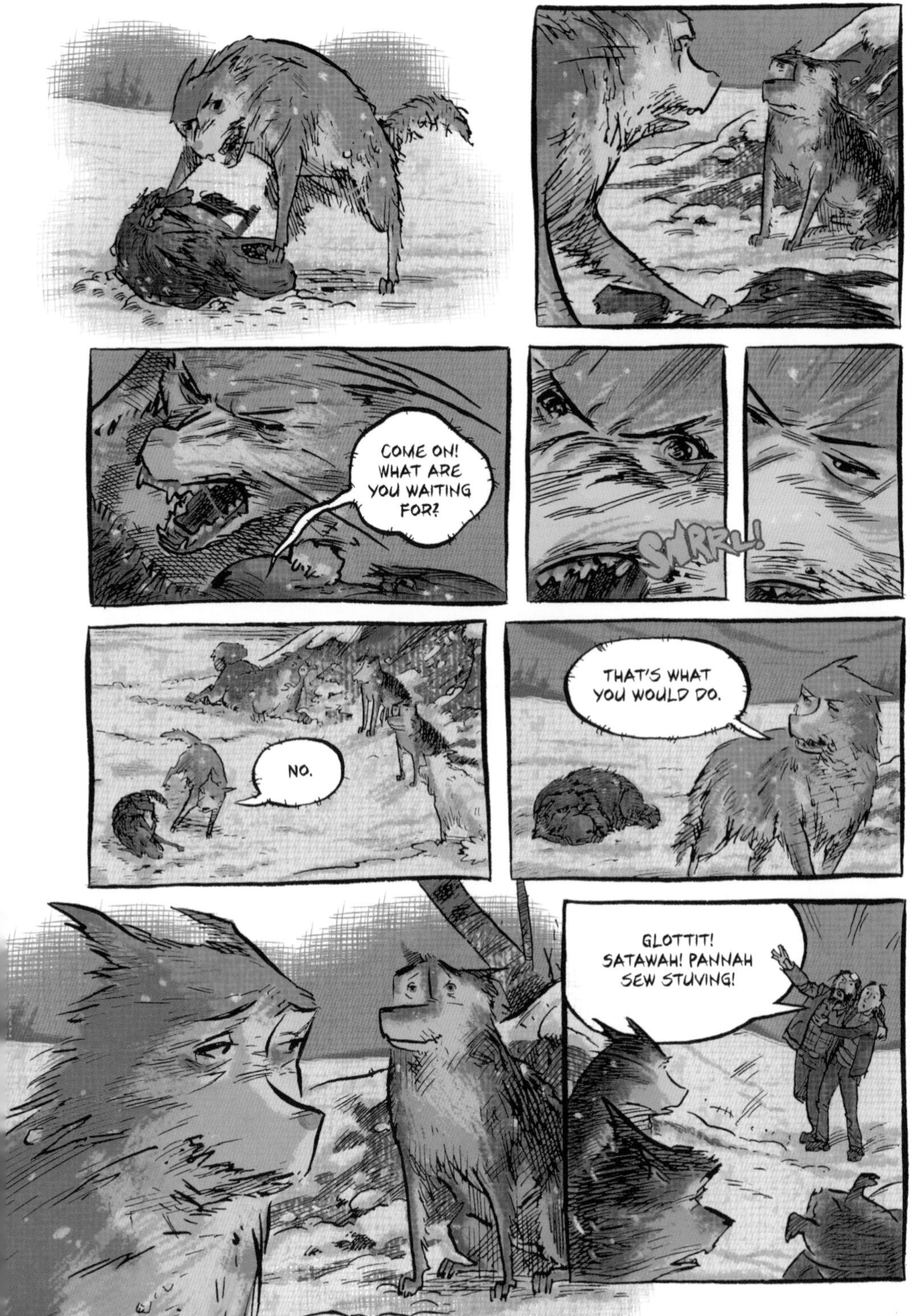
COME ON! WHAT ARE YOU WAITING FOR?
SNRRL!
NO.
THAT'S WHAT YOU WOULD DO.
GLOTTIT! SATAWAH! PANNAH SEW STUVING!

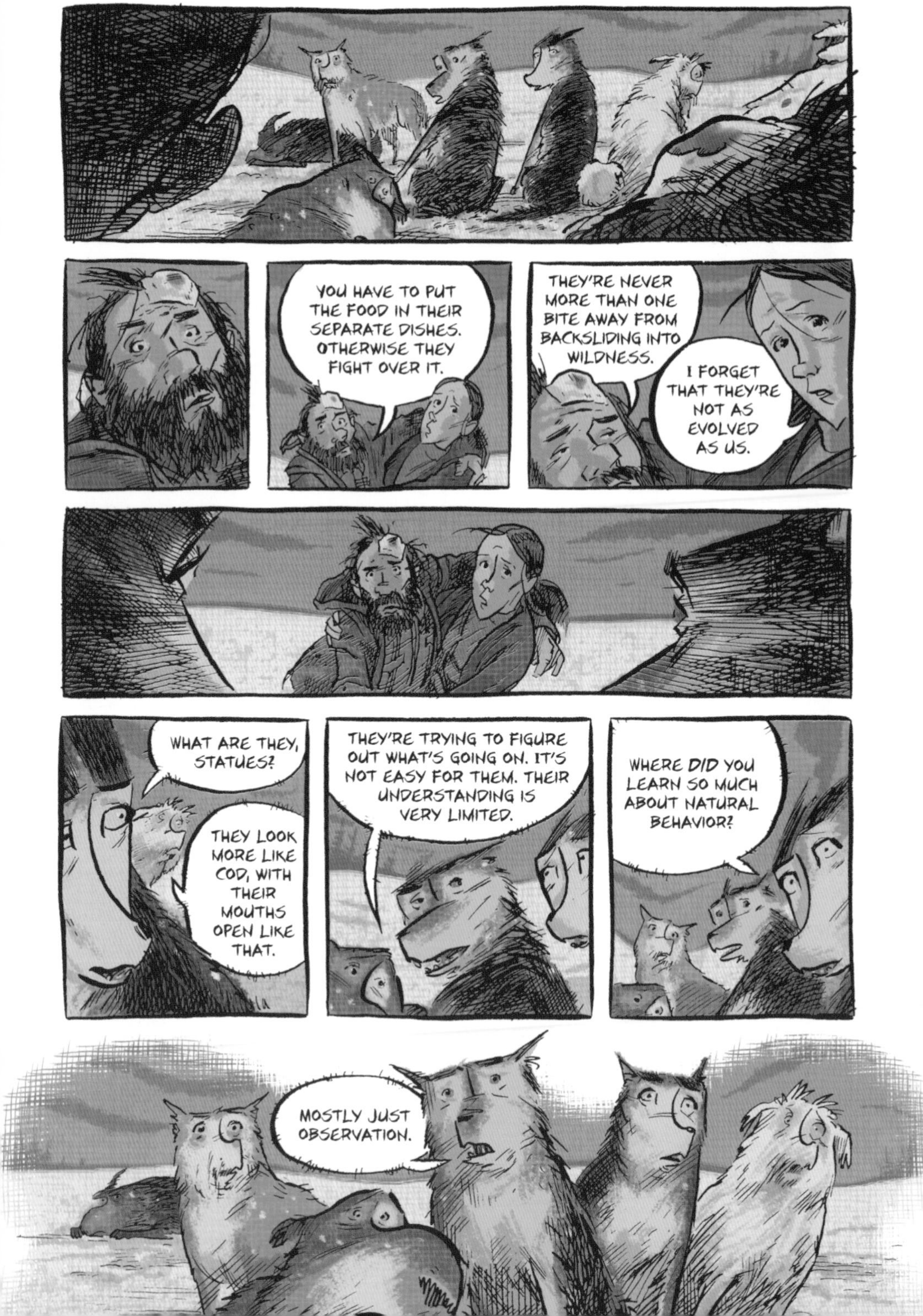
YOU HAVE TO PUT THE FOOD IN THEIR SEPARATE DISHES. OTHERWISE THEY FIGHT OVER IT.
THEY'RE NEVER MORE THAN ONE BITE AWAY FROM BACKSLIDING INTO WILDNESS.
I FORGET THAT THEY'RE NOT AS EVOLVED AS US.
WHAT ARE THEY, STATUES?
THEY LOOK MORE LIKE COD, WITH THEIR MOUTHS OPEN LIKE THAT.
THEY'RE TRYING TO FIGURE OUT WHAT'S GOING ON. IT'S NOT EASY FOR THEM. THEIR UNDERSTANDING IS VERY LIMITED.
WHERE *DID* YOU LEARN SO MUCH ABOUT NATURAL BEHAVIOR?
MOSTLY JUST OBSERVATION.

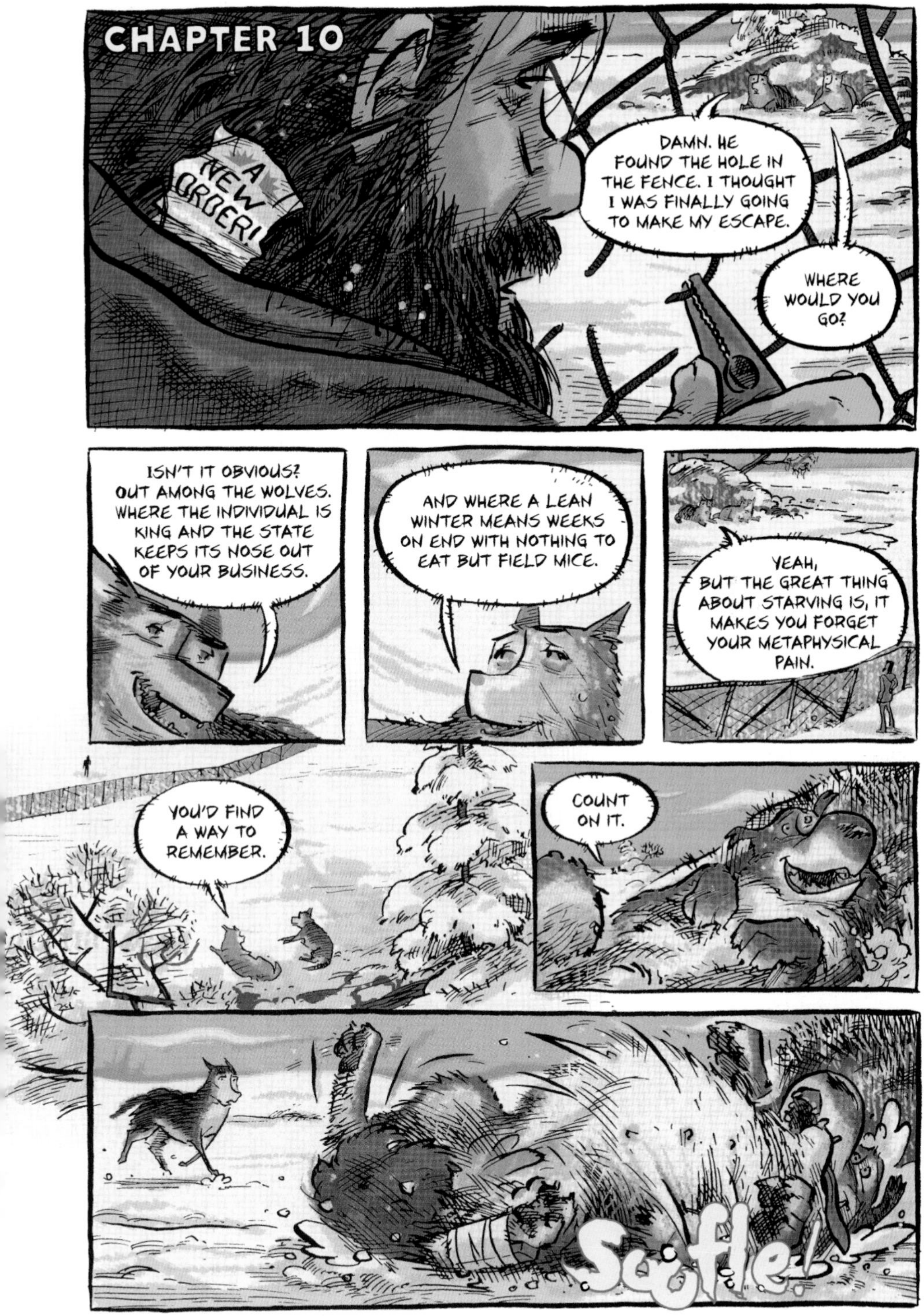

CHAPTER 10
A NEW ORDER!
DAMN. HE FOUND THE HOLE IN THE FENCE. I THOUGHT I WAS FINALLY GOING TO MAKE MY ESCAPE.
WHERE WOULD YOU GO?
ISN'T IT OBVIOUS? OUT AMONG THE WOLVES. WHERE THE INDIVIDUAL IS KING AND THE STATE KEEPS ITS NOSE OUT OF YOUR BUSINESS.
AND WHERE A LEAN WINTER MEANS WEEKS ON END WITH NOTHING TO EAT BUT FIELD MICE.
YEAH, BUT THE GREAT THING ABOUT STARVING IS, IT MAKES YOU FORGET YOUR METAPHYSICAL PAIN.
YOU'D FIND A WAY TO REMEMBER.
COUNT ON IT.
Scuffle!

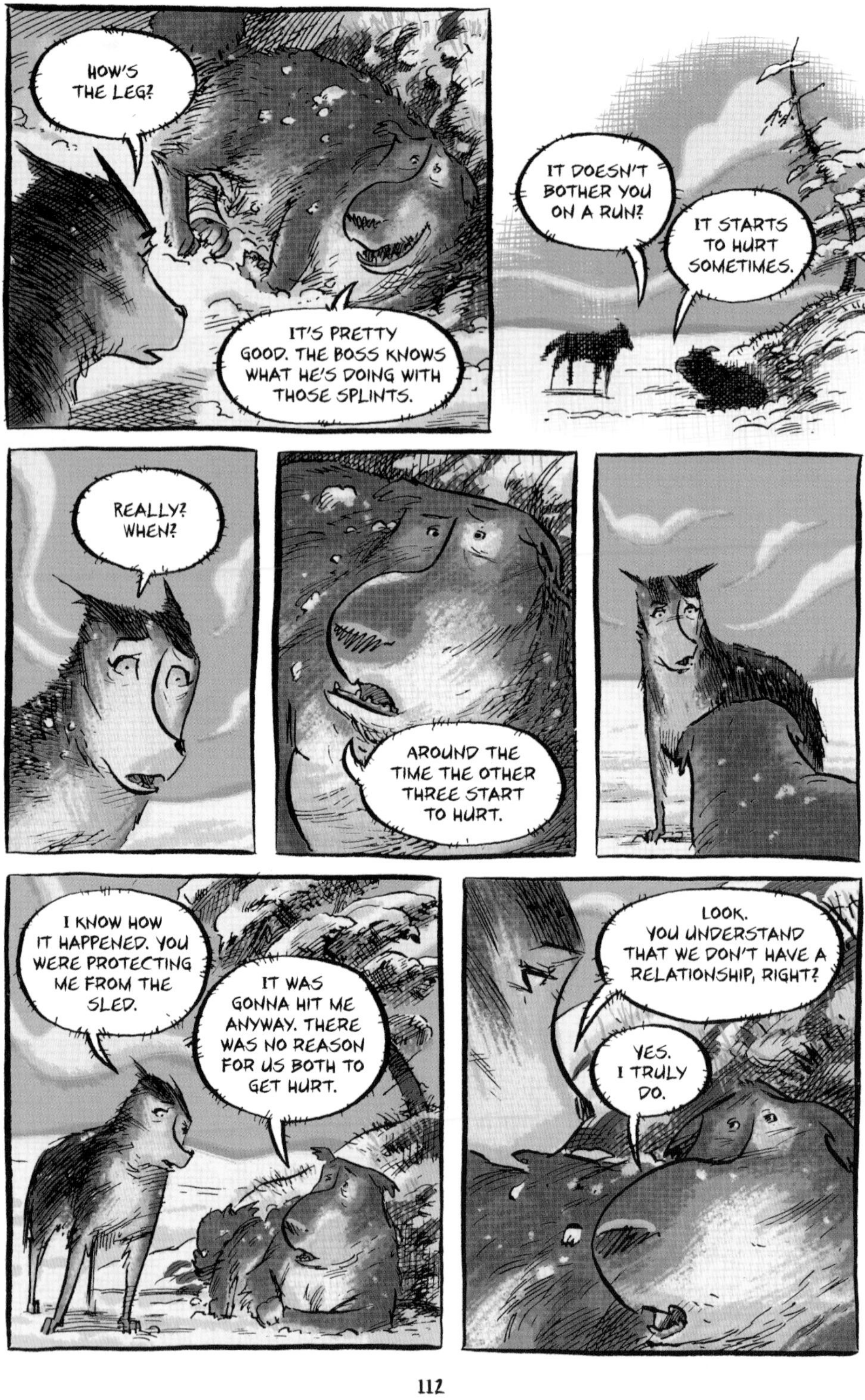
HOW'S THE LEG?
IT'S PRETTY GOOD. THE BOSS KNOWS WHAT HE'S DOING WITH THOSE SPLINTS.
IT DOESN'T BOTHER YOU ON A RUN?
IT STARTS TO HURT SOMETIMES.
REALLY? WHEN?
AROUND THE TIME THE OTHER THREE START TO HURT.
I KNOW HOW IT HAPPENED. YOU WERE PROTECTING ME FROM THE SLED.
IT WAS GONNA HIT ME ANYWAY. THERE WAS NO REASON FOR US BOTH TO GET HURT.
LOOK. YOU UNDERSTAND THAT WE DON'T HAVE A RELATIONSHIP, RIGHT?
YES. I TRULY DO.

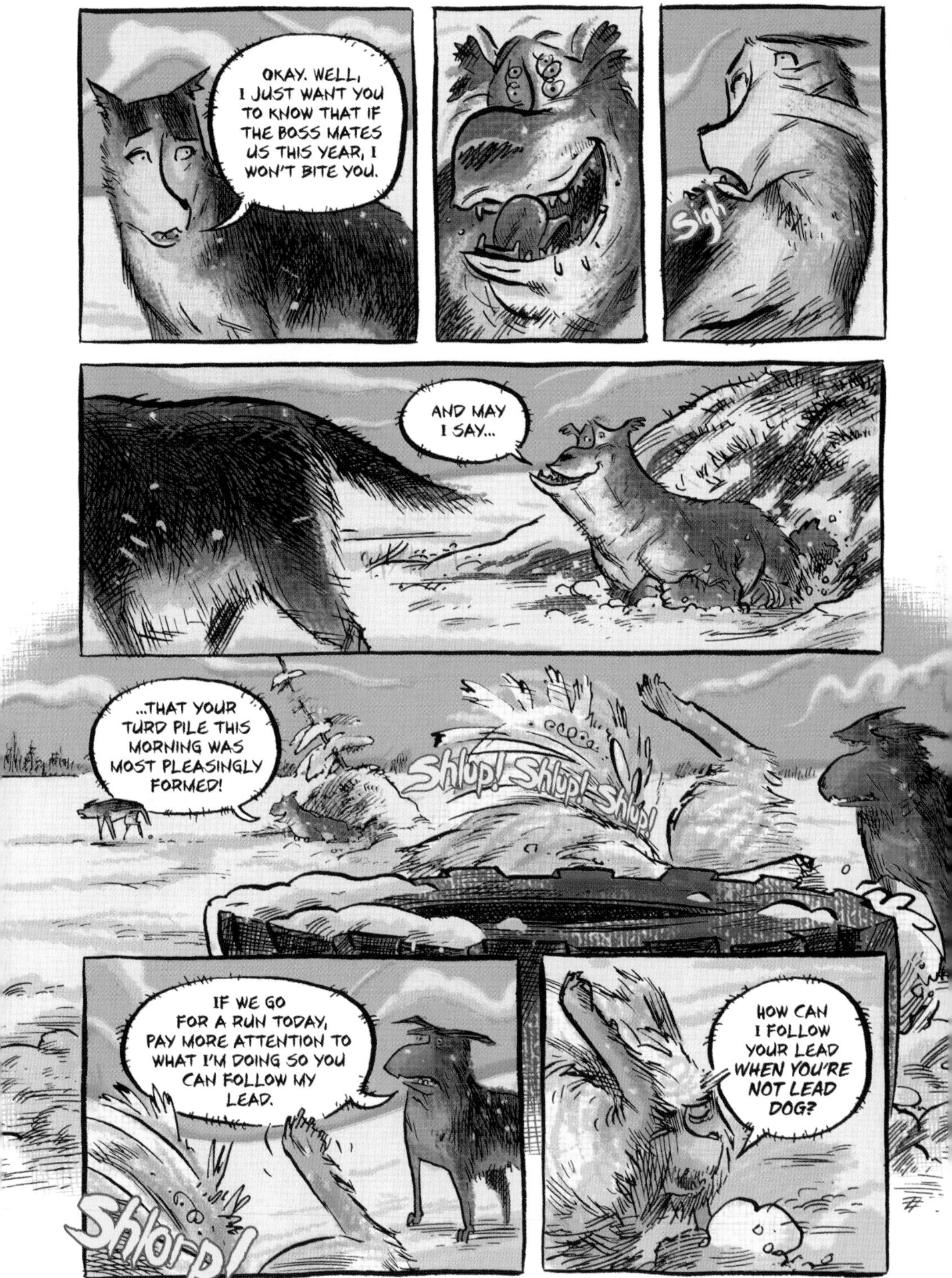
OKAY. WELL, I JUST WANT YOU TO KNOW THAT IF THE BOSS MATES US THIS YEAR, I WON'T BITE YOU.
Sigh
AND MAY I SAY...
...THAT YOUR TURD PILE THIS MORNING WAS MOST PLEASINGLY FORMED!
Shlup! Shlup! Shlup!
IF WE GO FOR A RUN TODAY, PAY MORE ATTENTION TO WHAT I'M DOING SO YOU CAN FOLLOW MY LEAD.
Shlorp!
HOW CAN I FOLLOW YOUR LEAD WHEN YOU'RE NOT LEAD DOG?

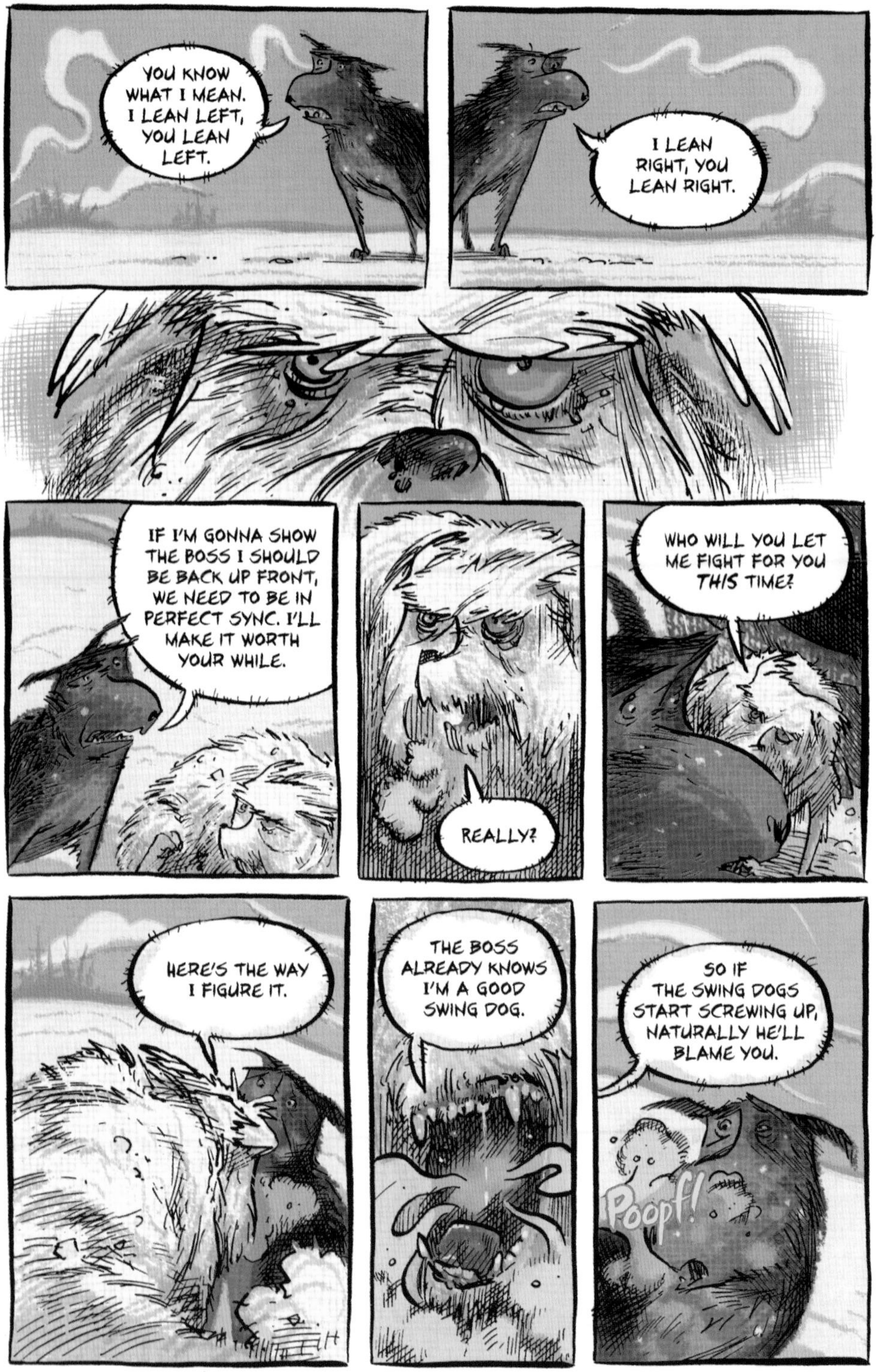
YOU KNOW WHAT I MEAN. I LEAN LEFT, YOU LEAN LEFT.
I LEAN RIGHT, YOU LEAN RIGHT.
IF I'M GONNA SHOW THE BOSS I SHOULD BE BACK UP FRONT, WE NEED TO BE IN PERFECT SYNC. I'LL MAKE IT WORTH YOUR WHILE.
REALLY?
WHO WILL YOU LET ME FIGHT FOR YOU *THIS* TIME?
HERE'S THE WAY I FIGURE IT.
THE BOSS ALREADY KNOWS I'M A GOOD SWING DOG.
SO IF THE SWING DOGS START SCREWING UP, NATURALLY HE'LL BLAME YOU.
Poopf!

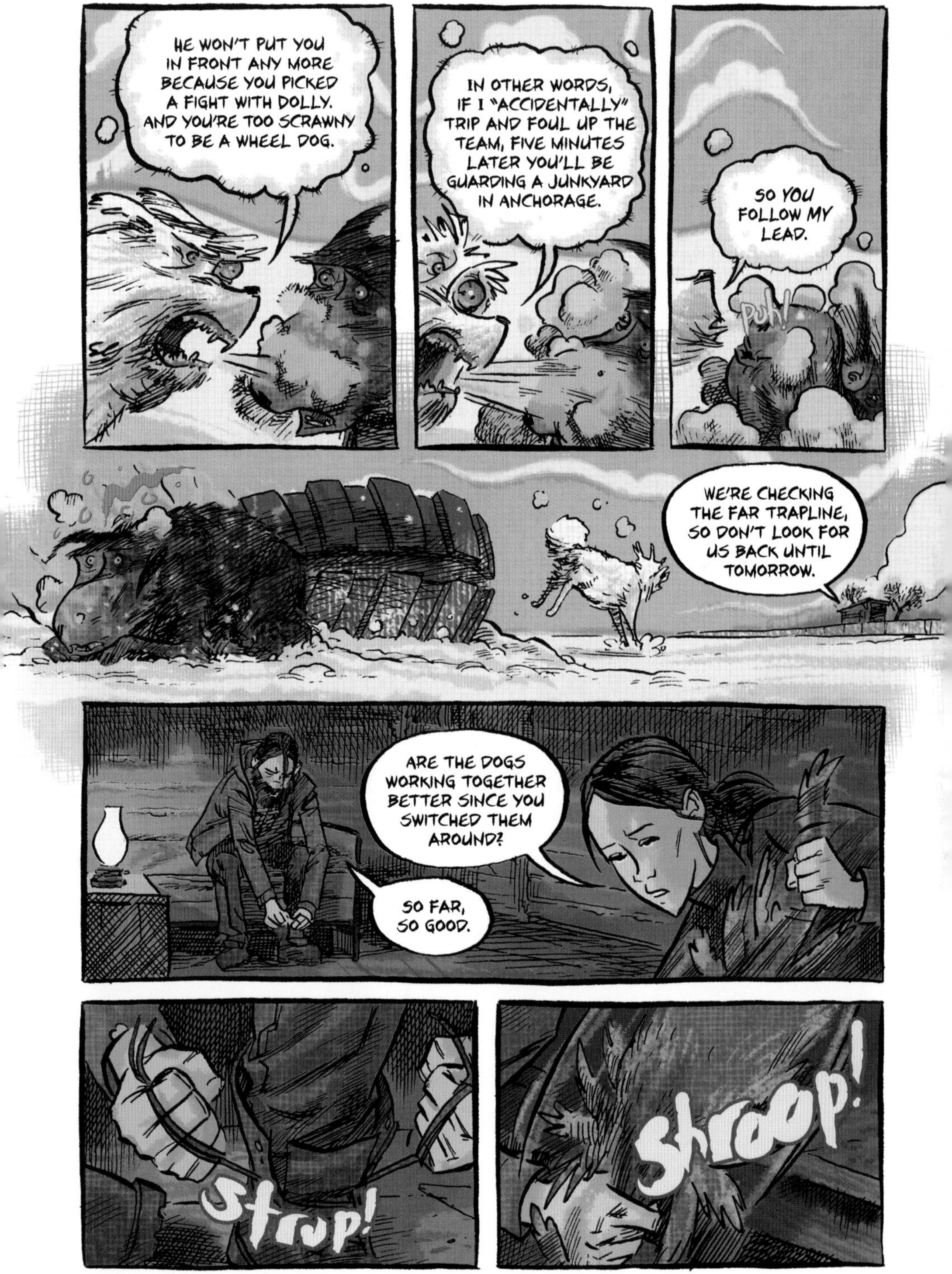
HE WON'T PUT YOU IN FRONT ANY MORE BECAUSE YOU PICKED A FIGHT WITH DOLLY. AND YOU'RE TOO SCRAWNY TO BE A WHEEL DOG.
IN OTHER WORDS, IF I "ACCIDENTALLY" TRIP AND FOUL UP THE TEAM, FIVE MINUTES LATER YOU'LL BE GUARDING A JUNKYARD IN ANCHORAGE.
SO YOU FOLLOW MY LEAD.
PUH!
WE'RE CHECKING THE FAR TRAPLINE, SO DON'T LOOK FOR US BACK UNTIL TOMORROW.
ARE THE DOGS WORKING TOGETHER BETTER SINCE YOU SWITCHED THEM AROUND?
SO FAR, SO GOOD.
STRUP!
SHROOP!

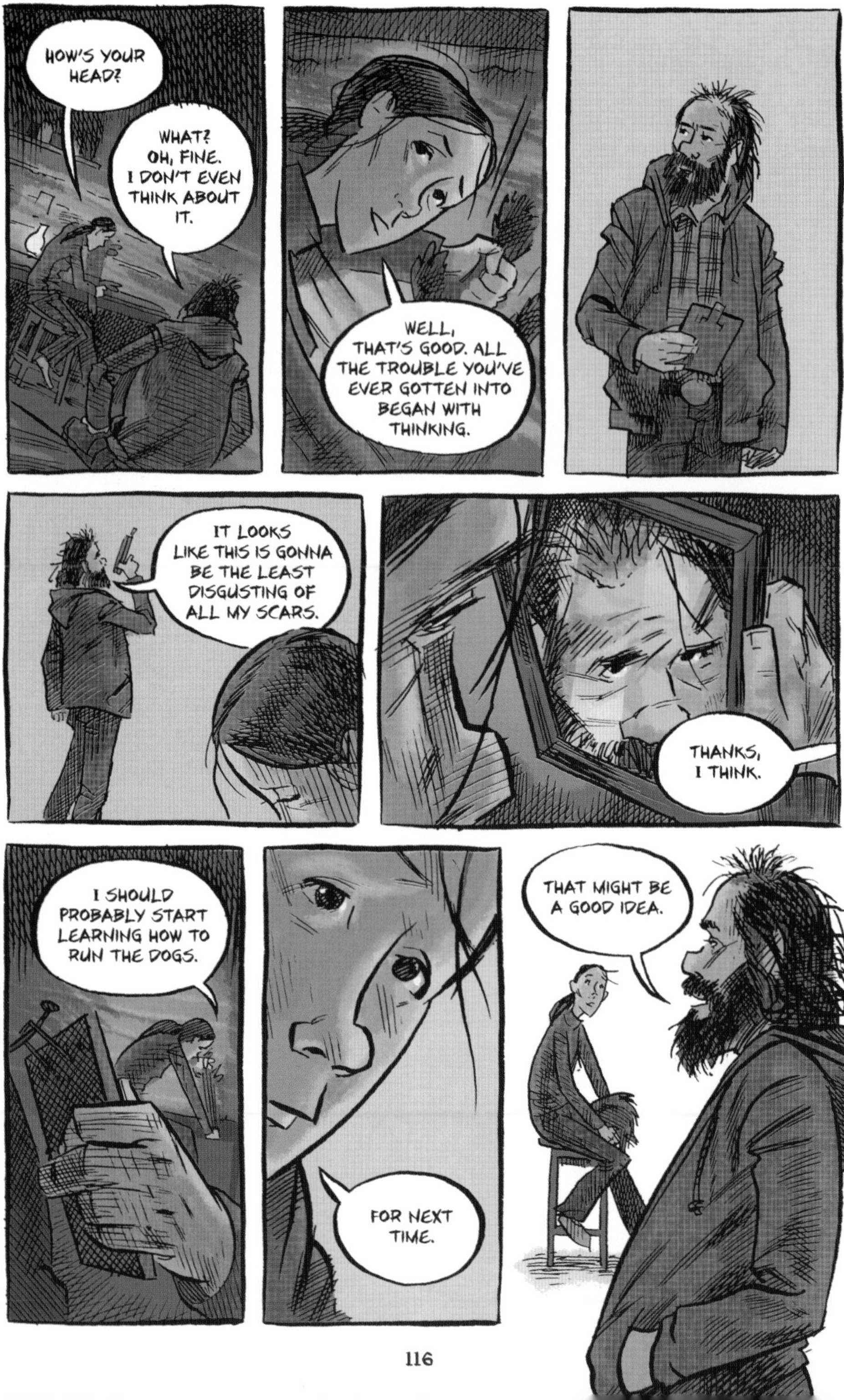

HOW'S YOUR HEAD?
WHAT? OH, FINE. I DON'T EVEN THINK ABOUT IT.
WELL, THAT'S GOOD. ALL THE TROUBLE YOU'VE EVER GOTTEN INTO BEGAN WITH THINKING.
IT LOOKS LIKE THIS IS GONNA BE THE LEAST DISGUSTING OF ALL MY SCARS.
THANKS, I THINK.
I SHOULD PROBABLY START LEARNING HOW TO RUN THE DOGS.
FOR NEXT TIME.
THAT MIGHT BE A GOOD IDEA.

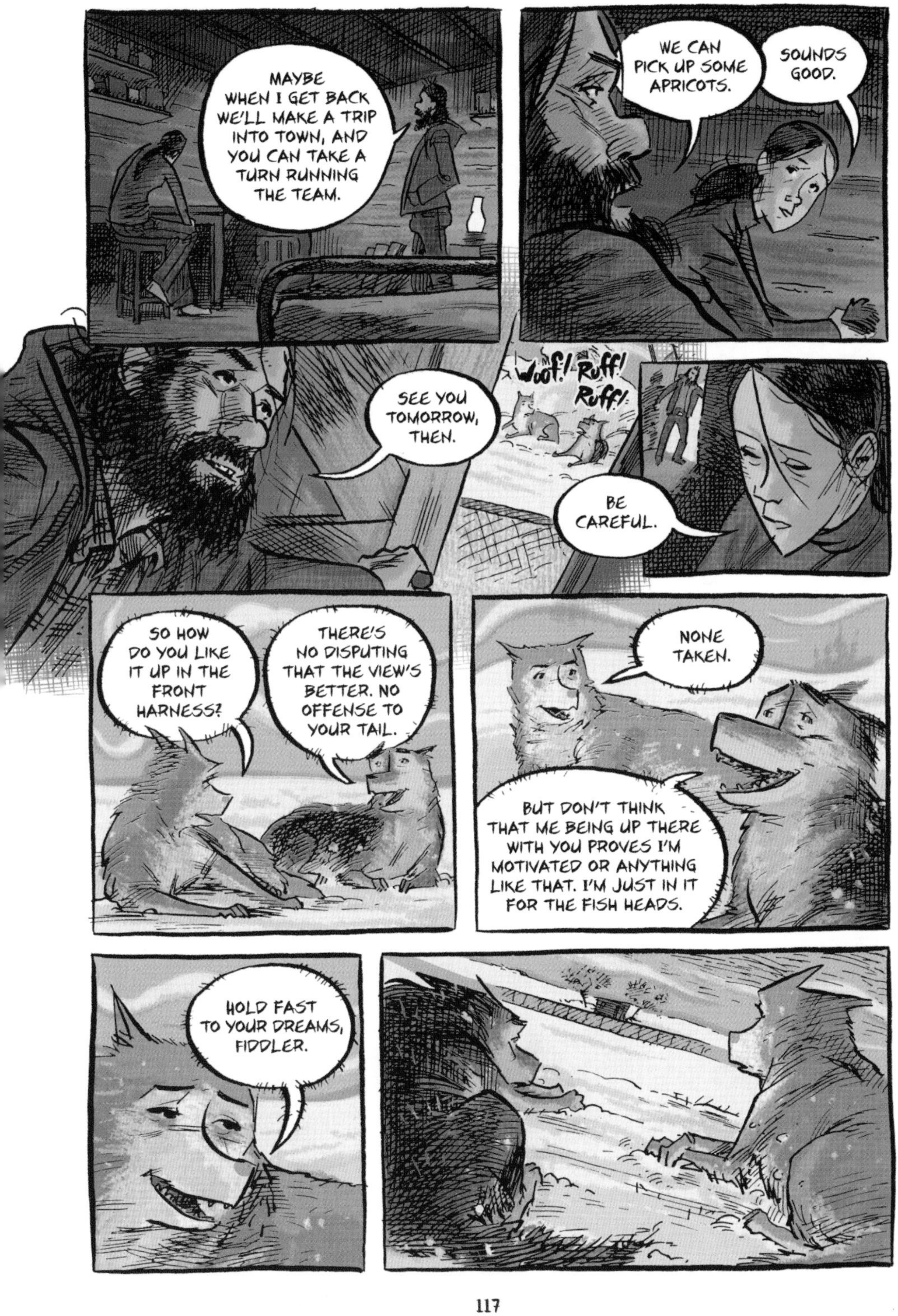

MAYBE WHEN I GET BACK WE'LL MAKE A TRIP INTO TOWN, AND YOU CAN TAKE A TURN RUNNING THE TEAM.
WE CAN PICK UP SOME APRICOTS.
SOUNDS GOOD.
SEE YOU TOMORROW, THEN.
Woof! Ruff! Ruff!
BE CAREFUL.
SO HOW DO YOU LIKE IT UP IN THE FRONT HARNESS?
THERE'S NO DISPUTING THAT THE VIEW'S BETTER. NO OFFENSE TO YOUR TAIL.
NONE TAKEN.
BUT DON'T THINK THAT ME BEING UP THERE WITH YOU PROVES I'M MOTIVATED OR ANYTHING LIKE THAT. I'M JUST IN IT FOR THE FISH HEADS.
HOLD FAST TO YOUR DREAMS, FIDDLER.

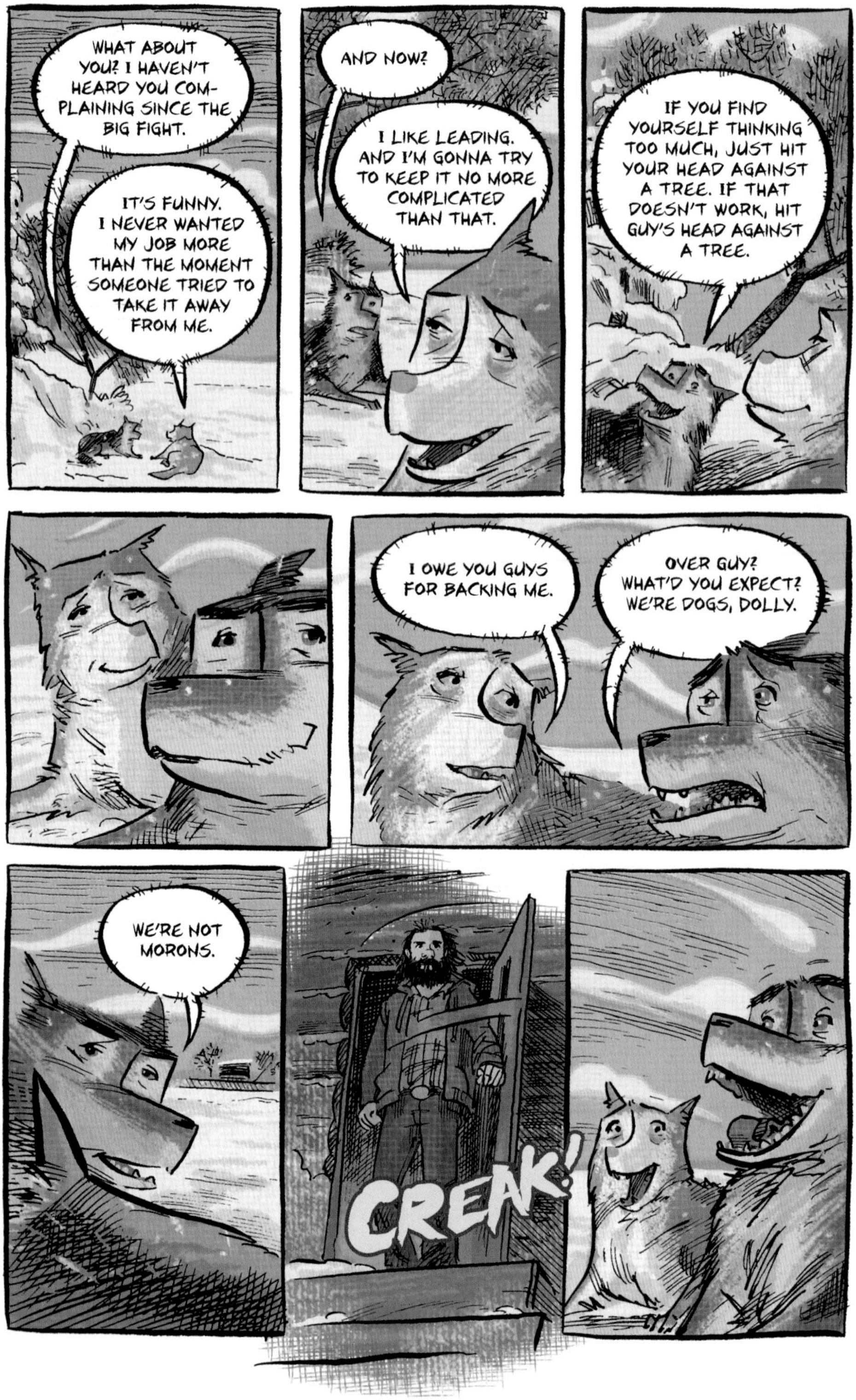
WHAT ABOUT YOU? I HAVEN'T HEARD YOU COMPLAINING SINCE THE BIG FIGHT.
IT'S FUNNY. I NEVER WANTED MY JOB MORE THAN THE MOMENT SOMEONE TRIED TO TAKE IT AWAY FROM ME.
AND NOW?
I LIKE LEADING. AND I'M GONNA TRY TO KEEP IT NO MORE COMPLICATED THAN THAT.
IF YOU FIND YOURSELF THINKING TOO MUCH, JUST HIT YOUR HEAD AGAINST A TREE. IF THAT DOESN'T WORK, HIT GUY'S HEAD AGAINST A TREE.
I OWE YOU GUYS FOR BACKING ME.
OVER GUY? WHAT'D YOU EXPECT? WE'RE DOGS, DOLLY.
WE'RE NOT MORONS.
CREAK!

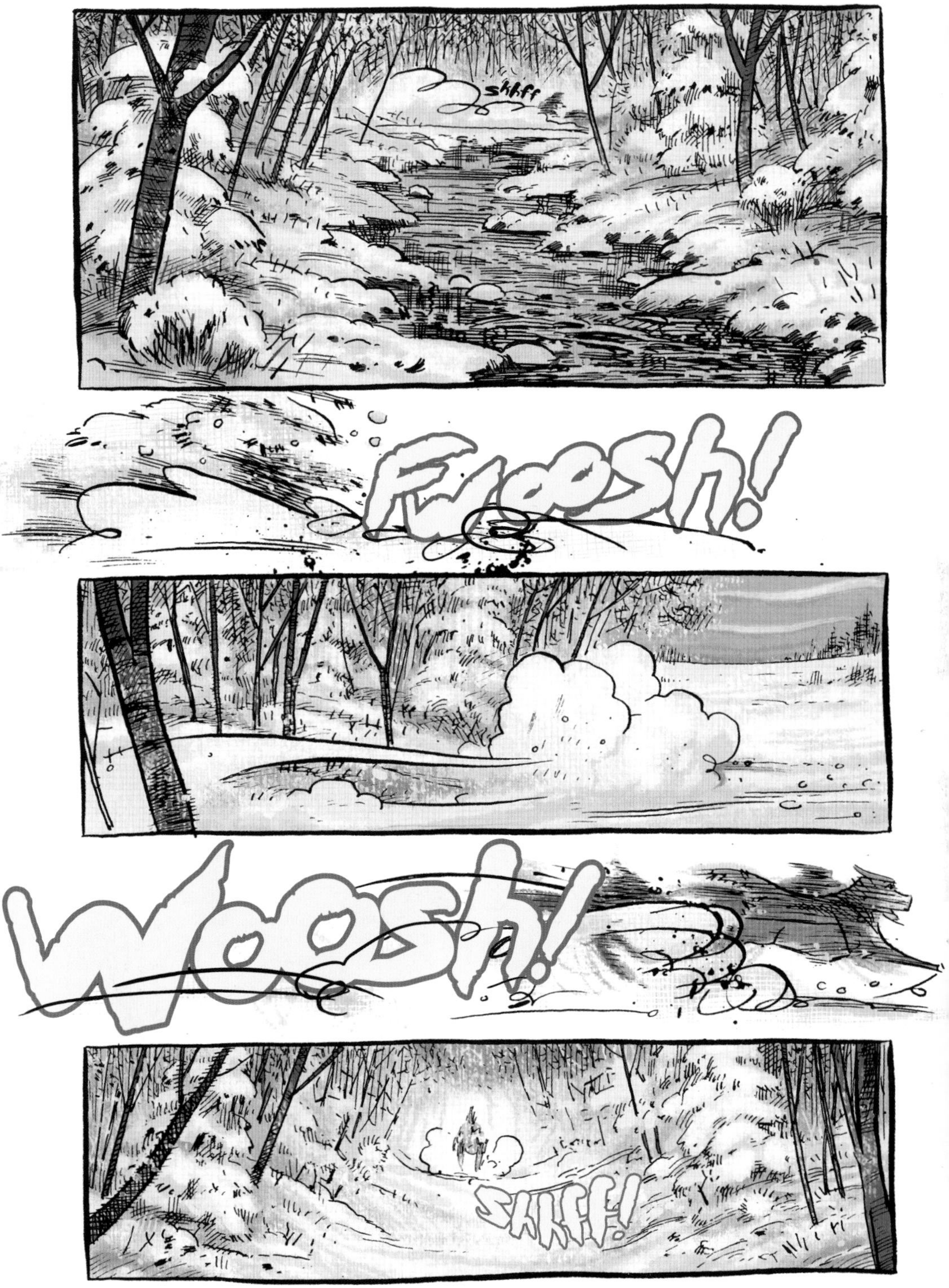
shhff
Fwoosh!
Woosh!
Shfff!

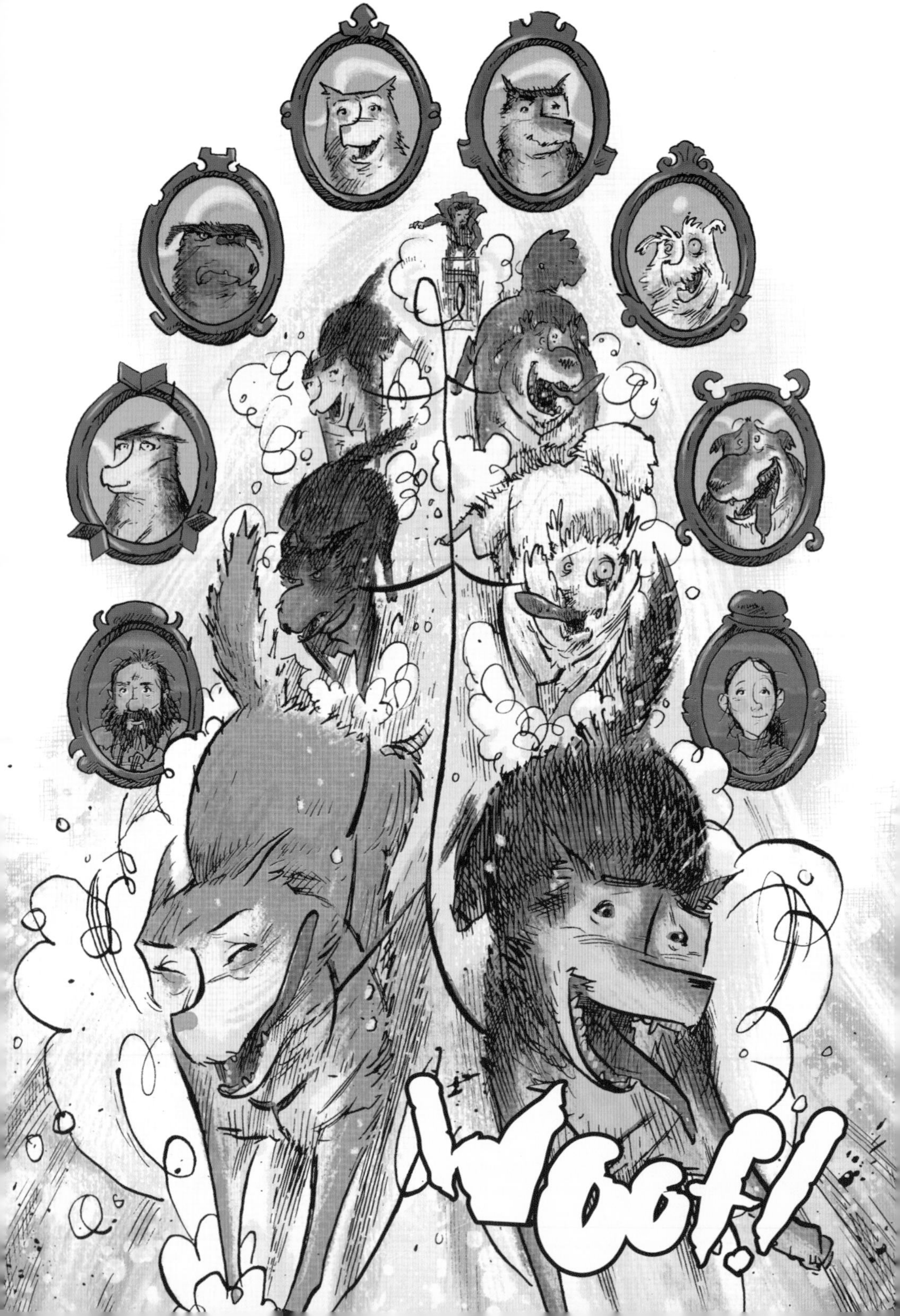
WOOF!!

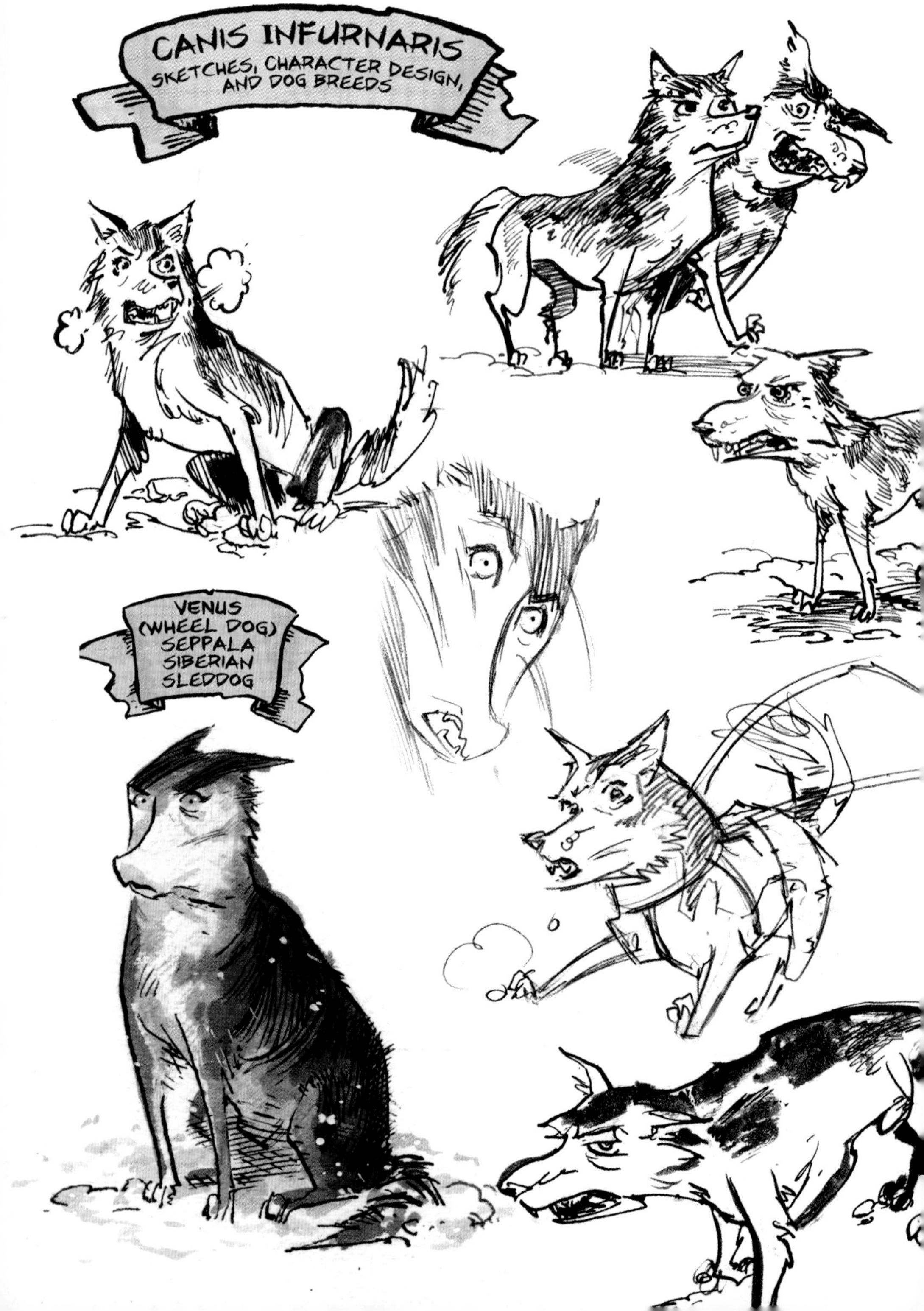
CANIS INFURNARIS
SKETCHES, CHARACTER DESIGN, AND DOG BREEDS
VENUS (WHEEL DOG) SEPPALA SIBERIAN SLEDDOG

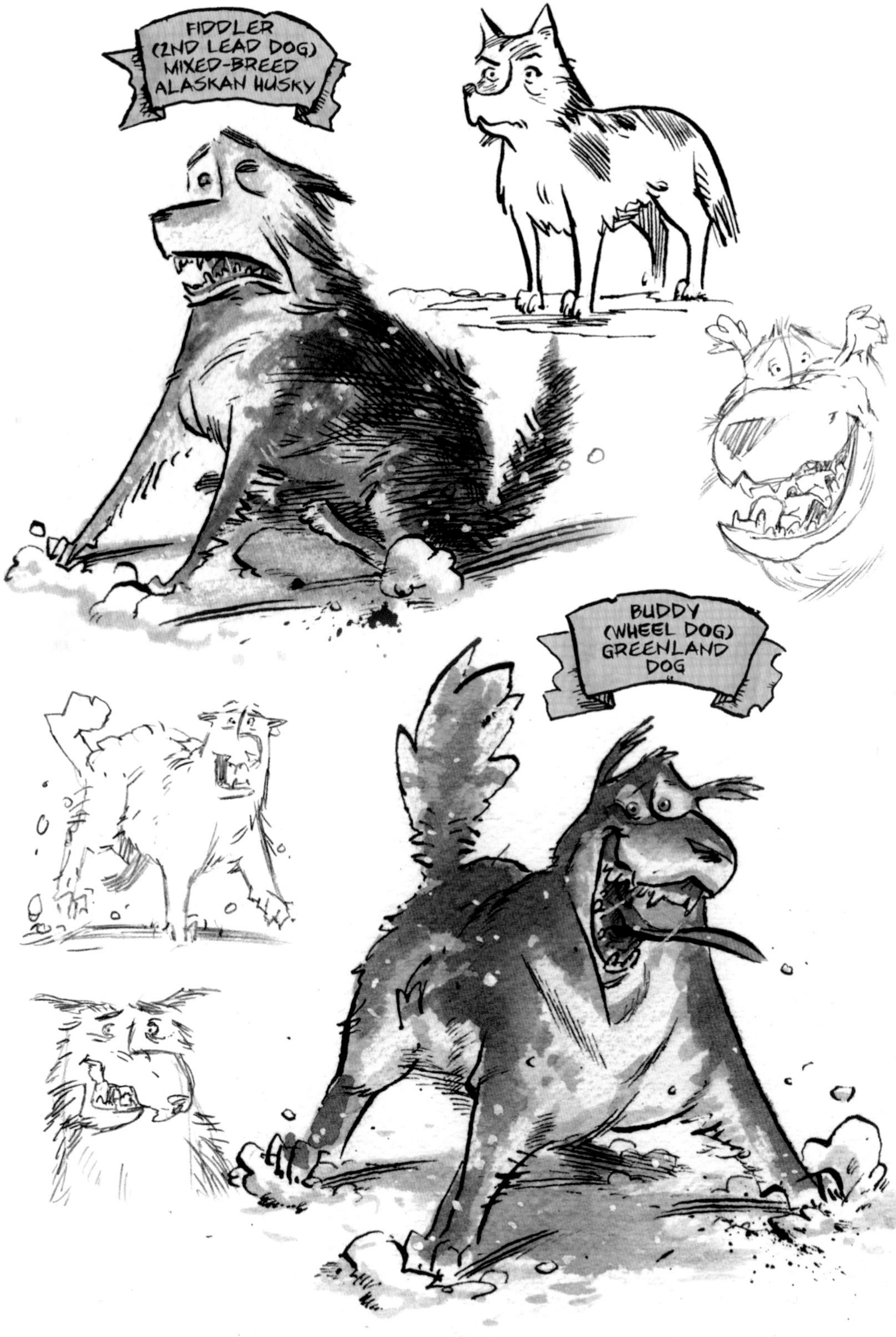
FIDDLER
(2ND LEAD DOG)
MIXED-BREED
ALASKAN HUSKY
BUDDY
(WHEEL DOG)
GREENLAND
DOG

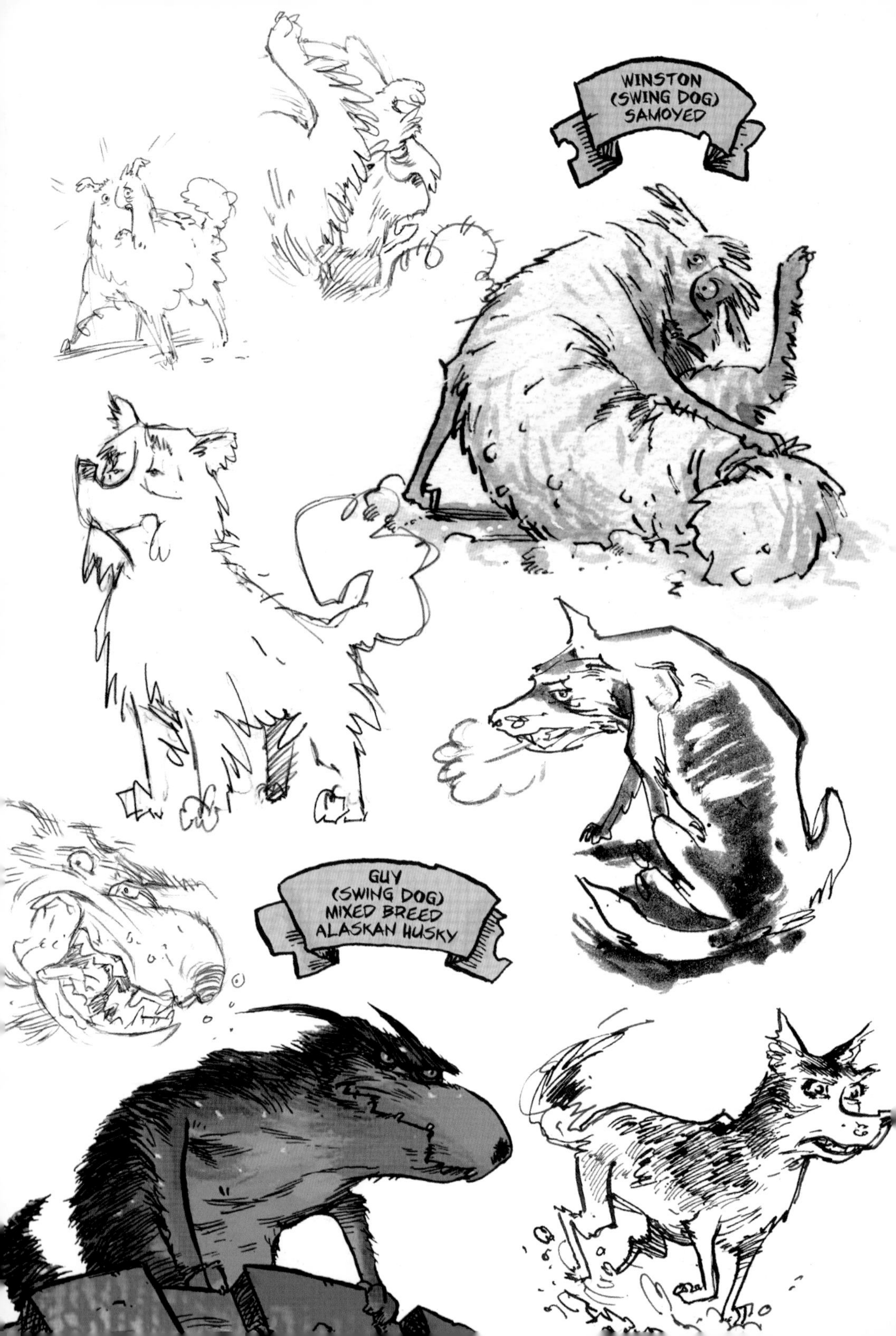
WINSTON
(SWING DOG)
SAMOYED
GUY
(SWING DOG)
MIXED BREED
ALASKAN HUSKY

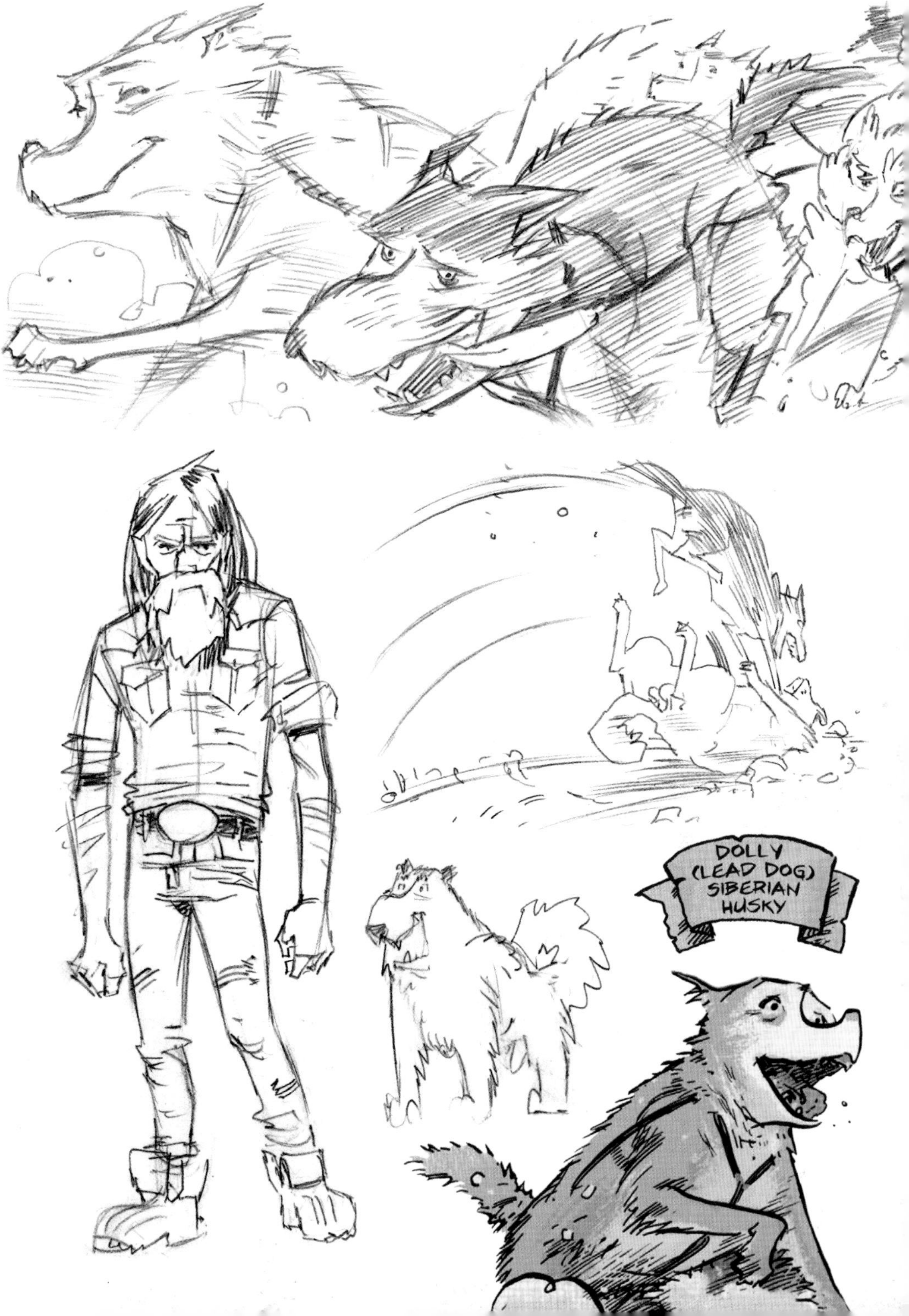
DOLLY
(LEAD DOG)
SIBERIAN
HUSKY

GLENN EICHLER WOULD LIKE TO THANK MICHELE, ALEX, AND CHLOE, AND THE DOGS WHO TALK TO HIM WHEN HE SLEEPS.

JOE INFURNARI WOULD LIKE TO THANK HIS PARENTS, JASON ROBERT BELL, JENNIE FISKE, GEORGE O'CONNOR, MIKE CAVALLARO, DEAN HASPIEL, ROB FAY, DEEPG, AND HYPOTHETICAL ISLAND STUDIOS.

**First Second**

New York & London

Text copyright © 2011 by Glenn Eichler
Illustrations copyright © 2011 by Joe Infurnari

Published by First Second
First Second is an imprint of Roaring Brook Press,
a division of Holtzbrinck Publishing Holdings Limited Partnership
175 Fifth Avenue, New York, New York 10010

Distributed in Canada by H. B. Fenn and Company Ltd.
Distributed in the United Kingdom by Macmillan Children's Books,
a division of Pan Macmillan.

Book design by Colleen AF Venable

Cataloging-in-Publication Data is on file with the Library of Congress

First Second books are available for special promotions and premiums.
For details, contact: Director of Special Markets, Holtzbrinck Publishers.

First edition 2011
Printed in China

10 9 8 7 6 5 4 3 2 1